MELVILL'S LECTURES.

LECTURES

ON

PRACTICAL SUBJECTS,

DELIVERED AT

St. Margaret's, Lothbury,

BY THE

REV. HENRY MELVILL, B. D.,

PRINCIPAL OF THE EAST INDIA COLLEGE, AND CHAPLAIN TO THE TOWER OF LONDON; AUTHOR OF
SERMONS PREACHED BEFORE THE UNIVERSITY OF CAMBRIDGE AND ST. MARY'S CHURCH;
SERMONS ON CERTAIN OF THE LESS PROMINENT FACTS AND REFERENCES
IN SACRED STORY, PREACHED ON PUBLIC OCCASIONS;
ETC., ETC., ETC.

PHILADELPHIA:
H. HOOKER, 911 CHESTNUT STREET.
1864.

CONTENTS.

LECTURE IV.

THE WITNESS IN ONESELF.

LECTURE V.

THE APOCRYPHA.

LECTURE VI.

A MAN A HIDING-PLACE.

LECTURE VII.

THE HUNDREDFOLD RECOMPENSE.

LECTURE VIII.

THE LIFE MORE THAN MEAT.

LECTURE IX.

ISAIAH'S VISION.

LECTURE X.

ST. JOHN THE BAPTIST.

LECTURE XI.

BUILDING THE TOMBS OF THE PROPHETS.

LECTURE XII.

MANIFESTATION OF THE SONS OF GOD.

LECTURE XIII.

ST. PAUL'S DETERMINATION.

LECTURE XIV.

THE SONG OF MOSES AND THE LAMB.

LECTURE XV.

THE DIVINE LONG-SUFFERING.

LECTURE XVI.

SOWING THE SEED.

LECTURE XVII.

THE GREAT MULTITUDE.

LECTURE XVIII.

THE KINSMAN REDEEMER.

LECTURE XIX.

ST. BARNABAS.

LECTURE XX.

SPIRITUAL DECLINE.

LECTURE I.

The Return of the Dispossessed Spirit.

MATT. xii. 43–45.

"When the unclean spirit is gone out of a man, he walketh through dry places, seeking rest, and findeth none. Then he saith, I will return into my house from whence I came out; and when he is come, he findeth it empty, swept, and garnished. Then goeth he, and taketh with himself seven other spirits more wicked than himself, and they enter in and dwell there: and the last state of that man is worse than the first. Even so shall it be also unto this wicked generation."

THIS parable has been before read to you in the second lesson of this morning's service. Its drift is much less evident than that of many of our Lord's parables; you may have often read it without attaching to it any definite meaning, or extracting from it any practical lesson. We think it well, therefore, to devote a sermon to its illustration. The words with which our Lord concludes, "Even so shall it be also unto this wicked generation," sufficiently show that the parable had a special reference to the Jewish people. But before considering it under this point of view, we should like, by a few general remarks, to guide you in applying the parable to yourselves. If you are observers, even the most cursory, of character, you must be aware that there is in every man a ruling passion, a master-disposition. Each individual amongst us is tempted by nature to some one kind of sin, which, according to St. Paul's expression, is "the sin which most easily besets him." And the great difficulty which religion has, is in the grappling with the master-passion, in the overcoming the besetting sin, whether it be a sin of the flesh, or a sin of the intellect. If an individual be a real subject of grace, having been truly converted, a new master-principle has been introduced into his heart—the love of God being most strictly his ruling passion, whatever the affection to which he had beforetime been captive. But though there is the introduction of this new master-principle, we cannot say that there is a thorough casting out of the old. We do not, of course, mean that there will be two master-principles. There cannot be two things which are both greatest of their kind. But whilst the love of God is the master-principle, what had formerly been the master-principle remains within, in a subdued, though not in a dominant, state ; and the great warfare of the Christian's life will result from the efforts of this principle to regain the lost ascendancy. If the voluptuous man be converted, his hardest after-task will lie in resisting the lusts of the flesh ; whilst the proud man, or the envious, will find his main battle must be waged with pride or with envy. The weak point before conversion will be the weak point after. And the devil, who once had undisputed possession of the man, and who knows therefore the quarter in which he is most assailable, will direct his temptations against the vulnerable point, and seek to make a breach where there had beforetime been the broadest highway.

So that the besetting sin, whatsoever it be, must, to the end of our days, occupy our chief vigilance and prayerful-ness. For we may take it as an ascertained fact, that, if we fall again under the dominion of evil, it will be through the re-entrance of that unclean spirit, which went out from its mastership, when we first knew Christ, and which, ever on the alert to recover its empire, will take advantage of our leaving the ground a moment undefended, to rush to its lost throne with a kind of sevenfold energy. In this way, the parable before us admits of a striking application to every renewed man. Conversion is virtually the casting out of a dominant passion, and the yielding up the soul to a new master-principle. But it often happens that men relax from their first strenuousness; and then the chamber, which was swept and garnished at the entrance of the new principle, becomes, in a certain sense, empty and untenanted. And thus there may be said to be given an invitation to the old ruling-passion, the unclean spirit, which the Divine word had cast out, but which has never ceased to hover round its original dwelling-place. And there being, as it were, an unoccupied house, and an unguarded avenue, this unclean spirit will hurry to take possession. And forasmuch as none sin with a greater vehemence than those who yield again to a renounced passion, or an abjured lust, there will be, for the time, such an energy of tyranny in the reinstated demon, that he shall seem to have associated with himself seven others, of greater strength and more desperate wickedness.

We want to make you aware of this, before we advance to the fuller explanation and application of the parable. Depend on it, the chief danger to the Christian is from the old master-passion, the sin which was his besetting sin before his conversion. He is far more likely to fall into that, than into any other form of evil. We adhere to the delineation of the parable: we tell every one of you, in whom, through the operations of grace, the love of God has become the ruling principle, that the unclean spirit, which went out from dominion, when the Holy Ghost entered and claimed sovereignty for God, is watching night and day to gain entrance into the mansion from which he was expelled—ay, and that if you yield to the unclean spirit, the old master-passion, it will be far worse for you than if you had been overcome by any other form of evil: it will be like taking back a habit, or moving back into a plague-stricken dwelling; and with so awful a despotism will the re-admitted spirit seize on every power of the mind, and every member of the body, that the appearance shall be as though he had ransacked the hosts of fallen angels, and selected seven of the mightiest from that terrible company, to aid him in retaining dominion, and annihilating immortality.

But we now turn to other and more complete illustrations of the parable. We may premise that "the seven spirits," which the unclean spirit is said to have associated with himself, may be considered as denoting only one very powerful spirit, or as figuring the mightier energy with which this one unclean spirit comes back equipped. You all know that the number "seven" is not used in Scripture as five may be, or six, to mark precisely an amount. It is rather a mystical number, applied whenever perfection or completeness is to be considered as existing. In the Book of Revelation, the Holy Ghost is undoubtedly described as "the seven spirits of God." "Grace be unto you, and peace from Him which is, and which was, and which is to come, and from the seven spirits which are before his throne, and from Jesus Christ." Hence we are not required, in expounding the parable before us, to produce a catalogue of seven evil spirits, associated with the cast-out one when restored: seven spirits is but a scriptural expression for one spirit of the very mightiest order; and may only denote that the master evil-passion, if allowed to return, will return with all its energies awfully strengthened by absence. This having been premised, we will now endeavour to show you the meaning of the parable as applied to the Jews; for, as we have before said, the words of our Lord, "Even so shall it be also unto this wicked generation," fasten it especially on that disobedient people.

Now Judæa had long been a well-watered land, whilst the phrase "dry places" described accurately every other district of the globe, considered in respect of its spiritual advantages. Though God had never left Himself without witness, even in the darkest times, and among the most barbarous tribes, the Gentile world was one vast moral desert, the refreshing showers of Revelation having been confined to one solitary people. But Judæa, thus favoured and fertilized, yielded no fruit in return for its privileges: a barrenness, general as that which marked the unwatered fields, deformed those which had the dew and the rain. Such was the condition of the human race, when the fulness of time came, and the long-promised Redeemer was born of a woman. The watered places, which were the Jewish people, yielded no harvest to the great proprietor of the soil; whilst the "dry places," which were the Gentile world, sent not up even that scanty produce, for which traditional religion, and the constant manifestations of

Godhead which occupy the universe, threw into the ground sufficiency of moisture. The whole world, in fact, if we may vary the image, was lying under the dominion of Satan; and this apostate leader, as the predicted season drew nigh, when the seed of the woman should bruise his head, touched the top point of sovereignty, and held the globe, with all its millions, in the foulest of vassalage.

And when Christ with his disciples moved through Judæa, proclaiming truths which had long been hidden from mankind, and ejecting the spirits which had seized on men's bodies, there was an assault, such as had never before been witnessed, on the empire of darkness; and the likelihood must have appeared great, even to evil angels themselves, that, so far at least as Judæa was concerned, there would be an overthrow the most complete of the long-endured despotism. And here comes in the representation of our parable. Disturbed by the preaching and the miracles of Jesus, the unclean spirits, who had tyrannized over the souls and bodies of the Jews, abandoned partially Judæa, and sought to establish themselves in the dry places of the Gentiles. We are, of course, profoundly ignorant of machinations and movements in the world of spirits, and cannot therefore pretend to ascertain, except from the simple statement of the parable, this departure of the powers of evil from amongst the Jews, and their attempted domestication in the dry places of the Gentiles. But we know that, over and above the discomfiture of Satan in the ejectment of evil spirits from men's bodies, there was made for the time a mighty impression on a great body of the Jews, so that there were moments when Jesus stood within a hair-breadth of being acknowledged as Christ. Therefore, morally as well as physically, there was a wide shaking of the empire of Satan; and we can quite understand, from the known condition of the Jews, that the effect of the ministrations of Christ and his Apostles had been the partial expulsion of unclean spirits from the land, and the consequent affording of a kind of breathing-time to the nation, that they might be free to receive or reject their deliverer.

And we learn, on the authority of the parable, that the spirits, thus disturbed and cast out, craved a new home, like those who asked leave to enter into the swine, and sought that rest amongst the Gentiles which they had had amongst the Jews. They walked through "dry places," seeking rest, but found it not. They were quickly pursued into the plains of heathenism by the emissaries of Christianity. There elapsed but a little time after the Resurrection and Ascension of Christ, before the first preachers of Christianity went forth to the assault of the idolatry and ignorance of a long-benighted world. They gave no quarter to the spirits of evil. Denouncing fearlessly every abomination, though all that was ancestral sanctioned and hallowed its mysteries, and prejudice and interest conspired to uphold them, these champions of truth would be content with nothing but the casting down of temples at whose altars unclean spirits presided, and the rooting up of groves, from whose recesses they breathed out their oracles. And though there was not an immediate demolition of the huge fabric of superstition, a success so marked attended this bold crusade against error, that multitudes in every land threw away their idols, and a contempt for false gods became visible even amongst those who still refused to acknowledge the true. And thus there was no rest in the dry places for the unclean spirits. There was a general unsettlement in men's minds. Thousand renounced the falsehoods of heathenism, whilst those who adhered to them were dissatisfied with the system. So that the demons felt that they had no longer a firm hold on the Pagan population. There were clear indications of a far-spreading revolution, which, though it might be delayed for a time, would finally substitute Christianity for heathenism. And therefore the unclean spirits, whom the preaching and miracles of Jesus had driven from Judæa, were now driven from the dry places of the Gentiles by the preaching and miracles of the Apostles. Whither then shall they resort? The parable represents them as determining to return to their houses whence they came out. They calculated that, possibly, they might again find that rest amongst the Jews, which they had sought in vain amongst the Gentiles. They hurried back, therefore, to examine their former dwelling; and they found it "empty, swept, and garnished."

The Jews had indeed crucified their Lord: but nevertheless the door of mercy was not yet closed: the proclamations of pardon were circulating through their land; and He, whom they had slain, "exalted to be a Prince and a Saviour," still offered, if they would acknowledge their wickedness, to shelter them from destruction. There had been, however, no general acceptance of the proffer; and the body of the people, who had been "swept," as it were, by awful warning and pathetic entreaty, and "garnished" with mercies which proved eloquently the long-suffering of God, refused to admit the Redeemer into their hearts, and thus stood "empty," unoccupied, and ready to receive back the ejected spirits of evil. And then came the final casting-off of the nation. The last and crowning attestation to the mission of Christ had wrought no conviction. The Spirit had been poured out, communicating to the preachers of the faith the most extraordinary powers, and thus witnessing, as it would have seemed, with irresistible force, to the truth of the proclaimed doctrines and facts. But the people resisted this testimony, with the same obstinacy with which they had resisted every other, and thus committed the unpardonable sin—unpardonable, not because any sin can literally overpass the forgiving mercies of God, but because, the last evidence to the truth of Christianity having failed to subdue infidelity, there lay a direct impossibility against the reception of Christ as a propitiation.

And now, therefore, "swept and garnished"—swept by the rushing of the mighty wind of Pentecost, and garnished with the trophies of baffled disease and vanquished death—the nation stood forth a nation of scorners; and whilst there went forwards in their streets the preaching of the Resurrection, and they were entreated to fill up with an Incarnate Deity the vast void which they felt in their undying souls, they blasphemously refused to admit the Mediator into the untenanted chambers, and thus left free the space to the incursions of the unclean spirits. With the noiseless but rapid march of the pestilence, the troop of demons, strengthened both in numbers and energies, rushed into the unoccupied dwellings, and grasped again the sovereignty from which they had been ejected. Expelled from the "dry places" of heathenism, they poised themselves, so to speak, on their raven wings, over the scene of their former dominion; and perceiving that the throne had been refused to the rightful Lord, they came down, thirsting for human blood; and, with the only laugh which fiends can laugh, the laugh at bringing others to share their fire and their shame, buried themselves in the nation's heart, and Judæa was their own. And, oh! indeed, the last state of that generation was worse than the first. If you consult the histories of the period between the Crucifixion of Christ and the destruction of Jerusalem, you will find the Jews presenting all the aspect of a possessed and maddened people, acting as though furies were gnawing at the vitals of society, and causing every member, from the highest to the lowest, to gnash the teeth, and wring the hands. Magicians and impostors overran the land, seducing thousands, and drawing upon them, as upon rebels, the vengeance of the Romans. The sword was never sheathed: and when foreign armies ceased, for a moment, to harass, civil discord blazed out, and each man's hand was turned against his fellow. Never was there, indeed, a more disastrous spectacle. You can give no explanation how a people could be thus torn, and distracted, and infuriated, except that there were harboured unclean spirits in their breasts; and that these demons, playing with the souls and the limbs of their vassals, proclaimed a carnival to war, and ghastliness, and suicide. And there were no signs of turning unto God. The nation writhed in agony, but bent not the knee in penitence. They answered to the awful description of the men, upon whom the fifth vial is poured, who are said to "gnaw their tongues for pain, and to blaspheme the God of Heaven because of their pains, and their sores, and to repent not of their deeds."

The end came on, and the unclean spirits girded themselves for their last revelry. Was it these spirits—for

Satan is the Prince of the power of the air—who caused the war chariots to career along the clouds; who hung the sword of fire over the city; who breathed mysterious sounds as of a multitude departing from the Temple, or of Divinity forsaking its shrine; and who produced all that series of prodigies, which even heathen historians describe as heralding the downfall of Jerusalem? It may be that demons delighted in thus causing alarm, when they knew that alarm would not lead to repentance. But, at all events, the siege of Jerusalem, ushered in with these fearful signs, gave opportunity to the demons to let loose all their madness. We speak not of the famine, though a demon must have seized on that mother, who slew her infant, and dressed it for food. We speak not of the slaughter, though their conqueror Titus was the mildest of men, and demons must have goaded them to the compelling him to carnage. We speak of the broad marks of a national madness, of a national demoniacal possession. Shut up in the city, the opposite factions filled even the Temple with slaughter, as though there had not been enough of foreign enemies. They destroyed the very granaries of corn which should have sustained them, and burnt the magazines of arms which should have defended them. With their own hands they set the first fire to the porticoes of the Temple, and taught their conquerors to desecrate the Sanctuary. And how account we for this strangeness of fury? What explanation can we give of such unparalleled infatuation? Oh, we can only say, that the unclean spirits had come back from the dry places of the Gentiles, and that they had entered into the Jews with a sevenfold mightiness; and that now, lashing the population into madness, and determined to have their fill of human agony, ere the devoted nation was ground into powder, and sprinkled over the globe, they were working out for all posterity a proof of the assertion, "The last state of that man is worse than the first."

But we cannot pursue further the application of our parable to the Jews. We think that we have said enough to show you the fidelity of the sketch; and we leave it to your own minds to fill up in greater detail the outlines. We proceed to apply briefly the parable to ourselves. We shall attempt nothing beyond grasping and illustrating the general idea; for undoubtedly it was the main design of the parable to convey one great lesson, though sundry minute circumstances are introduced into the allegory. We take this general idea to be, that conviction of sin, which does not end in conversion, hardens, in place of benefitting, a man. We will strive to exhibit this idea, and to demonstrate its truth by a few statements which all may comprehend. Now men will come up to the public preaching of the word, though the master natural-passion, whatever it be, retains undisputed dominion. And this passion may be avarice, or voluptuousness, or ambition, or envy, or pride. But however characterized, the unclean spirit is brought into the sanctuary, and exposed, so to speak, to the exorcisms of the preacher. And who shall say what a disturbing force the sermon will often put forth against the master-passion; how frequently the word of the living God, delivered in earnestness and effect, shall have almost made a breach in the strong-holds of Satan? If the demon ever tremble for his ascendancy, it is when the preacher has riveted the attention of the possessed individual; and after describing and denouncing the covetous, or exhibiting the voluptuary, or exposing the madness and misery of the proud, comes down on that individual with the startling announcement, "Thou art the man." And the individual will go away from the sanctuary, thoroughly convinced of the duty of ejecting the unclean spirit; and he will form, and, for a while, he will act on, the resolution of wrestling against pride, or of mortifying lust, or of renouncing avarice. So that the demon may be said to go out of the man, having yielded to the exorcisms of the preacher.

But then the individual, in whom conviction has been wrought, is acting in his own strength, and, having no consciousness of the infirmities of his nature, seeks not to God's Spirit for assistance. In a little time, therefore, all the impression will wear away. He saw only the danger of sin; he went not on to see its vileness; and the mind soon habituates itself, or soon grows indifferent, to the contemplation of danger, and, above all, when perhaps distant. He will therefore allow the conviction, which had not indeed penetrated below the surface, to be swept off. Nay, he will even garnish his soul with a sort of hardy persuasion that the preacher exaggerated the danger, and that the master-passion may be indulged with comparative impunity. And thus swept, and thus garnished, he returns to his old haunts. The unclean spirit, which had hovered round him during his brief hour of amendment, is reinstated in the sovereignty of the soul. And whether it be to money-making that he again gives himself, or to sensuality, or to ambition, he will enter into the pursuit with an eagerness heightened by abstinence;

and thus the result shall be practically the same as though the unclean spirit had leagued seven others with himself, and those too more consummate and more awful in their wickedness. And if the man, after this ejectment and restoration of the unclean spirit, come again to the sanctuary, and if again the preacher denounce with a righteous vehemence every working of ungodliness, and make a bold stand for God and for truth against a reckless and unbelieving generation, alas! the man who has felt convictions, and smothered them, will be more inaccessible than ever, and more impervious. He will be hardened by the process through which he has passed of the casting out, and receiving back, the master-passion. It will acquire a far mightier instrumentality than before to make the very lightest impression: a smothered conviction is like a triple band of brass round the evil spirit's throne.

We especially wish this application of the parable treasured up in your memories. Ye may learn from it the peril of trifling with convictions. The parable, when thus interpreted, is one of the most striking delineations which the Scriptures present, of a truth which should be always borne in mind, that he, who takes a step towards God, and then draws back, does not fall again into his old position; he will be further off than if he had never approached; if the advance was an inch, the retreat will be a league. And when you think that there the man is now sitting, unmoved by the terrors of the word; that he can listen with indifference to the very truths which once agitated him; and that, as a consequence on the re-entrance of the unclean spirit, he has more of the marble in his composition than before, more of the ice, more of the iron; and that thus the likelihood of his salvation is fearfully diminished; oh, you can need no proof of the justice of the verdict, that "the last state of that man is worse than the first."

Might not the parable before us admit of a national, as well as of an individual, application? It were, of course, easy to illustrate over again the general idea, just altering our language, so that nation might be substituted for individual. If a people be moved by the startling sermons of God's judgments—by pestilence, for example, or by famine—to humble themselves before Him, and to put away from them some fractions of their wickedness; and if, when health is restored, or plenty again smiles on their plains, they forget the Almighty, and return, every man, to his iniquities; why assuredly we have here, as well as with an individual, the casting out, and the taking back, of the unclean spirit; and we conclude, on precisely the same principles, that the last state of that land shall be worse than the first.

But we cannot conceal our persuasion that the parable sketches, with a still stronger pencil, the possible conduct and condition of a nation circumstanced like our own. We occupy so precisely the position which the Jews occupied as a peculiar people, that there is always an antecedent probability that what sketches nationally the one, may sketch also nationally the other. And if we look to England at the period of the Reformation, we find that men, raised up by God, and endowed of Him with singular boldness, and wisdom, and piety, exorcised the unclean spirit of Romish superstition, and ejected from amongst us the corruptions of Popery. It was a sublime moral revolution, and never did the human mind struggle free from a more oppressive shackle, never was there thrown off from a people a mightier weight, than when Reformers had won the hard-fought battle, and Protestantism was enthroned as the religion of these realms. But we should like to have it carefully considered, whether there have been no receiving back the unclean spirit. The human mind, long enslaved, was intoxicated with its freedom, and, in place of stopping at liberty, went on to lawlessness. Hence the overspreading of the land with a thousand sects and a thousand systems; as though, in casting out the one spirit of ecclesiastical tyranny, we had taken in the seven of ecclesiastical disunion. And over and above this melancholy disruption of the visible Church, Popery itself has too often found a home in our Protestantism: for whenever formality has insinuated itself into religion, or self-righteousness, or the substitution of means for an end, then has there been introduced the very essence of Romanism: the ejected spirit has come back, the same in nature, though less repulsive in appearance. We speak, of course, of the great mass of Protestants; and no one, who is acquainted with the English ecclesiastical history since the period of the Reformation, can call it an exaggerated statement, that the torn and shattered condition of Christians rent into a thousand parties, and the nominal Protestantism, which has taken the place of professed Popery, with a great mass of our community, furnish melancholy evidence, that, in place of being finally rid of the unclean spirit, he has found harbourage amongst us for himself and his allies.

And, as though this were not enough, have we not, of

late years, as a nation, ay, and even as a Church, tampered with Popery, almost as though we had sent embassages to the dry places, soliciting the cast-out spirit to return openly and undisguised? Therefore has it come to pass that we are in our present extraordinary predicament, obliged to rouse ourselves as though against the forces of an invader, menaced with the loss of that pure form of faith which we received from the Reformers, and with the re-establishment of the system which those venerated men lived, and which they died, to eject. There must be no relaxation in our resistance to Popery; the parable before us is most emphatic in its warning; if we receive back the evil spirit, he will come, having taken to himself seven other spirits more wicked than himself; and "the last state of that land shall be worse than the first." O England, honoured by the Almighty, as no other land hath been, a speck upon the waters, and yet chief amongst the nations, may not Christ speak to thee in something of the same sad, reproachful words with which He spake to Jerusalem: "How often would I have gathered thy children together, as a hen doth gather her brood under her wings, and ye would not." Not indeed that the "things which belong to thy peace are hidden from thine eyes." God be praised, we are not yet come to that! But we may be on the high road. We have had unexampled privileges: have we not neglected them? have we duly improved them? "What could have been done more to the vineyard that has not been done?" God raised up men to exorcise the evil spirit. But if we permit that, under one shape or another, the spirit shall come back; if we allow the marks and defences of true Protestantism to be "swept" from the land; if we "garnish" ourselves with that spurious liberality which would sink the difference of creeds, and represent the distinctions as unimportant between the Reformed and the Roman, why then, swept and garnished, we stand ready for a fresh surrender to the tyranny of Anti-Christ, whether in the form of Popery, or his last form of infidelity.

Then, truly, shall the last state be worse than the first. But we are not come to this. These are but words of warning, rather than of denunciation. Still, we must say, however hopeful the recent signs of vitality and vigour in the Protestantism of the land, Oh that the many mercies which are still continued to us as a nation, might lead us to consider well the return which God looks for at our hands! The parable before us has indeed a national, just as well as an individual, application. But, in neither case, even if there have been a receiving back of the evil spirit, even if he have returned with sevenfold might, in neither case is there necessity that we retain this spirit. We may, through God's help, eject it nationally; we may, through God's help, eject it individually. We may eject it nationally. We may put from us our sabbath-breaking, our covetousness, our pride, our indifference, and thus become Protestants in something better than name, living protests for truth, bold witnesses for God; and over a Protestantism such as this, even though no acts of Parliament should come to its aid, there is no power in Rome which shall ever ride rampant. And we may eject the unclean spirit individually. Whatever that unclean spirit be,—whether the spirit of avarice, or of lust, or of pride, or of malice,—which of you is compelled to continue harbouring this spirit? which of you is forced to give up his heart to be the temple of this spirit? who is necessitated to remain the miser or the sensualist? The unclean spirit can only stay whilst you make him welcome. "Resist the devil, and he will flee from you." There is a mightier than he proffering you assistance. And, oh! if a nation or an individual will do battle once more with the unclean spirit, in the strength of the living God, once more shall he be cast out, and forced to seek rest in the dry places of the earth; and of that nation, or that individual, it may yet be true, that though there have been a second state worse than the first, the last state shall be blessed, the last shall be triumphant.

LECTURE II.

Honey from the Rock.

DEUT. xxxii. 13.

"He made him ride on the high places of the earth, that he might eat the increase of the fields; and he made him to suck honey out of the rock, and oil out of the flinty rock."

"A LAND flowing with milk and honey," was the description of the Canaan promised to the Israelites. "A land flowing with milk and honey," describes also the Christian's present inheritance, and still more the possession reserved for him in Heaven. Our text occurs in the song of Moses, that sublime composition in which, ere he ascended Mount Nebo to die, the lawgiver reviewed God's dealings with his people, and foretold what should befall them, if they turned aside to the service of idols. It is in anticipation of their entrance into Canaan, that he speaks of their eating the increase of the fields, and sucking honey out of the rock; so that, whilst the past tense is employed, the passage must be regarded as prophetic. And forasmuch as the history of the Israelites is confessedly a typical or figurative history, sketching, as in parable, much that befalls the Christian Church in general, and its members in particular, we may expect that the prophecy before us will find its accomplishment in the experience of true disciples of Christ in every nation and age.

This is the use which, on the present occasion, we would make of the text. You can have no difficulty in understanding it in its primary application to the children of Israel. God emphatically made them "ride on the high places of the earth;" He "caused Israel, as a triumphant conqueror, riding in grand procession, to possess the fortified cities and inaccessible mountains, which the Canaanites thought secure from their assaults." "In this fertile land, the rocky parts which were the least valued, and which, in other countries, are generally unproductive, by the peculiar blessing of God, afforded them abundance of the finest honey and oil." Thus taken, the text is little more than an assertion of the extraordinary richness of the productions of Canaan,—productions to be enjoyed by the obedient, who should yield themselves unreservedly to the commandments of God. But, as we have already observed, every thing about the Jewish people was significative or emblematical: Canaan itself was a type of the condition, both here and hereafter, of the disciples of Christ. Whatsoever, therefore, the terms by which the richness of the literal Canaan is described, or the favoured condition of its inhabitants, we may justly suppose that these terms, metaphorically taken, are expressive of the provision made in Christ for His Church, of the privileges appertaining to those who love Him, and trust in Him, with all the heart, and soul, and strength.

There cannot, then, be any thing forced in the application which we shall make of our text, if we consider it as delineating what may be the happy portion of Christians. We say, what may be; for you are not to regard the verse as describing what all Christians enjoy, so much as what those may expect who are serving the Lord with the greatest devotedness. There is an evident indication in the text of struggle and conquest as preceding the possession of the rich produce of Canaan. This we wish you particularly to observe. The riding on the high places of the earth, is in order to, is preparatory to, the eating of "the increase of the fields;" as though that eating were in recompense of mastery won over the strong-holds of the enemy. This having been premised, let us go straightway to the considering the import of the promises which may be said to be contained in our text: the first, a promise, that when, through God's help, a Christian has wrestled with and overcome his enemies, he shall "eat the increase of the fields;" the second, a promise that he shall "suck honey out of the rock, and oil out of the flinty rock."

Now it is a truth, of which you should often be reminded, that Christianity, as it was not set up at once in the world, but left to make its way, by slow and painful struggles, towards a dominion which it has not yet attained, so it is progressive, and not instantaneous, in acquiring empire in individual cases. There may be no inconsiderable analogy between the history of Christianity in the world, and its history in the individual. Christianity, when first published, made rapid way, as though but few years could elapse ere every false system would vanish before it. Then came interruptions, backsliding, degeneracy; and afterwards, repentance, partial reformations, and heartier endeavours. But the consummation is still a thing only of hope; and Christ must re-appear in power and great majesty, ere his religion shall prevail in every household and every heart. In like manner, the converted individual devotes himself, at first, with the greatest ardency, to the duties of religion: after a while, too commonly, the ardency declines; duties are partially neglected, or languidly performed: then the man is roused afresh, and labours, in bitterness of spirit, to recover the ground so unhappily lost; but though, on the whole, he advances, there remains much land to be won by religion; and it will not be before "the day of the Lord" that he is "sanctified wholly in body, soul, and spirit." Nevertheless, the true character of religion in both cases is that of progressiveness; or rather, perhaps, we should say, of an inability to be stationary: it may not always be on the advance; but, if not on the advance, we may conclude it on the decline; for there is that in its nature which forbids the standing still. "To be perfect, even as our Father which is in Heaven is perfect," may not be looked for whilst we dwell in the flesh: but nothing less must be our desire, nothing less our aim; and it ought to suggest a thought, whether we have ever commenced in religion, if we feel content, though we have not attained to perfection.

The believer has all along to struggle with indwelling sin, to keep under the body, to study, that he may copy, the example of Christ, to labour at the cleansing himself of all the filthiness of the flesh and spirit, and perfecting holiness in the fear of the Lord. And beyond question, there is required, in order to this, much of painful and perilous effort. It is no easy thing to maintain war with the world, the flesh, and the devil; to be always on the watch for occasions of mastering ourselves, or on the alert to seize means for acquiring greater conformity to the image of our Lord. But if the duty be painful, it is in the highest degree profitable; for God hath so associated our happiness with holiness, He hath made us so dependent, both here and hereafter, for acquaintance with Himself, which is the soul's great joy, on our diligence in endeavouring to keep his commandments, that, if we thought of nothing but how to multiply our gladness and peace, we should labour at nothing but how we may destroy the remainders of sin, and cleanse thoroughly that Temple in which it pleases the Almighty to dwell.

And there is no respect in which the present advantageousness of unwearied diligence in our heavenly calling is more evidenced than in this, that, in proportion as we become more spiritually-minded, the beauties of Scripture are more and more unveiled. Not in vain is it said, "Blessed are the pure in heart, for they shall see God." It is not so much the darkness of the understanding, as the darkness of the heart, which prevents the view of God as revealed in his word: our evil passions weave the mist which obscures those high truths that are gathered into the statements of the Bible. And if we would know more and more of the precious stores which the sacred Volume contains, it is not so much by hard study, as by hard self-discipline, that we may hope to prevail: commentators may do something towards solving what is difficult, and elucidating what is obscure: but the best commentator is the mortifying sin, and the imitating

Christ. I should say that he who had just won some great victory over himself, or made some great sacrifice in the service of God, was better, more hopefully situated for unravelling the intricacies, and apprehending the secrets, of the Bible, than if he had suddenly gained acquaintance with the laws of criticism, and the illustrations of learning.

And may we not fairly say that something of this kind is figuratively asserted in our text, where the "riding on the high places of the earth" is made to conduct to the being fed with "the increase of the fields?" "The increase of the fields"—"Man doth not live by bread alone; but by every word that proceedeth out of the mouth of the Lord doth man live." Every word is precious, fitted for the nourishing of the soul, that immortal part which craves other sustenance than earth can furnish. But some portions of what the field yields are finer than others—declarations which are more expressive of the tenderness, the graciousness of God; doctrines which are less obvious, but richer in comfort; promises which breathe more of the depth, the intenseness of heaven—these are specially "the increase of the fields"—what it does not yield at first, but after time and tillage; and with these will God feed those who ride, so to speak, "on the high places of the earth," scaling, with the Israelites, the loftiest towers, that they may expel the Canaanite from his fortress, or sin from its lurking-place. A man, when he begins in religion, lives commonly, if we may keep up the simile, on the plainer parts of the Bible: the great facts of an Atonement, a propitiation for sin, reconciliation to God through the suretyship of a Mediator, these are his sustenance; and verily through his firm faith in these, he feeds on that bread of life which came down from heaven. But whilst such truths never cease to be sweet to his taste, and strengthening to his soul, he will, as he perseveres in righteousness, as he rides, that is, more and more on the high places of the earth—subduing the towering eminences of the world and the flesh—as he does this, he will, we say, discover and appropriate other truths—the truths, for example, of God's electing love, of the actual indwelling of God in the soul, of the present commencement and communication of heavenly joys, of such an union between the several parts of the mystical body as was intended by the Saviour when He prayed on behalf of his followers, "that they may be one, even as we are one." Such truths may be regarded as, in a special sense, "the increase of the fields"—what the land yields to the patient and persevering husbandman. There is such a thing, according to the Apostle, as the continuing in infancy, and being fed with milk: there is also such a thing as the advancing to manhood, and being fed with meat; and this is but another allegorical representation of what seems figured in our text, that some may eat of what the field yields of itself, whilst the choice increase is reserved for such as toil earnestly at subduing the land.

Not indeed that the higher truths are wholly different from the other; for Christ must be the staple in all food of the soul—they are rather the same truths, but in a more refined and exquisite state, prepared for those "who have tasted the good word of God, and the powers of the world to come." Oh, my brethren, let it never be regarded by you as the mere wandering of enthusiasm, nor resolved into the fancy of the mystic, that there is to be attained by man, in his sojourning upon earth, an intimate communion, or correspondence with his Heavenly Father, a real though spiritual intercourse, so that God shall discover his perfections to the soul, and manifest Himself "even as He doth not to the world." In place of regarding such seasons as only dreamed of in a heated and transcendental theology, we would press upon you the endeavouring to make them matter of personal experience, assuring you that, if you are going on, as you should be, towards perfection, you will find truth after truth unfolded to the mind, just as though the heavenly teacher were actually at your side, expounding to you the Scriptures, and making the heart burn within you, as He caused the magnificence of the invisible world to pass before you in glorious procession. This is not setting you to seek what is mystical and indefinite, rather than what is practical and palpable. For we tell you unreservedly that there is no way of acquiring these richer privileges of the believer, but the highway of holiness; and that, if you would enjoy the especial communications of God to the soul; if you would find delight in the deeper truths of Scripture, if you would anticipate the blessedness of heaven, your only course is perseverance in self-denial, the giving unwearied diligence to "adorn in all things the doctrine of the Saviour." Do this, this which, in the figurative language of our text, is the riding on the high places of the earth, and we may promise you that you shall not be always in doubt as to your final acceptance: you shall know something of "the full assurance of hope:" you shall find such precious truths as these brought home to the soul, "My sheep hear my voice, and I know them, and they follow me; and they shall never perish, neither shall any pluck them out of my hand:" "All things are yours, whether life or death, things present or things to come, all are yours, and ye are Christ's, and Christ is God's." And as you realize, in unwonted measure, the presence and preciousness of the Redeemer, and gather from the darker —(but only dark with excess of burning light)—the darker intimations of Scripture, how your salvation is wound up with all the attributes and purposes of Deity, you will thankfully confess, that, if the field yield food for the sustenance of all who follow Christ, there is special provision for such as follow Him with the greater constancy and devotedness, led by Him to successive conquests over foes entrenched in lofty strong-holds—and that of these it may be said, according to the image of the text, that God hath "made them ride on the high places of the earth, that they might eat of the increase of the fields."

We proceed to consider the second part of the prophecy or promise of our text, that which has to do with the obtaining honey from the rock, and oil from the flinty rock. This part perhaps goes even further than the first, in connecting the blessing with diligence in those on whom it is conferred. If honey be obtained from the rock, the rock must be climbed: and since it will not lie on the surface, every cleft or fissure must be carefully explored—so that the promise appears specially to presuppose labour, and therefore bears out what we have all along argued, that the text belongs peculiarly to those who are "working out their salvation" with more than ordinary earnestness.

But, however it may be supposed that bees might swarm in the clefts of the rocks, and that thus there might be literally "honey from the rock," there would seem to be a sort of opposition intended between the thing produced and the place which produces it: there is nothing congruous between the place and the production: a man may find shelter under a rock, or he may make a foundation of a rock; but "honey from the rock" is what he would perhaps never expect: he would not naturally go to the rock, if he were in want of honey; and we must not overlook this peculiarity of the promise, for it is full, as we shall find, of interest and instruction. You know that the figure of a rock or a stone, is very frequently employed in the Bible to represent the person or offices of our Lord. Indeed, a rock may be said to have been the standing type of Christ through the wanderings in the wilderness; for the people, as St. Paul says to the Corinthians, "drank of that spiritual rock that followed them, and that rock was Christ." And Christ is indeed emphatically that rock, in the clefts or fissures of which, so to speak, may honey be found: "it pleased the Lord to bruise him, and put him to grief;" "but he was wounded for our transgressions, he was bruised for our iniquities." The little apparent likelihood of the rock yielding honey is paralleled by the strangedess of the fact, that Christ conquered by yielding, or subdued death by dying. And if you take the rock as specially that typical rock which was smitten by Moses in Horeb, then the promise of "honey from the rock" may be as much a promise of peculiar privileges to such as are diligent in righteousness, as that of eating of the increase of the fields. Every believer draws water from the rock; but the honey may be reserved for those who "by patient continuance in well-doing" show forth eminently the praises of Him who "bare their sins in his own body on the tree."

And there is indeed a hidden preciousness in the Saviour, in that "Rock of Ages cleft for us," which is apprehended and appreciated more and more as the believer goes on confiding in Christ, and striving to magnify Him in all the actions of his life. It is not merely a general sense of the sufficiency of the Atonement which such men obtain, a persuasion that there is provision in the Mediator for the wants of sinners, even the very chief. They go deeper than this: they find in Christ such stores of consolation, such "treasures of wisdom and knowledge," that they are never weary of searching, as they are never able to exhaust. Every necessity, as it arises, is supplied from his fulness; every cloud scattered by his brightness; every desire either satisfied, or its satisfaction guaranteed, by "the unsearchable riches" of his work of Mediation. Christ, if we may venture to use the expression, grows on the believer; he has but little idea of what a Saviour He is, when he first trusts Him with his soul: but, as he continues "looking unto Jesus," "considering Him that endured such contradiction of sinners against Himself," meditating "the agony and bloody sweat, the cross and the passion," he comes to know more and more of his Lord, and is both amazed and delighted at successive discoveries of his suitableness, his wonderfulness, his tenderness, his immensity. It is honey, so to speak, which he now obtains from Christ, not merely sustenance, but the most delicious and delicate food; for, as the Saviour communicates more and more of his richness, exciting and gratifying an appetite which craves celestial nutriment, assuring him of his unchangeable love, and allowing him foretastes of the banquet that shall be spread at the marriage supper of the Lamb—indeed, the believer will often exclaim with David of old, "How sweet are thy words unto my taste! yea, sweeter than honey to my mouth."

And this honey is from the rock, from the clefts of the rock. I must go, as it were, to the wounds of the Saviour, if I would obtain this precious and ever multiplying provision. I must be much with Him in the garden and on the cross; for it is by studying his awful endurances, by putting, like Thomas, though with other motives than this doubting disciple, "my finger into the print of the nails, and thrusting my hand into his side," that I may hope to gain acquaintance with the mystery of Redemption, and to find it more animating, and more comforting, as I find it more majestically, more splendidly obscure. And surely we may confidently say that, if there be a fulness, a preciousness, in the Redeemer, which is ascertained, though left unexhausted, as his mighty sacrifice is contemplated, and the lessons which it furnishes are wrought into the practice; if there be this reward to meek, consistent, persevering piety, that it finds deeper and deeper abundance in the Saviour, a sweetness and a richness in his offices which give indescribable emphasis to the scriptural expression, "the chiefest among ten thousand, and the altogether lovely;" and if, moreover, it be Christ as bruised and broken, pierced and riven, like the vast mass of stone on which the thunderbolt has fallen, which yields these choice treasures, oh, then, it must be true, that the soul which hungers and thirsts after righteousness, is not only made to "eat of the increase of the fields," but permitted to draw "honey from the rock, and oil from the flinty rock."

But whilst this is perhaps the most correct interpretation of the metaphorical expression, there is no reason why we should not advance another which is full also of important and interesting truth. There is an apparent opposition, as we have already observed, between the production and the place where produced,—the production honey, the place the rock. Honey is not what you would naturally look for from a rock; and therefore the promise, in its spiritual import, may fairly be regarded as denoting that, out of what looks stern, harsh, and insuperable, God will extract for his people, not only what shall nourish them, but what shall be sweet to their taste. This idea is put yet more strongly in the concluding words of the text, "oil out of the flinty rock;" the addition of the word "flinty" giving a stronger image of ruggedness, and therefore making the place less promising for any choice and delicate product.

And what is denoted by the metaphor, when thus interpreted or applied, if not that affliction is made by God to minister abundantly to the strength and comfort of his people; so that, when brought by his Providence into wild and rough places, they are enabled to find there even choicer provision than in verdant and cultivated spots? We need not adduce lengthened proof, that the promise, thus interpreted, is verified to the letter in the experience of the Church. The testimony of believers in every age has been, that the season of affliction has proved a season of rich communication from above, a season when God's faithfulness and love have been more realized than they ever were before, at which texts of Scripture have assumed a new and deeper meaning, and truths that hitherto had dwelt only in the head, have made their way into the heart, and diffused there a peace passing all understanding. Ask the mourners of present days, or ask the mourners of past, and with one voice,—if indeed they have received the chastisement as from the hands of a father,—they will assure you that God has seemed to choose the hour of trouble as the hour in which to give the more penetrating assurances of the graciousness of his purposes, to elevate the affections above transient and perishable things, and not only to centre them more fixedly on everlasting joys, but to afford foretastes of those joys, such as were never obtained whilst earthly happiness was unbroken and bright. Then it commonly is, when sorrow after sorrow has come upon the believer, and one beloved thing after an other has departed, that the soul has the strongest sense of the worth of religion, of the superiority of the future to the present, of the exquisite adaptation of the Bible to the wants of humanity, and of the exuberant consolations which are laid up in Christ. The Christian, with whom every thing goes smoothly, and on whom every thing looks smilingly, knows comparatively but little of what God is, and what the sympathy of the Saviour with those whose nature He assumed, and whose iniquities He bore. His circumstances do not, as it were, bring out the tenderness of his Maker, nor put to the proof the fellow-feeling of the Mediator. There must be darkness and dreariness for this. But when the darkness and the dreariness come, it is as though God had been waiting for an opportunity to shine beautifully on the soul, and Christ had reserved the manifestations of his compassionate care and regard, till their want would be most felt, and therefore also their worth. We need not enlarge upon this.

The experience of the righteous is so decisive in its testimony to the fact of affliction yielding rich spiritual sustenance, that it were but wasting time to employ it on proof. Honey from the rock—yea, the rock may be that which is hewn into a sepulchre, but even then may honey be found in its clefts. They who consign their friends, their children, their kinsmen, to the grave, believers if they be in Him who is "the Resurrection and the Life," "sorrow not even as others which have no hope," but draw sublime consolation from the receptacle in which they deposit their dead. Never have they so much felt the magnificence of the Mediator's triumph, as in surveying the triumph of death. The opened grave is to the eye of the Christian like an avenue, through which he can look into the invisible world, and discern the stupendous results of the victory won by the Captain of his salvation. And if you ask for an explanation of what may often be observed, that mourners seem elevated by acquaintance with death and the grave, as though, in scenes from which nature recoils, they had found the material of high growth in spiritual-mindedness, in consciousness of the saving power of Christ, in admiration of his work, in anticipation of its glorious consummation in their own happy experience, oh, there is nothing to be said but that it is God's ordinary course to discover Himself most to his people, where, on every human calculation, there is least to minister to their joy, and thus to make good the very expressive and comprehensive promise of their not only eating of the increase of the fields, but of their being made "to suck honey from the rock, and oil from the flinty rock."

Such, my brethren, are some of the privileges of true religion. The meaning of our text, as just explained or applied, is much the same as that of a passage in the writings of Hosea: "Behold, I will allure her, and bring her into the wilderness, and speak comfortably unto her; and I will give her vineyards from thence." The wilderness is not the place where we should naturally look for vineyards, no more than is the rock for honey. But God promises vineyards from the wilderness, and honey from the rock—indicating, under both figures, that those dispensations which have in them most of the painful and severe, the dreariness of the wilderness and the hardness of the rock, are both designed and adapted to yield to their subjects an abundance of the very choicest of spiritual provision. Yea, you must go to the wilderness for vineyards, and to the rock for honey. Not that there are no vineyards except in the wilderness, and no stores of honey except in the rock. The vine will grow in the sunny vale, and the bee find and deposit her treasures in the luxuriant garden; for religion is adapted as much to prosperity as to adversity. But we take, comparatively, little note of the vine amid a hundred other tokens of fertility, and the honey is perhaps almost untasted where every luscious fruit is offering itself abundantly. The worth of the vineyard is felt, when met with in the wilderness, and the honey, to be appreciated, must be found in the rock.

Such, then, we repeat it, are some of the privileges of true religion. And perhaps even yet our text may not have been fully expounded. For if, in its primary application to the Jews, it denoted the sustenance to be afforded them in Canaan, as applied to ourselves, it may relate to the provision laid up for us in Heaven, of which Canaan was the type. When God shall have "made us ride on the high places of the earth," and exalted us to his Kingdom above, the promise before us may be always receiving accomplishment. God shall be always communicating supplies from his own fulness, as age after age of expansion or enlargement passes over the redeemed. And these supplies may be still supplies of honey from the rock. There will be no exhaustion of Christ and Redemption. Never shall glorified spirits be weary of searching into the mysteries of grace, or leave those mysteries as thoroughly explored. Keep up, if you will, the metaphor of our text, and eternity shall be spent in contemplating and examining the Rock of ages: every moment shall discover a fresh cleft—the clefts in this rock (most strange, but most true) fitting it to bear up the universe; and every fresh cleft yielding fresh store of honey to satisfy desires which shall but grow with their supply.

But we must leave these contemplations, leave them however with the exclamation of the Prophet—an exclamation perhaps but too suitable to many now present—"Wherefore do ye spend money for that which is not bread, and your labour for that which satisfieth not?" Think not, be not so vain as to think, that you can find satisfaction in any finite good. Ye are not to be so cheated. Your souls are so constituted that they can find no resting-place except in God, nor that except through Christ. Alas! "man walketh in a vain shadow, and disquieteth himself in vain." "He feedeth on ashes," he pursueth shadows, and, all the while, there is bread which hath come down from Heaven, and everlasting realities solicit his acceptance. Be admonished, then, ye who seek happiness in something short of God, that you seek what is impossible. It is the cavity which might hold a planet seeking to be filled with a sand-grain. But look for happiness in God, and look for it through Christ, and God shall make you here "eat of the increase of the fields," for this may specially mark the believer's portion upon earth; and hereafter shall He satisfy you with "honey from the rock," for this may specially mark his portion through Eternity.

LECTURE III.

Easter.

1 PETER i. 3.

"Blessed be the God and Father of our Lord Jesus Christ, which according to his abundant mercy hath begotten us again unto a lively hope by the resurrection of Jesus Christ from the dead."

THERE are many characters under which God may be surveyed by the sinful, but only one under which He may be surveyed without fear. I may think of God as Creator; and very noble is the contemplation, as immensity, with its troop of worlds, opens itself before me, and every where reveals the work of one hand. I may think of God as the moral Governor of the Universe, and then, again, it is a magnificent contemplation, that one Being should be sending out his inspections over whatsoever liveth, and that, neither overcome by magnitude, nor perplexed by multiplicity, He should note every action, and register it for judgment. Or I may survey God in his several attributes; I may consider Him as omnipotent, and marvel at a power to which there is nothing great, and nothing small; I may regard Him as omniscient, and amazement may well possess me, as having "about my path and about my bed" the very Being who is occupying the furthest corners of infinite space; I may think of God as just, for how otherwise shall He judge the world? I may think of Him as holy—the very Heavens are not clean in his sight; I may think of Him as benevolent—the countless tenantry of earth, sea, and air, attest that his mercies are over all his works.

But what is it to me, a transgressor from the womb, that, as Creator, God has strewed immensity with his workmanship? Can I bless Him as Creator, when I may have been created only to be miserable? What is it to me that He should sit as universal King, and trace upon his book all deeds and all thoughts? Can I bless Him as moral Governor when what He observes of me must all help to condemn me? What is it to me that He is omnipotent? Can I bless Him for a power which it is impossible to escape? What that He is omniscient, what that He is just, what that He is holy? Can I bless Him for a knowledge which must extend to my every failing, for a justice which must pledge Him to visit every offence, for a holiness which must cause Him to regard the sinful with aversion? And even if I think of Him as compassionate, and full of loving-kindness, I may indeed well bless Him and praise Him for opening his hand, and showering down upon me mercies. But when I remember that his love must be limited and regulated by other attributes, and that these attributes are ranged against me as a sinner, how am I to bless Him even as benevolent, whilst I feel that benevolence is no security against my having to endure everlasting wretchedness?

It is thus, as we have often found occasion to tell you, that the disciples of natural theology can see nothing divine in which to take refuge. We are able, without the Bible, to see ourselves lost; but, oh! take away that Book, and who shall know how he may be saved? Thus creation may be glorious: every star may burn with Deity, every flower display his skill, every insect own his care; and God may be wonderful in his every attribute, his perfections commanding our admiration, each by itself, and, immeasurably more, in the harmonious combination; but who, nevertheless, amongst the children of men, is to arise and call Him blessed; who is to regard Him without terror; who, yet more, is to make Him the object of love? But Revelation has come in; the Gospel has been published: and now there is a character, under which this great, this awful, God may be viewed with emotions of exultation and thankfulness. We cannot fall before Thee, Father of Heaven and earth, and call Thee blessed, as Creator, though thine hand reared the architecture of the universe, and thy breath gave it animation. We cannot call Thee blessed, because of thy magnificent attributes, blessed as omnipotent, blessed as omniscient, blessed as omnipresent. But, dust and ashes though we be, conceived in sin, and shapen in iniquity, deserving thy wrath, and lying justly under thy heavy condemnation, we can exclaim, with the Apostle, in our text, "Blessed be the God and Father of our Lord Jesus Christ."

You may remember that St. Paul introduces his noble prayer on behalf of the Ephesians, in the same manner as St. Peter his lofty thanksgiving: "For this cause I bow my knees unto the Father of our Lord Jesus Christ." And we may suppose you well convinced, though you cannot be too often reminded, that there is no other character under which God can be approached with hope by the sinful. Except as we come to Him through a Mediator, except, that is, as we address Him as "the Father of our Lord Jesus Christ," we have no plea to urge why He should answer our prayers, or listen favourably to our praises. And at this most joyful season, we commemorate an event, which is our standing proof that He, who undertook the office of Mediator, was sufficient to the mighty work, and did indeed restore that access to God which human transgression had fatally interrupted. At this season did He, who had assumed our nature, on purpose that He might therein undergo the penalties provoked by our sins, and render that obedience to the law which was required, but hopelessly, at our hands, come forth from the grave, into which He had descended as our surety, not having seen corruption, though He had submitted to the original curse. And the Apostle, in our text, would evidently refer to the resurrection of Jesus, as, in some great sense, the cause of whatsoever spiritual blessings are now within our reach; for he commemorates it as having been through this resurrection that God hath "begotten us again to a lively hope." In the succeeding verses, indeed, he speaks in yet larger terms, declaring us begotten, not only to "a lively hope," but "to an inheritance incorruptible, undefiled, and that fadeth not away,"—thus making our entrance into Heaven altogether dependent on the resurrection of our Lord; so that, if, in discoursing on our text, we should take a large range, and gather within the consequences of what the Church has just commemorated, all our privileges as Christians, we shall evidently be borne out by the context, and not overpass the meaning of St. Peter.

We address you, then, in the words of the angels to the women: "Come, see the place where the Lord lay." Come and gaze on the deserted sepulchre, as on the scene where your victory was won, and your immortality secured. Come and see whether results were not effected, or consequences entailed, through the breaking forth of the Redeemer from the tomb, which may well urge you to chime in with the words of triumph which constitute our text. We desire that our Easter meditation may be animating, but simple; and we think that St. Peter's anthem—for such it might be called—will furnish the precise matter which this double object requires. Let us divide the anthem into its component parts: there is a thing done; there is the agency through which it is effected; there is the thankfulness which it ought to elicit. The thing done, is our being begotten again to a lively hope; the agency, through which it is effected, is the resurrection of Christ; and when these have been briefly considered, we shall be in a position to inquire, whether there be not abundnnt cause to exclaim, with St. Peter, "Blessed be the God and Father of our Lord Jesus Christ!"

Now we shall not insist at any length on the expression 'begotten again," which is here used by St. Peter. It is much the same with that employed by our Lord in his discourse with Nicodemus, when He asserted the necessity of a new birth, or a birth from above, in order to an entrance into the kingdom of Heaven. We would only desire to impress on every one present, that to be truly religious, implies a moral change too great to be effected by ourselves; but hardly to be mistaken, when once wrought by God. It must be great, too great for human power, if it can only be described as being "begotten again." But if thus great, it must be perceptible; if it may be wrought in secrecy, it must, when wrought, become palpable. And ye must seek the evidence of your being "new creatures," in the bent of your desires, in the tenor of your pursuits, in the objects of your affections; not in your external privileges, and not in your acquaintance with the scheme and doctrines of Christianity. The grand design of Christianity, so far as you are personally concerned, is the making you "new creatures;" and so long as this great design is not wrought out in you, you may be familiar with the bearings of the Gospel, and professed admirers of its beauties; but you derive nothing from your knowledge, but increased condemnation, a condemnation which you could not have incurred, had you been born in a heathen land, or never grafted into a Christian Church.

But we wish now principally to insist on its being "a lively hope" to which you are begotten, and to treat of the agency, or instrumentality, through which, according to St. Peter, this new creation is effected by God. We therefore turn at once to the event which the Church at this time commemorates, and will examine how the resurrection of Christ stands associated with the change on which we have spoken. You will observe at once that the resurrection of our Lord must have been regarded by the Apostle as giving, in some sense, all its efficacy to the Mediatorial work, seeing that he ascribes to this single event what we are wont to ascribe to the whole process of redemption. We regard it, and that, too, most justly, as owing exclusively to the interference of Christ, to his assuming human nature, and working out in that nature our reconciliation to God, that we can pass from a position of death to a position of life, and be received into that family from which we were banished by sin. It is to no solitary part of the Mediatorial work, but to that work as a whole, that we trace the mighty alteration in the condition of human kind,—an alteration such, that whereas, independently on the suretyship of Christ, there remained nothing for the race but the enduring, through eternity, the deserts of its sins, in and through that suretyship pardon has been made possible to all, yea, re-admission to the happiness, and to more than the happiness, which Adam forfeited for himself and his children. And, therefore, if we were called to define the instrumentality, through which the Creator has rekindled the quenched light of this creation, or revivified fallen humanity, we should assign the whole scheme of vicarious substitution, and endeavour to explain from it, how God can be just, and yet a justifier of sinners. How, then, is it that St. Peter, in stating the instrumentality which God has employed, should confine himself altogether to the resurrection of Christ? for it is exclusively to this that he attributes regeneration, the being "begotten again to a lively hope."

There is but little difficulty in answering this question. You must all be aware, that, so long as Christ lay in the grave, no evidence was afforded that his sacrifice had been accepted. He was still under the power of the curse, detained as a prisoner, so that the curse was not exhausted, nor "captivity led captive." When, however, He came forth from the grave a conqueror over death, then was there given incontestable proof that justice had no further claim upon man, because it had none upon his surety. The resurrection proclaimed to the universe, that the oblation made on Calvary, had sufficed to the taking away sin, and that, in thorough consistence with every attribute, God might now extend mercy to a race of transgressors. It is not that the virtue lay in the resurrection, rather than in the sacrifice; but that the resurrection proved the virtue of the sacrifice, attested its acceptance, and so made a clear way for the application of its merits. It may therefore, with the strictest truth, be affirmed that it was in raising his Son from the dead, that God restored hope to this fallen creation. By that act He declared that He had reconciled the world unto Himself, and so caused a new era to break on mankind. Neither is this all: for we learn unequivocally from Scripture that, had not Christ risen and ascended, the Holy Spirit would never have come down to renew the face of the earth. This Spirit was to descend as one of the results of Christ's Mediation: his manifold gifts were to be vouchsafed as the purchase of the Redeemer's death and passion, and dispensed by that Redeemer, exalted to the right hand of God. It might then be accurately said, that through Christ's resurrection was there secured to mankind that agency through which alone the lost image of God can be re-impressed on the soul, and any thing of moral renewal pervade the globe which sin has profaned. And if it were through the raising of his Son from the dead, that God stood ready to communicate the renovating influences of his Spirit, influences, without which there could be no renewal, but through which the waste and desert places may blossom as the rose, it follows, with the greatest precision, that God may be said to have begotten us again "through the resurrection of Christ." The resurrection of Christ obtained for us, and secured to us, the influences of the regenerating agent; and therefore it may literally be affirmed, that through this resurrection we are born anew of God.

Neither do we think it needful, in contemplating the results, or rather the efficacies of the resurrection, to limit the expression, "begotten again," to those cases of renewal which it ordinarily denotes in theological language. By speaking of our being begotten again to "a lively," or a living, "hope," the Apostle would seem to indicate something of an universal change as having passed, through Christ's resurrection, over this earth and its inhabitants. And such a change did actually pass: there was substituted a living hope for a dead, throughout every department of this creation, amongst its irrational as well as its rational tenants. It was not that heretofore there had been no hope whatever: for man is so constituted that he cannot live without hope: he must follow a meteor, when there is no star on the firmament. There was hope amongst men, even when truth had almost departed, and ignorance of God pressed heavily on all countries and classes. There was a hope that Deity might be propitiated; that, in some better world, the disorders of the present might be rectified, and goodness gain the ascendency for which here it had struggled in vain. Reason did something, in the midst of the ponderous night, to keep men from quite parting with the expectation of immortality, and, combining the teachings of conscience with the lingerings of tradition, caused a spectre of hope—for indeed it was never more substantial—to flit to and fro amid the cloud and the tumult. Yes, a spectre of hope; a dead thing; though, at times, it appeared amongst the living, and wore something of the hue which had belonged to the fresh and beautiful visitant, that had gladdened the earth whilst yet unstained by sin. But they who followed this spectre did but find themselves conducted into deeper darkness, and deserted where they most needed guidance. The spectre, which, to a superficial glance, presented all the brightness and motion of life, had only to be gazed on intently, or through the glasses of patient meditation, and it grew fainter and fainter, till at last it faded into air, and left the observer in increased gloom and perplexity. A living hope, a hope that should not merely perform some of the actions, but possess all the energies of life, that should not merely beckon onwards, but wait to be examined and handled—this never sprang from the reveries of philosophers, but eluded the searchings of those who laboured most bravely to open up a path to happiness hereafter. This hope, this living hope, paradoxical as it may sound, could only be generated through death, and spring only from the grave. It required, in order to its creation, in order to its existence, that a Mediator should die, and, by dying, sweep away the entailments of disobedience. And when, therefore, the vast debt was paid, and each of those obstacles to our forgiveness removed, which natural theology had in vain striven to displace, the spectral thing vanished, and the substantial arose. The Redeemer burst the sepulchre; and hope, living hope, which had been entombed there since the fall, and must have remained there, had not the mighty one entered to dissolve the spell, sprang gloriously forth, and gleamed and glanced over the long-darkened earth.

I know not what there was into which this living hope did not enter. The inanimate creation confessed its presence, and has ever since expected a day when new heavens, and a new earth, shall succeed into the place of the old, and a richer than the lost loveliness mantle all the scene of human habitation. The dust of buried generations might have been said to own its revival; for henceforward the dead awaited the sound of a trumpet, at which they must arise and put on incorruption. And the soul of man, heretofore perplexed by shadows, and beguiled by meteors, felt that the way into the holiest was indeed re-opened; and that, notwithstanding the many offences which had seemed to preclude it from fellowship with God, there were provided for it wings on which it might soar, and a plea which would be sure to prevail to the obtaining for it entrance into the heavenly city. Was it not then hope, living hope, which followed the Redeemer as He brake away from death, which sprang with Him from the sepulchre, as though it had waited that the stone should be riven, in order that it might emerge and re-visit the earth? We have confessed already that there was a spectre of hope, even when there was no knowledge of Christ, a lingering form which haunted the globe, and cheated the weary and the lost. But hope itself was in the grave: the spectre is of the dead, not of the living: who shall lay the spectre, by reviving the departed? This, again and again be it said, was the work of the Mediator: He scattered the shadows by revealing the substance. His was the office, his the achievement, of destroying the works of the devil, and reinstating the earth in the place whence it fell. What He undertook, He accomplished: his resurrection both completed and attested the accomplishment: but, nevertheless, it was living hope, rather than exterminated evil, which was the immediate result and trophy of his victory. He did not at once annihilate death, though we know Him to have abolished it: He did not sweep away sin, He did not banish sorrow. To a superficial observer, the resurrection might seem to have wrought no difference in the face of this creation, the same dark trains of guilt and grief appearing to traverse it in undiminished force. But the alteration was wrought in hope: hope started from the dust, put on her beautiful garments, spake to the prostrate, and pointed them to days of glory and triumph. It may be that death yet reigns: but hope, standing by the tomb of the Redeemer, can smile even at death, and be most alive in the midst of dissolution. "Iniquities prevail against us;" but hope, resting on the finished work of mediation, anticipates their forgiveness, and full deliverance from their power. The traces of devastation are yet around us: the whole creation groaneth and travaileth in pain: tears are still shed, hearts are still wrung: but hope, hope that cannot make ashamed, because its life is from Him whose word cannot fail, hope walks amid the wide desolation; peoples it with all the imagery of restitution and gladness; and in the magnificence of a firmament, of which the Lord God Almighty Himself shall be the sun, and in the splendours of an inheritance into which shall enter nothing that defileth, beholds exultingly the incontestable evidences of the complete spoiling of principality and power.

This, this, it is, which was instantly effected through the resurrection of Christ: other results are yet future: but hope rose with Him from the tomb, and remained, when He ascended, to animate those whose path is through misery, and whose struggle with corruption. And we may well, therefore, give our assent to the accuracy of the representation contained in our text. Setting aside, for a moment, the peculiar sense in which the being "begotten again" was to be taken with respect individually to believers, who will not allow that the whole earth leapt, as it were, into a new existence, an existence of hope, of living hope, when the Mediator, in the strength of his divinity, returned from the dead? I could imagine the step of the risen Conqueror heard in the solitude, heard in the crowd—in the homes of the living, and among the silences of the dead—by things animate and things inanimate—but every where wakening hope, as though the mysterious sound broke a fatal spell, and freed the enthralled spirit. And I could suppose our text uttered by as many, and as varied, voices as pealed on the ear of St. John, when there rose the universal ascription of honour to God and the Lamb—"every creature which is in Heaven, and on the earth, and under the earth, and such as are in the sea, and all that are in them," joining in the confession, that they had been "begotten again to a lively hope by the resurrection of Jesus Christ from the dead."

And, surely, after having thus engaged you with proof, that whatever of regeneration has yet passed over the earth, and whatever may be looked for in future days, ought distinctly to be traced to the resurrection of Christ as a cause, we need not adduce lengthened argument to show that we have reasons, at Easter, for exclaiming with the Apostle, "Blessed be the God and Father of our Lord Jesus Christ." Who that thinks on the provision which has been made for the opening of the kingdom of Heaven to all believers, for the restoration of the lost glories of this earth, for the extirpation of evil from the universe, for the destruction of death by a general resurrection, and refers all this, as it ought to be referred, exclusively to the fact, that, having died unto sin once, Christ is alive for evermore—can require to be urged to join in an anthem, whose chorus shall be, "The Lord is risen, the Lord is risen indeed?"

But let us select one blessing from the throng, that which Easter should specially commend to our thoughts; and let us inquire whether any will keep silence, when praise is being woven, because there shall yet be brought to pass the saying that is written, "Death is swallowed up in victory?" We are not sure whether this great article of Christian faith, the resurrection of the body, obtains its due share of attention and affection, even amongst those who "love the Lord Jesus in sincerity." We rather think that there are many, who, wearied with long struggle with the corruptions of the flesh, and accustomed to regard and find the body as nothing but an incumbrance in the highest duties of religion, derive scarcely any delight from anticipating the Resurrection, and would hardly be conscious of much change in their hopes and expectations, were there to come a sudden intimation that no trumpet will sound to wake up the dead. There is a sort of an unacknowledged, but prevalent feeling, as though there were a necessary opposition between what is material and what spiritual, and as though, in getting quit of the body, we should become fitted for the purest and most refined happiness. And, of course, the question is not whether God, if He pleased, might make the soul, in her separation from the body, the recipient of a very lofty and exquisite felicity. We may admit without detriment, that the soul might be unspeakably happy, were God pleased that it should remain, throughout eternity, dissevered from the body; so that, even were there no Resurrection, a Christian might confidently anticipate a portion of vast glory and blessedness. There is, however, all the difference between the believing that God could make the soul ineffably happy, if it pleased Him to leave the body for ever in the grave, and the separating, in any measure, the soul from the body in our expectations of happiness, now that God hath appointed and revealed their lasting re-union. The question is not, whether the soul might be happy without the body: the ascertained fact is, that the soul is to be united to the body; and that, whatever its enjoyments and occupations during the season of separation, the full glories and felicities of the justified will not be attained until that which is sown in corruption shall have been raised in incorruption. And, therefore, if we attach little worth to the doctrine of the Resurrection; if, regarding the body as a clog, we fix our thoughts on a purely spiritual happiness—purely spiritual in the sense of having no alliance with what is material—it is manifest that we are but substituting our own fancies for the truths of Revelation.

We do not then attempt, by any abstract reasoning, to prove to you the importance of the resurrection of the body; we fasten you to the fact, that the body is to be glorified as well as the soul, that the happiness of the soul will be incomplete, until re-united to the body; and from this we require you to learn, that you have an incalculable interest in the great truth that the dead shall live again; and that it is no mere speculation, which might safely be spared from your creeds. And so soon as you thus give its due place to the resurrection of the body, and regard matter as well as spirit as redeemed by the Saviour, you will rise in your estimate of "the earthly house of this tabernacle," and shun the employing it to base and low ends. The body cannot be an ignoble thing, which it is emancipation to quit, and a privilege to throw aside, if the Lord of glory shed blood for its redemption, and if He now hold the keys of Hades and of death, that He may guard every atom of its dust, when dissolved, and broken up through separation from the soul. And I can join in the exclamation of our text, and pronounce, "Blessed be the God and Father of our Lord Jesus Christ," when it is simply our own resurrection which is regarded as the regeneration wrought through the Mediator's. I can bless God that this mortal is to put on immortality. I know not of what a disembodied soul may be capable: but I know, that, as originally created in the image of his Maker, man was a compound being, matter and spirit; and I conclude it, therefore, essential to his perfection, that he should be this compound through eternity. And this makes me thankful that the body is to rise: without this, the second Adam cannot have won for me all that the first Adam lost. I am thankful moreover for the Resurrection, because, of all motives to the subduing and keeping under the body, and to the presenting it a living sacrifice unto God, there is none comparable, in its intenseness, to that derived from its future appointments. It puts a sort of sacredness on the body, to regard it as destined, with the soul, to the spiritualities of eternity, not to be thrown aside, when its inhabitant has broken away, and soared to a purer land, but only to be purified, that it may again receive that inhabitant, and be its dwelling-place in the burning light of God's presence.

Not, we say, to be thrown aside. It is very easy, and very specious, to enlarge on the folly of paying any honour to that which must become the prey of the worm, of conveying, with something of state, to the grave that which is turning into a mass of corruption, and then perhaps erecting a monument to mark the resting-place of a certain portion of dust. If we knew nothing of a Resurrection, if we believed that the body was to be given over for ever to corruption, we might come to regard it as a worthless and dishonoured thing, and to consider that the showing it any respect, in its lifelessness and loathsomeness, were unworthy of the rational and degrading to the religious. But not whilst we believe in the general Easter of this creation. Not whilst we believe that the grave is but a temporary habitation, and that what is sown a natural body is to be raised a spiritual. The funeral ceremony attests and does homage to the doctrine of the Resurrection. It is not in honour of the body, as mouldering into dust, that a decent state should attend its interment; but in honour of the body, as destined to come forth gloriously and indissolubly reconstructed. I have no affection for the tablet and the monument, if it were only to mark where the foul worm hath battened: but I look with pleasure on the recording marble, as indicating a spot where the trumpet of the Archangel shall cause a sudden and mysterious stir, and Christ win a triumph as the Resurrection and the Life. And we again say that the thought of what the body is reserved for should lead to our giving due honour to the body, and our shunning the employing its members as instruments of unrighteousness. I should feel an awe on entering a Temple which might be shattered and soiled, but of which I knew, that, through a divine power, it was to be splendidly rebuilded, and made as a shrine in whose depths the very Deity would abide. I could not turn that Temple to common uses: I could desecrate it neither to the businesses nor the revelries of life; but, as I passed along its ruined arches, or marked how its columns were stained, I should seem to hear the approachings of the Divinity, as He came to possess and preside; and I should be too full of reverential dread to do aught that might defile a structure that was yet to be so hallowed. The body is such a Temple—shattered, if you will; soiled, if you will—but destined to be rebuilded, and visibly occupied by Godhead. Shall I then pollute it? Shall I throng its courts with the sheep and the oxen? Shall I burn on its altars the fires of base passion? Oh, the man, whose thoughts are much on the Resurrection of the body, will be also the man whose efforts are much towards the subjugation of the body; and if it were only, that, from knowing to what flesh is appointed, he feels nerved to the wrestling with those lusts which war against the soul, he will gladly exclaim with St. Peter, contemplating his own Resurrection as insured by that of Christ, "Blessed be the God and Father of our Lord Jesus Christ."

Blessed indeed, for ever blessed be God, that He hath not left us in our low estate, but hath raised up a horn of Salvation for us in the house of his servant David. Blessed, for ever blessed, be God for the Gospel of his Son Jesus Christ. But let us see to it that we have scriptural warrant for appropriating to ourselves the provisions and promises of this Gospel. Let us diligently remember, according to the inference which we deduced from the peculiar phraseology of our text, that a great and vital change must pass over the man who is truly a believer in Christ. "If any man be in Christ, he is a new creature." How striking is that expression of our Lord to Nicodemus, "That which is born of the flesh is flesh, and that which is born of the Spirit is spirit." It is as much as to affirm that man is all flesh through his first birth, and all spirit through his second. There is no distinction allowed between soul and body; the soul is spoken of, in the one case, as assimilated to the body, and therefore fleshly; the body, in the other case, as assimilated to the soul, and therefore spiritual. We can have very little difficulty in assenting to the accuracy of the first representation; but the best amongst us may well be staggered by the second. There is no debate that the human soul becomes, through transgression, of apparently the same nature with the body, earthly in its desires and attachments; so that, notwithstanding its ethereal origin and properties, it might be designated fleshly. But, alas! how little is there amongst

Christians, from which we could infer, that if, in the natural man, the body has dragged down the soul to the level of the flesh, in the renewed man, the soul has elevated the body to the level of spirit. How few have the body in such subjection to the soul, that the dominant principle is not carnal, but spiritual. Yet it is evident from the striking words which we have quoted from the discourse of our Lord, that the regeneration of our nature ought to effectuate this result, or be evidenced by it; and that we stop short of what new birth is designed to produce, so long as the soul obtains not the ascendency, and makes not the body its minister and auxiliary.

Let us see to it, if we profess ourselves true disciples of Christ, that we labour incessantly as showing forth in the life this renewal of our nature. May the words, which are addressed to you in this place, stimulate you to the righteous endeavour. We preach, and you listen, for Eternity. Oh then, with what faithfulness should the minister speak, and with what meekness should the hearer receive, the engrafted word. We can but add an earnest prayer, that the Lord of all power and might, without whom nothing is strong, nothing is holy, would give his blessing with his Gospel as here feebly, but affectionately, uttered. We know that nothing is to be done but through the influence of God's Spirit. Men are not to be converted, and, when converted, not confirmed and edified, through processes of argument or laboured appeals. The work must be of God; through God, and through Him alone, are our weapons mighty to the casting down of strong-holds. But we may expect his blessing, if you on your part, and I on mine, seek it by diligent prayer. And having this blessing, we may look for great things. When the last, the great Easter-day breaks on this creation, and thousands are being gathered to sing the song of Moses and the Lamb, there may be some who, as they join the mighty orchestra, shall remember thankfully the Gospel as heard in this place, and bless the God and Father of our Lord Jesus Christ, for having here begotten them again to a lively hope.

LECTURE IV.

The Witness in Oneself.

1 John v. 10.

"He that believeth on the Son of God hath the witness in himself."

A Christian minister should often press upon his hearers the difference between historical and saving faith, and entreat them to take heed lest, to the ruin of the soul, they confound things which are so essentially distinct. We may wonder indeed that the confusion should be made; for it is quite clear that historical faith is, in no sense, influential; and a faith which is not influential, can hardly be suspected of being saving. No man's conduct, for example, is at all affected by his belief in the actions which are ascribed to Julius Cæsar. If a new history of ancient days is put into his hands, he may store his mind with fresh incidents, but not his heart with fresh motives: he will never dream of giving to his faith in the death of some great leader or philosopher of antiquity, any uniform dominion over his actions and conversation. He has no personal concern with the worthies of whom he reads: they are nothing to him, and he is nothing to them, except as the possession of a common nature makes a link of association. The chasm of many centuries separates between himself and the heroes or sages of olden times; and though this chasm may for a while be overleaped, whilst he ponders their achievements, or studies their writings, yet there is no such thing as the bringing down antiquity into present being, annihilating the interval of days, and walking side by side with the dead through existing scenes and occupations.

And you will hardly require proof, that faith of this kind is not the faith which we are called on to put in the Gospel of Christ. If the Bible be dealt with just as we deal with the volumes of history, satisfying ourselves first, on external evidence, of the authenticity and credibility of the work, and then assenting, by a cold act of the understanding, to the veracity of the facts alleged in its pages; certainly we shall never believe with what the Bible itself calls belief; for the truths, to which we have assented, become not the heart-springs by which our actions are guided. The seat, in short, of historical faith is the head; whilst the requisition of the Almighty is, "My son, give me thine heart;" and the head and the heart, if not far removed in the body, are widely separated in all that relates to vital religion.

We introduce our discourse with these few remarks on the difference between saving and historical faith, in order that we may point out to you the difference between the evidences by which the two are supported. The historical faith requires nothing but what are popularly called the evidences of Christianity; and a volume from the hands of such writers as Paley or Chalmers, gathering to a point with industry and intelligence the scattered testimonies to the divine origin of our religion, suffices, with every inquiring mind, to produce a conviction that the Bible is no "cunningly-devised fable." But saving faith, whilst it does not discard the evidences which serve as out-works to Christianity, possesses others which are peculiar to itself; and just as historical faith being seated in the head, the proofs on which it rests address themselves to the head, so saving faith being seated in the heart, in the heart dwell the evidences to which it makes its appeal. There has often been given melancholy proof, that men may be thoroughly acquainted with the evidences of Christianity, and yet be completely ignorant of its vital truths. And the caution can never be out of place, that we confound not the historical with the saving belief; nor conclude that, because we can demonstrate the inspiration of Scripture, we have felt its power, and yielded to its authority.

It is essential that we bear these considerations in mind, as we proceed to review the assertion of our text, "He that believeth on the Son of God hath the witness in himself." The character, to which the Apostle refers, is unquestionably that of a true believer in Christ, one who believes to the saving of the soul, and not merely with the assent of the understanding. Hence, according to our foregoing remarks, he is one who must be possessed of an evidence widely differing from that which goes to the establishing historical faith; and, consequently, we find that St. John affirms the existence of such evidence, saying, "He that believeth on the Son of God hath the witness in himself;" in himself, so that the witness can have nothing whatever in common with the logic of the Schools, or the deductions of analysis, but is a secret, though indelible thing, graven upon tablets which are not to be surveyed by the natural eye. The context of the passage might indeed warrant our confining the witness to points immediately associated with the great truth that Jesus is the Christ. For the Apostle begins the chapter with stating, "Whosoever believeth that Jesus is the Christ is born of God;" and the strain of his after argument has a clear and continued reference to this first announcement. But there is no necessity, that, in discoursing on the passage, we should confine ourselves to this or that portion of the Gospel. The Messiahship of Jesus is a kind of centre, whence emanate those various truths, through belief in which we become raised from the ruins of the fall; and no man can have faith in Jesus as the Christ, the anointed of God, except so far as he has faith in the life-giving doctrines which he was anointed to proclaim. Come, then, with us to a survey of sundry of these doctrines. The whole Bible may be epitomized as exhibiting man's state by nature, and his state by grace—let us seize on these two grand divisions; and let us labour to show you, that he that "believeth on the Son of God hath the witness in himself," first, to the ruin consequent on transgression; and secondly, to the rescue perfected by redemption.

Now, it is the result only of spiritual perception, that man beholds and recognises in himself a fallen being. He cannot indeed wholly shut his eyes to the ravages which sin has made in our creation; and he must be an infidel as to the first principles of even natural theology, if he think that the scathed and stricken globe, on which he dwells, is the fair unspotted world which the Almighty regarded with infinite complacence. The traces of wrath are too manifest throughout the provinces of the earth, to allow of doubt in any reflecting mind, that some fearful apostacy has divided us from God, and that we stand not in the rank which we occupied, when the Omnipotent fashioned man after the image of Himself. But, individually considered, the great result to ourselves of the fall of Adam has been such a prostration of moral power, that we have no ability of turning unto God, or of doing things that shall be pleasing in his sight. We are so fallen as to be unable to rise; and herein it is that we maintain the need of spiritual perception; for the carnal, whilst it may distinguish, accurately enough, the lineaments of decay which demonstrate the introduction of evil, looks upon man only as he "lieth in wickedness," and therefore discerns nothing of his incapacity to rise. The effort must be made, before the incapacity can be displayed; and the making the effort presupposes the operations of a higher agency than human; so that, with all the confession which is generally and frankly put forth, of the tremendous consequences of early rebellion, of the loss of birthright, and of the degenerate and sunken estate of our race, the heart of the apostacy is never approached, and the man of historical faith cannot, in strict truth, know himself fallen, because mere historical faith will never lead him to strive to rise from his degradation.

But how different with the man who truly "believeth on the Son of God." He "hath the witness in himself." He has been subjected to the workings of the Spirit of the Lord. He has passed through the successive processes of conviction and conversion. He has, it may be, long resisted the motions which would have led him to Christ, and gone about to "establish a righteousness of his own;" and not until his own insufficiency has been practically proved to him by repeated stumblings, when, in his own strength, he attempted to turn unto God, has that full change been effected which left him "a new creature," born again of an incorruptible seed. And we ask you whether it will not necessarily come to pass, that, when this renewed man looks into himself, and finds, in his own experience, accumulated proof of the desperate alienation of our nature from God—proof which has been furnished by vain endeavours at saving himself, and bold resistance to the teachings of the Holy Ghost—we ask you whether it will not come to pass that this man will so thoroughly understand the doctrine of original sin, that he may be affirmed to have "the witness in himself" to the moral ruin which followed on transgression?

And not only so; but the man in question is a believer in Christ Jesus as the High Priest of our profession, who hath "put away sin by the sacrifice of Himself." We often have to tell you that no correct estimate can be formed of sin, unless we measure its enormity by the greatness of the satisfaction which was required for its pardon. And only so far as the heinousness of sin is discovered, can the fearfulness be felt of our condition by nature; and therefore we may justly maintain that he alone understands rightly the fall of man, who understands rightly the evil of transgression. But external testimony will never satisfy us of this evil. Not indeed that it is impossible to gather, from such testimony, a confused and general estimate of sin. We may look at its palpable and pestilential consequences, and hence infer its destructive and appalling properties; so that a mind, over which none of the renewing influences of God's Spirit have passed, may picture to itself the lengthened trains of disease and sadness and death which have darkened creation, and fix upon sin as the desecrating cause which ushered in the retinue. Yea, the natural mind may advance even a step further than this: it may have an occasional dread of approaching wrath: it may attain a consciousness, and that, too, a painful and almost paralyzing consciousness, that an eternal penalty is annexed to transgression of God's law, and that all who die at enmity with the Most High, must, in recompense of their sinfulness, be visited with fiery indignation.

But, with all this, there is nothing which can strictly be called knowledge of sin; there is no faith in the sacrifice which has been offered for sin; whereas, he who "believes on the Son of God," "hath the witness in himself," to the immensity of sin, for he has, in himself, a vigorous perception of the mysterious and awful things of the Atonement. Just think what it is to gaze, with an eye of faith, on the Redeemer of mankind, during his career of self-denial and suffering. At each point of that career, He stooped beneath the weight of imputed transgression; and though He was infinitely delighted to execute the will of the Father, yet so stern and crushing was the pressure of guilt, when laid on spotless innocence, that the Apostle declares that even Christ "pleased not Himself" in the work which He had undertaken to achieve. His whole life was one continued oblation; and from the moment in which the divine nature coalesced with the human, up to that in which, amid the heavings of creation, the Mediator breathed out his soul in agony, yet in love, the reconciliation of the sinner to a holy God was going gradually forwards; and no pang could have been spared from the anguish, without rendering the reconciliation incomplete. What, then, must be the heinousness of sin, if its pardon could be procured by nothing short of this costly and complicated endurance! The man, who believes in the Son of God as baptized, for our sakes, with the baptism of woe and of blood, will individualize, as it were, the atonement. He will feel that Christ Jesus, by his agony and passion, redeemed all; but he will also feel that the same agony and passion would have been indispensable in order to redeem one. Had he himself stood alone upon the earth, yea, and had he offended only in one solitary tittle, still the same stupendous instrumentality must have been employed; Godhead and manhood must still have combined; and the complex person, the man Jesus Christ, must have wrestled, and toiled, and wept, and died; otherwise the lonely offender must have sunk beneath the vengeance due to his lonely offence, and not have been the less stricken by the wrath of the Almighty, from being the single object that had roused it into action.

And it is essential to true faith in Christ as our surety and sacrifice, that apprehensions such as these should be entertained by the believer. Sin is beheld through the wounds of the Saviour; and, thus beheld, its lightest acting is discerned to be infinitely dishonouring to God, and infinitely destructive to man. But it is "in himself" that the believer finds the witness. Faith brings Christ into his heart; and then the mysteries of Calvary are developed; and the man feels his own share in the Crucifixion; feels, as we have already described, that his own sins alone were of guilt enough to make his Salvation impossible without that Crucifixion. And if such internal feelings be the necessary accompaniment, or, rather, a constituent part, of saving faith in the Lord Jesus Christ, is it not undeniable, that "he who believeth on the Son of God hath the witness in himself" to the heinousness of sin; in other words, "hath the witness in himself" to the ruin consequent on transgression?

Or, if we push the inquiry further, we may still reach the same conclusion. The fall has entailed upon man corrupt affections and impaired faculties; and much of the moral ruin, with which the earth is overspread, results from the legacy thus fatally bequeathed. But until there is conflict in the heart—and conflict there will be none until the opposing principle of grace is introduced—man remains comparatively ignorant of the actual bias and tendency of his nature. When, however, he "believes on the Son of God," then he finds "a witness in himself" to the truth of all which Scripture testifies concerning the imbecility and iniquity of man. Is the heart characterized as "deceitful above all things, and desperately wicked?" Believing on Christ, he hath "the witness in himself;" for though he "keep the heart with all diligence," yet does he find it continually "starting aside like a broken bow," and plotting treason against the Saviour. Is it asserted that "the flesh lusteth against the Spirit, and the Spirit against the flesh?" He hath "the witness in himself;" for he finds, with St. Paul, "a law in his members warring against the law of his mind, and bringing him into captivity to the law of sin, which is in his members." Are we told that "we are not sufficient of ourselves to think any thing as of ourselves?" He hath "the witness in himself;" seeing that the review of every day covers him with confusion, showing him, that, however much may have been attempted, little or nothing has been done, in the work of secret communion with God. Is the Christian's life represented as a battle? is the power, possessed by apostate spirits, described as tremendous? is the scriptural delineation of the believer that of a stranger and pilgrim, journeying painfully through a moral waste, and surrounded on all sides by malignant foes? Why, to all this, he hath "the witness in himself." So long as he did not believe on the Son of God, every thing went smoothly: he was not conscious of the power of indwelling corruption, for he attempted no resistance to that power; he knew nothing of the might of evil spirits, for he had waged no war with these spirits; he felt not the earth to be a wilderness, for he had made it his home, and was enamoured of its desolations. But, believing on the Son of God, every thing is changed. He has been required to "crucify the flesh with its affections and its lusts;" and he hath "the witness in himself" to the strength of the carnal despotism. He has been sent into the field to "wrestle with principalities and powers;" and he "hath the witness in himself," that their might is only rivalled by their subtlety. He has had his hopes turned on "a city which hath foundations, whose maker and whose builder is God;" and the contrast between what is promised, and what is possessed, has given him "the witness in himself," that the things of earth are unsatisfying and vain.

So that we may safely affirm, that, whatever the statements which Scripture advances in relation to the condition and circumstances entailed upon man by the fall, the believer in Christ does not turn to any external sources, in order to gain assurance of their truth. He goes into himself. Just as it is certain that blessings must be taken from us before we can fully appreciate their beauty and worth, so also, in spiritual things, we must be delivered from curses, before we can rightly estimate their depth and their terror. It is not the man who is asleep on the edge of a precipice, who is conscious of the awfulness of the gulph—wake him, and his wild look, and thrilling cry, measure to you the danger from which he finds himself delivered. We know comparatively nothing of our natural condition, until rescued from it; the fetters are too polished to grate, and too transparent to be commonly discerned—break them, and we learn, by the fragments, the number and thickness of the links. Thus it is the believer alone who can have just apprehensions of the consequences of early apostacy; he gains those apprehensions, as we have endeavoured to show you, from operations carried on within the sphere of his own heart. And, therefore, take the survey, how you will, of the evil of sin, of the degradation of man through transgression, of the blight which has passed over his powers, of the eclipse which hath darkened his happiness—oh, books will give you nothing adequate, philosophy will be found at fault, a mere historical faith will leave you without any convincing demonstration, any sufficient exhibition; but this proposition remains firm and unshaken, "He that believeth on the Son of God hath the witness in himself."

We hasten to the second, and perhaps more obvious truth—namely, that "he, who believeth on the Son of God, hath the witness in himself" to the rescue perfected by Redemption. Now we think, that, when St. Paul styled himself "the chief of sinners," he used language which ought not to be explained by reference to the persecution and blasphemy, of which he had been guilty in the days of his ignorance. It would be hard, or rather impossible, to show that Saul of Tarsus was a sinner "above others," because, out of blind love for the law of Moses, he raged furiously against those who, as he thought, were subverting that law. He sinned grievously; but he sinned ignorantly; and the readiness with which, when better taught, he espoused the cause which he had striven to destroy, proved incontestably, that, however mistaken and misdirected his zeal, he had not been actuated by any obstinate enmity to truth and its author. We rather think, that, in calling himself "the chief of sinners," St. Paul used language which every renewed man would be equally disposed to adopt. We should question whether there could be genuine conversion, apart from this honest appropriation of pre-eminence in sinfulness. The man may not have been a murderer; he may not have been an adulterer; his conduct may never have been deformed by the grosser workings of ungodliness. If the extent of sinfulness is to be computed by direct and flagrant breaches of the precepts of the second table, there may be many of his fellow-creatures to whom the title of "chief" is palpably more appropriate. But the principle on which this computation proceeds, is manifestly incorrect. If we may fairly talk of degrees in sinfulness, the circumstances of the sinner must be taken into account—his means, his opportunities, the godly motions which he has resisted, the admonitions he has despised, the warnings he has neglected. And then only can one man be fairly proved to be a greater sinner than another, when, having received as much in assistance, he has rendered back less in obedience.

But this is a calculation which we have no power of making. Known unto God alone are the strivings of the Spirit with the hearts of the children of men; and whilst each amongst us may be able to answer for himself, as to his own resistance to the motions of heavenly grace, it is not possible that he should answer for his neighbour: we can never tell whether the same amount of obstacle have been placed in the path of other transgressors, as we know to have been set before ourselves in the career of waywardness and evil; and, therefore, neither can we tell whether another have sinned against as much of light, and as much of grace, as we feel that we ourselves have resisted: so that, if sinfulness be rightly estimated, estimated by what has been done, placed in juxtaposition with what has been withstood, we maintain that every renewed man is bound, by that charity which "hopeth all things," to account himself "the chief of sinners,"—not reckoning by the fact that his misdoings have been less flagrant than those of another, but proceeding on the supposition that his privileges may have been greater.

And if it be a necessary result of conversion, or of believing on the Son of God, that a man should feel himself "the chief of sinners," then think what "a witness he hath in himself" to the glorious truth, that "the blood of Jesus Christ cleanseth from all sin." Faith has been implanted in his heart; and faith is that stupendous principle which gathers forgiveness, and propitiation, and intercession into our homes, and makes them, as it were, our own property, and admits us into the actual possession of mercies, known hitherto only by name, and rumour, and discourse; and hence the Gospel, which, when heard, was, at best, only a pleasing sound, like that of music on the waters, becomes, when believed in, an ample charter consigning to us a magnificent eternity. And if it be only remembered, that, as a consequence on this appropriation, which is effected by faith, the man becomes assured of the forgiveness of sins, and of the complete revocation of that edict of banishment which had gone forth against him, in common with the countless myriads of Adam's posterity, why, whither shall he turn, except to himself, when he would seek evidence of the majestic plenitude and power of redemption? He examines his own criminality; and he is forced to the verdict that he is "the chief of sinners." And yet he is pardoned, reconciled, accepted—he, the chief; he, whose case might therefore have been pronounced the most difficult, the least hopeful; his sins are blotted out, and the blood of atonement has prevailed to the bringing him nigh unto God. Where, then, shall the case be found, which the virtue of Christ's passion will not reach? Where the individual, whose offences are so complicated, whose resistance to the Holy Spirit has been so protracted and obstinate, that he is utterly excluded from the ranges of mercy, and thrown too far from God to be brought back by the Mediator's blood? The believer hath "the witness in himself" that "the chief of sinners" is forgiven. But if the greatest have found mercy, every other may find mercy. Therefore he "hath the witness in himself" to the unbounded freedom with which the compassions of God extend to the whole of human kind. He needs not argument; he requires no curious and well-arranged proofs; he looks into himself, himself a monument of distinguishing grace, himself a brand plucked out from the burning—and, oh! he will not ask the theological critic, or the polemical divine, to unfold to him the greatness of salvation: he will rather declare, with tears of gladness and thankfulness, that he "hath the witness in himself" that "this is a faithful saying, and worthy of all acceptation, that Christ Jesus came into the world to save sinners."

And, besides all this, the doctrine of the influences of the Holy Ghost is a prime characteristic of the Gospel scheme; and great are the offices of this third person in the Trinity in the work of human salvation. But the believer has himself been made the subject of these offices; and he can therefore feel, "in himself," the clearest testimony to their reality and extent. The Spirit is represented to us as effecting such a renovation of the creature, that, from a lover of sin, it becomes a lover of God, and is clothed with something of the same garniture as Adam was when he tenanted Paradise. The believer looks into himself, and he finds himself "a new creature;" "old things are passed away: behold, all things are become new;" and thus he "hath the witness in himself" to the renewing power of the Holy Ghost. And it is, further, the office of the Spirit to lead on the new creature from one degree, both of holiness and knowledge, to another; not suffering him to be stationary, but training him continually for "the inheritance of the saints." Of this office, also, the believer "hath the witness in himself." His growth may be slow: often may he be tempted to question whether any progress is made; still, let there be a fair comparison of different periods of the Christian life, and marks of advance will certainly be discernible: the workings of sin are more detected; the eye is more single; the objects of earth are less attractive; prayer is more earnest; praise is more fervent; and therefore it will necessarily come to pass that he "hath the witness in himself" that the Spirit sanctifieth all the elect people of God. The connection between justification and sanctification, between faith as the producing cause, and works as the necessary fruit, is thus found amongst those fundamental truths to which the inward witness testifies. The believer looks within; he feels that he would not barter for the universe the persuasion that salvation is wholly of God, and that no righteousness of his own can help forward his acceptance with his Creator. But then he also feels that the amazing love, which is displayed in this free redemption, binds him to God by ties a thousand times stronger than those of legal obedience; and that the fact of nothing being required in the way of merit, is an inducement, the most powerful, that every thing should be attempted out of filial affection.

We enter not now on any proof of this indissoluble connection between simple faith, and active zeal. We refer to believing experience; we appeal to its records. Has it not always been found that the strongest faith is accompanied by the warmest love; and that, in the very proportion in which the notion has been discarded of works availing to justification, have works been wrought as evidences and effects of justification? The believer feels and finds the truth of this "in himself." His whole soul is drawn out towards God. As to "continuing in sin, that grace may abound," this presupposes that he takes pleasure in sin; whereas it is the very constitution of his nature to hate sin; and, therefore, Antinomianism would be to him a kind of crucifixion: he has crucified the old nature, through the assistance of God; and now you would make him crucify the new, in opposition to God. No; rather he will love much, because much has been forgiven; and whenever he feels the heart stirred within him at the memory of the unlimited and unconditional mercies of which he is the object, and the soul warmed into ecstasy at the contemplation of blessings received, and longing to show her dedication to her Almighty Benefactor by expatiating, with tender solicitude, over a sinful and suffering world, surely it may be said of the believer that he hath a "witness in himself" to the illustrious truth, that, where the Spirit implants faith, it makes that faith the stimulus to holiness.

We might, therefore, associate our text with the words of St. Paul in writing to the Romans: "The Spirit itself beareth witness with our spirit that we are the children of God: and if children, then heirs; heirs of God, and joint heirs with Christ. So that the secret and inward testimony, on which we have spoken, is no imaginary thing: the believer "hath the witness in himself" by having the Spirit in himself; and if we mention briefly some few points in his experience, we may dismiss as proved our second proposition. A believer, for example, has received, at various periods of his life, clear and distinct answers to prayer—therefore he "hath the witness in himself" that God is a God that heareth prayer. He has obtained many victories over the world, the flesh, and the devil—therefore he "hath the witness in himself" that there are "more for him than there are against him." He has found the darkness of affliction cheered by the light of his Maker's countenance—therefore he "hath the witness in himself" of God's faithfulness to his covenant engagements. He has experienced delight in communion with God—therefore he "hath the witness in himself" that "there is now no condemnation to them that are in Christ Jesus." He perceives that his affections—though there be still much of leaning to earth—are set on heavenly things—therefore, he "hath the witness in himself" that he is "risen with Christ;" and, if "risen with Christ," (O mighty testimony, O illustrious evidence!) then he hath also "the witness in himself" that he, too, shall rise; that this corruptible shall put on incorruption; this mortal assume immortality; and that materialism, freed from all the dishonours with which sin has burdened it, shall be beautified into a worthy dwelling-place for the pure and perfected soul. Nay, the witness stops not here. It goes beyond the Resurrection. It brings within its range the kingdom of the saints. Often, amid the sufferings of this his probationary state, there are vouchsafed to the believer foretastes of joys laid up at God's right hand. His soul, rapt into the future, holds converse with the glorious company which Heaven hath already gathered into its capacious bosom. He asks not that eloquence should pour itself forth on an attempted description of Paradise; or that the notes of human music should weave themselves into melody emulous of the harpings of angels; or that the scenery of fair landscapes should be spread before him, figuring, by faint images, the pastures that are watered by the river of life. He has himself gone up into the promised land. He has brought down clusters, like those of Eschol; and, suspending these in his soul, he "hath the witness in himself" that it is a rich and goodly portion which the Lord hath provided for his people. Thus, believing on the Son of God, he "hath the witness in himself" on every point of Christian doctrine, and every point of Christian privilege: nothing is omitted by this inward testimony: from the first pulse of spiritual life to the full consummation of blessedness; from adoption into God's family on earth to admission within the circles of cherubim and seraphim; all that is to be learned, all that is to be done, all that is to be enjoyed, the witness speaks audibly concerning these; and we trust that, as we before showed that "he that believeth on the Son of God hath the witness in himself" to the ruin consequent on transgression, so now have we proved of the rescue effected by redemption, that it is equally and gloriously true, that "he which believeth on the Son of God hath the witness in himself."

We have little to add, except to call on you not to think it strange, that, weak and polluted as man is, he should carry in himself so sublime a witness as that on which we have been speaking. We bid you elevate your apprehensions of a converted and renewed man, of a true believer in the Lord Jesus Christ, in order that, if yourselves converted and renewed, you may know your high calling; and if not, may be stirred to earnestness in desiring and seeking that great change without which shall no man enter into the kingdom of Heaven. True, indeed, it may be said of the believer, he is a frail thing, a wasting thing, a sinful thing. But, nevertheless, he is a Temple of the Lord God Omnipotent. Remember the question of St. Paul, "Know ye not that your body is the Temple of the Holy Ghost, which is in you?" And, moreover, is not Christ expressly said to dwell in the believer's heart, and to be found in him, and to be one with him? And is it not also promised of the Father, that He will come with the Son, and make his abode with every faithful disciple? Behold, then,—this frail thing, this sinful thing, is actually inhabited by Deity,—the very Trinity of Godhead possesses, occupies, and fills him: oh, then, where is the marvel, that he, who hath such guests within himself, should have within himself such a witness as that which we have described!

Yes, it is on this account that the witness is so decisive and so comforting. It is the witness of an indwelling Saviour, the witness of Christ formed within us, the hope of everlasting glory. And I would have you all aspire to the possessing this witness. I would have every one of you able boldly to affirm, "I have the witness in myself to splendid destinies coeval with eternity." And if it be said, "Child as thou art of sinfulness, heir of corruption, whence comes it that thou canst have such witness in thyself?" God grant that this may be your reply, "I have Christ in myself, Christ who is styled 'the true and faithful witness.'" Why, then, shouldst thou marvel at my saying that I have "the witness in myself?" Only, dear brethren, remember that, as all assurance is the fruit of God's Spirit, it must be darkened and weakened by any indulgence in sin. Alas! if the believer be not diligent in mortifying corrupt passions, and waging war with the world and the flesh, he will have "the witness in himself;" but it will be a witness to the melancholy truth that God's Spirit may be grieved, and that, when grieved, there happens what the Psalmist has so pathetically described, "Fearfulness and trembling are come upon me, and a horrible dread hath overwhelmed me."

LECTURE V.

The Apocrypha.

2 PETER i. 21.

"Holy men of God spake as they were moved by the Holy Ghost."

THE Church, during this portion of the year, appoints that the first lessons for her daily service should be selected from the Apocrypha. It is not usual to take texts from the Apocrypha, and therefore we do not attempt to follow the public service in choosing our subjects of discourse. We say "not usual," though in the printed volumes of many of our eminent divines you will find sermons on texts in the Apocrypha, so that we should not be without precedent if we addressed you on passages from these uncanonical books. Though our Church differs widely from the Roman Catholic in regard of the Apocrypha, refusing wholly to recognise these books as inspired, she does not authorize their being treated with that neglect which they now commonly experience from Protestants. These books are appointed to be publicly read: but then, to prevent its being on this account supposed, that they are to be accounted of equal authority with the canonical, you find it expressly stated in the Articles, that "the

Church doth read them for example of life, and instruction of manners, but yet doth it not apply them to establish any doctrine."

Yet if texts from the Apocrypha may not be used to establish any doctrine, they may often be subservient to the instruction and comfort of the Christian. How curious and how interesting is what is related of himself by a man as great in genius as in godliness, John Bunyan, the author of the "Pilgrim's Progress." "I was now," says he when describing a season of great spiritual darkness, "I was now quite giving up the ghost of all my hopes of ever attaining life, when that sentence fell with weight upon my spirit, 'Look at the generations of old, and see; did ever any trust in God, and were confounded?'" The words enlightened and encouraged him: he went home; he searched his Bible; but they were no where to be found; he asked first this good man, and then another; but they could give him no information. "At this," says he, "I wondered that such a sentence should so suddenly, and with such comfort and strength, seize upon my heart, and yet that none could find it; for I doubted not but that it was in the holy Scriptures. Thus I continued above a year, and could not find the place: but at last, casting my eye upon the Apocryphal books, I found it in Ecclesiasticus, 'Look at the generations of old, and see; did ever any trust in the Lord, and was confounded? or did any abide in his fear, and was forsaken? or whom did he ever despise that called upon him?'" Bunyan describes himself as at first somewhat daunted at finding that words which had been so useful to him were only in the Apocrypha. But this feeling wore off, "especially," as he says, "when I considered that, though it was not in those texts that we call holy and canonical, yet forasmuch as this sentence was the sum and substance of many of the promises, it was my duty to take the comfort of it; and I bless God for that word, for it was of good to me; that word doth still ofttimes shine before my face."

Yet whilst arguing from this instance that the Christian may, at times and most lawfully, derive comfort from the Apocrypha, it will not often happen to him to confound, as did Bunyan, the Apocrypha with the canonical Scriptures, or to suppose that what was quoted from the one might be found in the other. There is generally no mistaking the Apocrypha for the inspired word of God. They are so distinguished that you can tell at once, on first hearing, which is which. And this is the first fact on which we mean to speak to you to-day—the sameness which there is throughout the Bible, and at the same time the marked difference which there is between the Bible and every other book. The text which we have taken from St. Peter will account for this, though nothing else will. The writers of the Bible, "holy men of God," "spake as they were moved," not by their own disposition or ability, but "as they were moved by the Holy Ghost"—there may well be sameness, if there were but one mover. But when this shall have been done, we should like to show you in some particular instances, of what use and worth the Apocryphal books may be, so that you may accord them that measure of respect which is prescribed by the Church. Such, then, is the plan of the remainder of our discourse. We wish to show you that there are advantages to be derived from reading the Apocrypha;

but we must first show you how broad a separation there is between the Apocryphal books and the Canonical, and how such a separation is to be accounted for by the fact, that we may apply to the one, though we cannot to the other, the words of St. Peter in our text, "Holy men of God spake as they were moved by the Holy Ghost."

Now we may venture to assert of the Bible—that is, of what you commonly mean by the Bible, the Canonical Books of the Old and New Testaments,—we may venture to assert of the Bible, that, though its several parts were composed in different ages, and therefore also by different writers, it is an uniform book, presenting throughout the same truths, though with great variety of exhibition, and marked throughout by a surprising similarity of style. What does this prove, but that the Bible must throughout have had the same author, however that author may have employed various scribes? It is, we think, one of the most beautiful of contemplations, this of the sameness of authorship which may be traced in Holy Writ. That men, separated from each other by long intervals of time, should have taken up successively the lofty topic of our Redemption, and, whether in the effusions of poetry, or the enactments of legislation, or the anticipations of Prophecy, or the narrations of history, should have told the same truths, and announced the same mercies—and this in a manner so peculiarly their own, that you cannot meet with a page of their writings, from the Book of Genesis downward to the Book of Revelation, and not instantly recognise it as a page of the Bible—we say of this, that it can be accounted for on no supposition, but that of each having been moved by the same divine Spirit, so that to deny the Inspiration of Scripture is to make its composition more marvellous than when considered superhuman. I seem always to hear the same voice, whether the volume before me is informing me how the unshapen Chaos resolved itself, at the Creator's bidding, into symmetry and life; or men, familiar with the future, are gathering centuries into sentences; or a lawgiver is arranging the ceremonies of a mystic ritual; or historians are discoursing of battles and captivities; or Evangelists describe the institution, and Apostles unfold the doctrines, of Christianity. I seem always to hear the same voice; as though the words of John, the exile in Patmos, were the echo of those of Moses, the leader of Israel. There is a vast difference in the subjects successively touched on. But, nevertheless, there is a tone which I always recognise, and which always impresses the feeling, that I am hearkening to the same speaker. There seems to be no change in the instrument, though continual change in the sound; as if, at one time, a whirlwind swept the chords, that I might be startled by the treadings of wrath and devastation; and, at another, they were touched by an angel's hand, that I might be soothed by the melodies of mercy.

And whilst the same voice is breathed from every page of Scripture, it never issues from any other composition. The Commentator cannot speak in the same tone as the Prophet or the Evangelist. What poet could forge a Psalm which should pass with us for David's? What preacher construct a sermon which might be received as delivered by Peter or Paul? Look at the Apocrypha. You perceive that the scriptural style is imitated, but that there is only imitation. We defy a man to write like the

Bible, and yet all the writers in the Bible write alike. We say, they write alike. Their styles are very different. You have the gorgeous and the simple, the didactic and the argumentative. But still they write alike. Whenever you meet a scriptural quotation, you know it to be Scripture, though not acquainted with the passage. And we affirm that there is an evidence, which ought to be irresistible, in that sameness of authorship which alone will account for what we thus observe in the Bible. We know no plausible explanation, if you reject that of the Inspiration of Scripture, of the facts to which we have referred, the facts that the same truths are delivered in the figures and predictions of the Old Testament, and the realities and occurrences of the New; the same scheme carried on by the wanderings of patriarchs, the sacrifices of priests, the ambition of kings, the sufferings of martyrs; the same style preserved by the poet in his hymns, the Prophet in his visions, the lawgiver in his codes, the historian in his annals—so that, as though the author never died, but appeared at one time in one character, and at another in another, the Bible comes to us as the dictate of one mind, and the writing of one pen—Inspiration accounts for this, but we can imagine no other solution.

This, you will observe, is the solution which, on the teaching of the Church, we can derive from the saying of St. Peter in our text. Not recognising the Apocryphal books as inspired, we can indeed read with great interest the histories which they contain, we can derive wisdom from the sentential maxims wherein they abound; but we are noways surprised that there should be in every part a marked inferiority to those portions of the Canonical Scriptures, which are most closely copied, so that they cannot be passed upon us as belonging to that volume which we regard as the utterance of the Lord God Himself. On the other hand, we admit it indeed for a marvellous fact, that a book, whose authorship is spread over so many centuries, and attributed in some sense to so many writers, as we may affirm of the Bible, should bear on it so earnestly the impress of one man, and the trace of one pen, that its every verse, wherever met with, wherever heard, is recognised by us as taken from the Bible—still the fact, however surprising, admits of a ready explanation: we expect in the Bible the appearance of a sameness of authorship, though we know of a diversity of authors: we expect to find a something which shall belong equally to Moses, and Isaiah, and Matthew, and Paul, though there shall also be much which shall widely distinguish these writers the one from the other; for we know, that, however different they might have been in those varied qualities which give a varied character to the productions of the pen, still, according to the assertion of our text, "Holy men of God spake as they were moved by the Holy Ghost."

Now we might insist at greater length on the remarkable differences between the Apocryphal books and the Canonical—differences which are well worth your most attentive consideration, inasmuch as they furnish a strong argument for the Inspiration of Scripture. There is an internal evidence in the books themselves, as compared the one with the other, which can hardly be resisted—showing how readily our text may be accepted as true of all the writers of the Canonical books, but how it would lose its force and convincingness, if we attempted to apply it to the writers of the Apocryphal. We have said enough, however, to prevent your giving too high a standing to the Apocrypha, or assigning to it the same worth and weight as you assign to the Canonical Scriptures. We would now rather engage you with some evidence of the excellence of the Apocryphal books; for there is perhaps more danger of your underrating than overrating these books; and as the Church bids us now read them to you in her week-day services, it may be well that we show you, in one or two instances, how profitable they may be to the scriptural student.

The remarkable fact, which we adduced from the life of John Bunyan, will show that, though in the general, the verses of the Apocrypha may at once be distinguished from those of the Bible, still they will sometimes act with all the force and all the persuasiveness of inspired sayings. In one of her most solemn services, the administration of the Holy Communion, the Church directs the reading of some sentences from the Apocrypha; and possibly there may be those amongst the hearers who scarcely know that they are not taken from the Canonical Scriptures. When, as the alms are being collected, the officiating minister utters the words, "Give alms of thy goods, and never turn thy face from any poor man; and then the face of the Lord shall not be turned away from thee;" or, "Be merciful after thy power; if thou hast much, give plenteously: if thou hast little, do thy diligence gladly to give of that little; for so gatherest thou thyself a good reward in the day of necessity"—there may be some whom such strong sayings stir to charity towards their destitute brethren, but who never think that the Book of Tobit, not any book which they are wont to reckon scriptural, furnished the words which plead so effectually the cause of the poor.

And God forbid that we should for a moment imply, that there is any want in the Canonical Scriptures of blessed and consolatory passages, which the clergyman may adduce, when he takes his pastoral round, and visits the house of mourning, where stricken relatives are bewailing the dead. Indeed there is "balm in Gilead;" the promises and assurances of the Bible are as precious as numerous; and he can find no grief, for which he may not adduce a soothing word in season. And yet he might sometimes take words from the Apocrypha, and find that they too would come home to the sorrowing heart. I do not know more striking words than these from the Book of Wisdom, "But the souls of the righteous are in the hand of God, and there shall no torment touch them. In the sight of the unwise, they seemed to die, and their departure is taken for misery and their going from us to be utter destruction; but they are in peace. For though they be punished in the sight of men, yet is their hope full of immortality." A "hope full of immortality"—how often are these words used! how seldom, perhaps, is it remembered, that they are not Scriptural, but Apocryphal!

Then, again, how exquisitely touching are the sayings of the Book of Wisdom in regard of early death: "For honourable age is not that which standeth in length of time, nor that is measured by number of years. But wisdom is the gray hair unto men, and an unspotted life is old age. He pleased God, and was beloved of Him; so that, living among sinners, he was translated. Yea, speedily was he taken away, lest that wickedness should alter his understanding, or deceit beguile his soul. He being made perfect in a short time, fulfilled a long time. For his soul pleased the Lord; therefore hasted He to take him away from among the wicked."

Then, again, the historical Books of the Apocrypha give much important information as to events which befell the Jews after the Canon of the Old Testament had been closed. And we shall now go at some length into the details of one particular occurrence, because we may thence show you how a passage in the Apocrypha will occasionally help to illustrate the inspired Scripture.

You may remember that, in the eleventh chapter of his Epistle to the Hebrews, that noble chapter wherein he recounts so many of the exploits of faith, St. Paul has these words: "Women received their dead raised to life again; and others were tortured, not accepting deliverance, that they might obtain a better resurrection." Now to what women does the Apostle refer? he is bringing forward the worthies of earlier times, whose histories are given in the Old Testament; but amongst these, what women were there, whose faith brought back the dead; or who, anticipating a better resurrection, submitted to tortures, and rejected a deliverance whose price was apostacy? There is no difficulty in answering this question, so far as relates to women who received back their dead. You have two notable instances, that of the poor widow of Sarepta, whose son was restored to her through the intercession of Elijah; and that of the Shunammite, who, when her boy died, hastened to Elisha upon Carmel, and had the reward of her faith, when the Prophet stretched himself upon the child, and "the flesh of the child waxed warm," and "the child opened his eyes." But where are we to find a woman who answers to the second part of the Apostle's description, "others were tortured, not accepting deliverance, that they might obtain a better resurrection?" The mention of a Resurrection would lead us to search for the parties, to whom St. Paul refers, in some late period of the Jewish history, seeing that there is good reason to question, whether this great article of faith were distinctly revealed in earlier days. It is evident, that, at the time of our Lord's appearance upon earth, there was a general persuasion amongst the Jews of the Resurrection of the body, only the Sadducees dissenting from the popular belief. But it does not appear that this general persuasion had been of long standing; it can hardly be said that the writings of the Old Testament contain explicit statements on which such persuasion might be grounded; and the probability, therefore, is, that it was during the period which elapsed between Malachi and Christ that it gained its hold on the Jewish people.

And it is to occurrences during this period that the best commentators agree in referring the latter part of the Apostle's statement. There is no history in the Old Testament which will bear it out; you cannot, that is, fix on any narrative, which sets before you individuals, submitting to be tortured for the sake of religion, and sustained by their belief in a better Resurrection. But what the Canonical books do not supply may be found in the Apocryphal; and if you look at the marginal references to the passage in question, you will find yourselves directed to the seventh chapter of the Second Book of the Maccabees. There, indeed, is a beautiful and thrilling history, which illustrates to the very letter the words of the Apostle, setting before us those who "were tortured, not accepting deliverance, that they might obtain a better Resurrection." Possibly the history will be quite new to many of you; it cannot fail to be deeply interesting to all; listen, then, whilst we endeavour to show you how the writings of one whom we do not believe to have been inspired, may illustrate the words of an Apostle, a writer who is assuredly to be reckoned amongst those who may be described by such a saying as this, "Holy men of God spake as they were moved by the Holy Ghost."

Now the Second Book of Maccabees is chiefly occupied with accounts of the fearful persecutions of the Jews by Antiochus, who lived about one hundred and fifty years before Christ. And the seventh chapter presents us with an extraordinary narrative, bearing out most precisely the statement which we seek to elucidate. The story is that of a mother and her seven sons, who, in one day, suffered death by exquisite torments, rather than act contrary to the law of their God. Of course, it would not suffice for the illustration of the passage, that we could thus point to a whole family submitting to a cruel death for the sake of religion. We must be able to show, that, in undergoing tortures, and refusing deliverance, they were animated by the hope of a better Resurrection—otherwise we clearly fail to produce an exact case in point. But you will find the mother and her seven sons expressing, most distinctly, their hope of a Resurrection, and thus fulfilling, with the greatest accuracy, the description given by St. Paul. Let us go to the place of execution—for never were martyrs more worthy of being observed; never was finer heroism displayed; and never were the last words of witnesses for God and for truth more deserving of being listened to with eager attention.

The parties brought before the tyrant are, as we have said, a mother and her seven sons; and the thing which they are required to do, is to taste swine's flesh, and thus to break the ceremonial law. They might have argued, with some show of probability, that, since it was but the ceremonial law, and not the moral, which they were required to infringe, it might be lawful for them to purchase life by compliance. But these were not persons who could be satisfied with an evasion or subterfuge. They knew, that, under the dispensation beneath which they lived, every tittle of the ceremonial law was indissolubly binding; and that they should be as verily guilty, if they wilfully infringed it in a solitary particular, as if they neglected the weightiest duties which the moral law enjoined. And therefore, though "tormented with scourges and whips," yet did they strenuously refuse to obey the cruel tyrant—one of them exclaiming, in the name of the rest, "What wouldst thou ask of us? we are ready to die, rather than to transgress the laws of our fathers." Upon this, the enraged king gave orders that he, who had spoken for the others, should be put to death in the most barbarous way; but his mother, and six brethren, though compelled to be spectators of his excruciating sufferings, looked on with unshaken constancy, and did but exhort one another to die manfully.

And then was the second son given over to the rack: but, when at the last gasp, he gathered up his shattered limbs, and thus addressed the tyrant, "Thou, like a fury, takest us out of this present life; but the King of the world shall raise us up, who have died for his laws, unto everlasting life." See ye not here that it was the hope of a better Resurrection which kept the martyr steadfast? The third son next refused, as his dead brothers had done, to obey the tyrant's command, and, stretching forth his hands that they might be cut off by the executioner, boldly exclaimed, "These I had from Heaven, and for his laws I despise them; and from him I hope to receive them again." He too, you observe, had his thoughts on a Resurrection. His limbs might be mangled; but he was persuaded that this corruptible would put on incorruption, this mortal immortality.

And now is not Antiochus satiated with blood? will not the heroism, displayed by the three, prevail on him to dismiss the others? Alas! no. The fourth son advances: he braves the same torments, and is supported by the same hope. Hear how he speaks, when just ready to die, "It is good, being put to death by men, to look for hope from God, to be raised up again by him: as for thee, thou shalt have no resurrection to life." Still, you see, it was a Resurrection to which the martyr looked. And the fifth died in like manner, and then the sixth—each displaying invincible fortitude, and each expressing an unshaken reliance upon God. What did the mother all this while? The ground is strewed with the mangled bodies of her sons—is she not, woman as she is, convulsed with grief? does not her courage give way, as child falls after child? is she not ready to entreat the survivors to yield? or will she not at least unman them by her tears and her anguish?

Wonderful mother! Well may the writer say of her, that she was marvellous above all, and worthy of honourable memory. In place of counselling her sons to apostacy, in place of even distressing them with her grief, "she exhorted every one of them in her own language," and animated to martyrdom. Noble, very noble, are the words which she is represented as using, and they are words which speak of the better Resurrection. "I cannot tell how you came into my womb; for I neither gave you breath nor life; neither was it I that formed the members of every one of you. But doubtless the Creator of the world, who formed the generation of man, and found out the beginning of all things, will also, of his own mercy, give you breath and life again, as you now regard not your ownselves for his law's sake."

There remained now but one son, the youngest; and even Antiochus, bloodthirsty as he was, seemed reluctant to order his execution. Seeing terrors had no power, he tried what bribes would do, promising the lad that he would make him a rich and happy man, if he would but turn from the law of his fathers. But the young man indignantly refused; and then the king, still wishing to overcome his constancy, called the mother, and exhorted her to counsel her son to save his life. It was a hard trial. He was the sole survivor of a flourishing family, the youngest moreover, perhaps also the dearest. I see the mother, after repeated expostulations from Antiochus, consenting to counsel her son: she approaches him, bows herself towards him, and addresses him in the speech of her country. Is she subdued at last? has her courage given way? are they words of cowardice which she whispers in his ear?

You would almost think so from the manner in which she begins, "O my son, have pity upon me that bare thee." But what pity does she ask? We may well again exclaim, "Wonderful mother!" She asked her son to have pity upon her, by making her childless, by scorning the tyrant, and braving death. "I beseech thee, my son, look upon the heaven and the earth, and all that is therein, and consider that God made them of things that were not; and so was mankind made likewise. Fear not this tormentor: but, being worthy of thy brethren, take thy death, that I may receive thee again in mercy with thy brethren." Her heroism, and her hope, communicate themselves to her son. He longs to lie with his slaughtered brothers: he upbraids the tyrant, predicts his doom, and then expires undaunted, in the midst of yet fiercer tortures than had racked the rest.

We are not told in what way the mother died. We read only the fact—"last of all, after the sons, the mother died." But we cannot doubt, that, having counselled courage to her children, she was not faint-hearted herself. Indeed the hardest part of her trial was already over: she had seen her sons die; what was it now to die herself? What attractions had life to offer her? There they lay, a ghastly pile, the brave and the beautiful, over whom she had watched from infancy, who had hung upon her breast, who had been nursed on her knee, and who, as they grew towards manhood, had gladdened her heart by their filial kindness, and, yet more, by their devotedness to God. She would not survive them: she would not be left behind. Their spirits seemed to beckon her; and, with a soul full of the expectation of a resurrection unto life, she must have scorned the deliverance proffered her by the tyrant, and welcomed the torments which were to free her from the flesh. Thus was the bloody tragedy completed: the mother and her seven sons fell together, choosing the most excruciating death in preference to disobeying God, and having such faith in a Resurrection unto life, that they despised the fire, and the rack, and the axe. Who does not look with veneration on the martyred group? Whose heart burns not, as the matron dashes away the tears which the agonies of her sons must have forced to her eyes, and points, with majestic air, those already dying to a bright world above, and urges those, whose trial is yet to come, to defy the malice and the cruelty of the persecutor? Who feels not the greatness of the faith that was displayed? and who then can marvel that an Apostle, eager to exhibit the noblest triumphs of the principle of faith, should not have confined himself to the Patriarchs and warriors, whose stories are told by inspired writers, but, going down into more private life, should have selected the family which was massacred in one day by an infamous tyrant, and have added its members to his illustrious catalogue, though he found the record in a book whose author is not reckoned amongst those described by our text, "Holy men of God spake as they were moved by the Holy Ghost?"

Now we have thus wished to show you that the Apocryphal Books, which are being read at this time in the public services of the Church, though not inspired, may be referred to with advantage, and made serviceable to the Christian. You are especially to observe that our Church does not use them to establish any doctrine. The

Roman Catholic does; and so loose, if not erroneous, are many of the statements of these books, that they can be employed to the giving sanction to some of the worst errors of Popery. But this is not to prevent our giving to the Apocryphal books their due measure of respect, extracting from them historical information, and venerating the noble maxims with which they abound. Surely the history which we have given you of the mother and her sons is one which is well adapted to nerve to constancy in a righteous profession. We cannot do better, in concluding our discourse, than exhort to imitation of the faith so signally displayed. Yes; such is faith, such its power, and such its reward. And though we do indeed feel that the crown of martyrs, the crown won at the stake, or on the scaffold, may be a crown of extraordinary lustre, we will not suppose that, because our days are days of peace, and not of persecution, we may not ourselves attain distinguished glories at the resurrection of the just. There is a martyrdom, less conspicuous, indeed, but hardly less real, than that undergone by the mother and her sons, and in which we, as Christians, are all summoned to have share. It is a martyrdom in which we are not only to be the sufferers, but also the executioners. I call it martyrdom, that, if the right hand offend us, we must cut it off; if the right eye, we must pluck it out; that the flesh must be crucified with its affections and lusts, and the body be presented, a living sacrifice, unto God. And I know not whether there may not often be required a more active and energetic faith for this slow and protracted immolation of ourselves, than for the going boldly to the place of execution, and there enduring cheerfully all that malice can devise. The dying daily, the perpetual self-mortification, the patient submission to injuries, the incessant effort to promote God's glory,—these may be, at least, as arduous, and ask as much moral strength, as the facing an oppressor, and the surrendering even life, rather than abjure our religion.

I know not, then, why we, too, may not share the better resurrection. At all events, by making greater sacrifices for God, by attempting a more rigid self-denial, by striving after higher and higher degrees of Christian virtue, we may undoubtedly outstrip others who are running the same race, and thus obtain a nobler portion from the Judge of quick and dead. Christian men, and Christian women, parents and children, ye are not called to stand before Antiochus, and to choose between denying your God, and surrendering your lives. But, "holy men of God, who spake as they were moved by the Holy Ghost," have told you that ye are called to witness in the face of a scornful world, and to choose between losing your souls, and mortifying evil passions. We conjure you to accept not deliverance. Be ye bold, as were the mother and her sons, of whom ye have now heard; and resolve, in the strength of the Lord, that nothing but death shall set you free from warfare and suffering. Binding yourselves to the altar, and offering up yourselves by daily and hourly sacrifices, in obedience to God, ye may gain honours, like those which martyrs are to wear, and rise, at last, in that better Resurrection, which shall include those who are to shine as stars in the firmament.

LECTURE VI.

A Man a Hiding-place.

ISA. xxxii. 2.

"And a man shall be as a hiding-place from the wind, and a covert from the tempest; as rivers of water in a dry place, as the shadow of a great rock in a weary land."

THERE is little or no debate amongst commentators, as to the personage described in these words. It is probable, indeed, that the prophecy, in which they occur, had a primary reference to Hezekiah, who, as successor to the iniquitous Ahaz, restored the worship of God, and re-established the kingdom of Judah. The very signal deliverance, vouchsafed by God to his people, in the reign of this monarch, when the swarming hosts of the Assyrian fell in one night before the destroying angel, may justly be considered as having been alluded to by the Prophet, in strains which breathe high of triumph and redemption. And when a king is spoken of as reigning in righteousness, and there is associated with his dominion all the imagery of prosperity and peace, we may undoubtedly find, in the holy and beneficent rule of Hezekiah, much that answers to the glowing predictions. But the destruction of the army of Sennacherib may itself be regarded as a figurative occurrence; and Hezekiah, like his forefather David, is but the type of the Lord our Redeemer. There are to be great and fearful judgments, ere Christ shall finally set up his kingdom on the earth; and the Assyrians, miraculously slaughtered, ere Jerusalem could be at rest under its pious monarch, may but vividly foreshow how the wicked shall consumed by the brightness of Christ's coming, and thus way be made for the universal reign of righteousness and truth. If, in our text, Hezekiah is to be understood by the "man," of whom such great and glorious things are affirmed, you will unavoidably feel as if the employed language were too bold and comprehensive: you will have to explain it in a reduced and qualified sense, interpreting it as full of Eastern metaphor, which must not be too rigidly understood. But apply the words to our blessed Saviour, and there will be found nothing of strain or exaggeration: in their largest sense, they come short of the greatness and preciousness of his offices; and the effort of the interpreter must be, rather, to prove them in any measure adequate to what they describe, than to bring up what they describe to their compass and extent.

When, indeed, the prediction has thus been interpreted of that righteous King, in the describing of whom language, the most magnificent, is necessarily weak, you may apply it, in a very qualified sense, to Hezekiah; but we ought not to think that Hezekiah is primarily intended; for this is to accuse the prophecy of exaggeration; and exaggeration is too nearly akin to falsehood to be ever found in the word of the Lord. We shall not, then, think it needful, in our present discourse, to give heed to any interpretation of the text, but that which refers it altogether to Christ. We shall consider it as containing descriptions, metaphorical undoubtedly, but not the less comforting and instructive, of what the Redeemer is to the Church; and dismissing all regard to kings or kingdoms, which may have prefigured the sovereignty of Jesus, shall examine only how this man is "as a hiding-place from the wind, and a covert from the tempest; as rivers of water in a dry place, as the shadow of a great rock in a weary land."

Now the first thing, which may justly strike you as remarkable in this description of Christ, is the emphasis which seems laid on the word "man." "A man" shall be this or that; and Bishop Lowth renders it, "the man," as if He were man in distinction from any other, which is, indeed, St. Paul's statement, when he thus writes to the Corinthians: "The first man is of the earth, earthy; the second man is the Lord from heaven." As though there had never been but two men—the first Adam and the second—every other, as having been born in sin, and the heir of death, appearing to the Apostle undeserving the name. The verse, preceding our text, runs thus: "Behold a king shall reign in righteousness, and princes shall rule in judgment." But this mention of a king, and of princes, only makes more memorable the mention of "a man:" there is the more evident design of fixing attention on the fact of its being a man, who was to bear certain offices, or perform certain deeds; as if we were likely to overlook this fact, or, at all events, to lay on it less stress than it was intended to bear. You readily perceive, that, if the prediction had been, "And this king shall be as a hiding-place from the wind," it would not only have seemed to follow more naturally on the foregoing verse, but, by keeping up the mention of royalty, would have suggested an agency adequate perhaps to the great things predicted. Whereas, by suddenly changing the title, by dropping the king, and speaking merely of the man, the Prophet must be considered as directing us especially to the truth, that the king should be a man; yea, and that it should be in consequence of his manhood, that He would prove Himself a hiding-place and a covert.

There is thus, in the prediction before us, when applied to Christ, the strongest possible assertion of the human nature of Christ, and of its being that nature which renders Him a Saviour suited to our wants. There is no exclusion of the great doctrine of the divinity of Christ; rather, by changing the title of a king for that of a man, the Prophet may be considered as expressing a fear, that we might dwell on Christ as divine, till we came comparatively to forget Him as human: what need to remind us so emphatically of the king being man, if He were nothing more than man, if He were not also God, and therefore likely, in this his higher nature, to draw off unduly attention from Him in his lower? But whilst it is thoroughly consistent with the truth of Christ's divinity, that his humanity should be so explicitly mentioned—nay, whilst so explicit a mention may even be taken as an argument for our Lord's having been the Son of God, as well as the Son of man—there can be no debate that it is the humanity of Christ, to which our text gives the prominence, that it is this humanity to which seems ascribed the suitableness of Christ for the offices prophetically assigned. Before, therefore, we examine these offices in detail, we ought to pause on the fact of our Lord's being man, and consider its indispensableness to the whole scheme of our redemption.

And this indispensableness is quickly perceived, forasmuch as what our blessed Saviour undertook was the reconciliation of our offending nature to God; and this, it is perhaps hardly too much to say, could not have been effected in any nature but itself. In the nature which had sinned, must suffering be endured and obedience perfected; otherwise, so far as we can see, there could have been no satisfaction made to the violated law: that law, having been imposed upon man, and broken by man, must have had demands against man which no angel, no being acting in any other nature but that of man, would seem to have been capable of answering. We do not, of course, mean that any mere man could have made satisfaction to justice on our behalf: it was the divine nature in the person of Christ, which gave infinite worth to the endurances of the human, and made the single sacrifice immeasurably more than a ransom for the world: but we do not see (though let us speak with all humility on such mysterious things) how the junction of the divine nature with, for example, the angelic, in the person of the Redeemer, would have qualified Him to act as our surety: what was done and suffered in the angelic nature might have procured the reconciliation of fallen angels to God, but could have had no discoverable connection with that of fallen man. It is then the fact, that the eternal "Word was made flesh," that He who was "the brightness of the Father's glory, and the express image of his person," consented to be born, in the fulness of time, of a pure virgin, and thus to be "found in fashion as a man," on which we ground our confidence that the curse is removed, that we are no longer necessarily under condemnation, but that God is willing to welcome us, as the father welcomed back his prodigal son. Forasmuch as He was man, I can feel of the Mediator, that He suffered and obeyed in my stead: I have found a being who, in regard of God and of myself, is what Job, in the infancy of Revelation, seems vainly to have sought for, pathetically exclaiming, "Neither is there any daysman betwixt us, who might lay his hand upon us both."

And, of course, if it be indispensable to the general scheme of Redemption that the Mediator should be man, you cannot take, as our text does, detached parts, or separate views of the work, without bringing in Christ's manhood as essential to each. He must have been man, in order to his making the atonement: and He must have been man, in order to his entering into all our wants, understanding our circumstances, and having a fellow feeling with us in our infirmities. And we need hardly point out to you, that, in giving such prominence to the fact of Christ's manhood, our text not only insists on that without which the Gospel could not meet our necessities, but exhibits the feature which, of all others, is adapted to comfort and encourage us. The weak and the sinful, like ourselves, shrink, and must shrink, from absolute Deity. So soon at least as we become convinced of our wickedness and danger, there is so thorough a feeling of the vast distance at which we stand from God, and the barrier interposed by his righteous and immutable attributes, and of the necessity that He be always "a consuming fire" to the rebellious and unholy, that, to tell us of our Creator, and not to tell us of our Mediator, is but to cover us with confusion, or to drive us to despair. It is the man who is still spiritually blind, who can think without apprehension of God, or regard Him as a Being to be approached and entreated. Where the spiritual eyesight has been in any measure purged, God will be viewed as terrible in his majesty, a Being whose holiness renders Him so awfully inaccessible to the sinful, that it were even better to attempt the fleeing from his presence, than to dare the endeavouring to address Him with petition. And if there had been made to us a Revelation, that God was willing to receive and pardon the penitent, no specification being given as to the nature of the arrangement, but the simple fact being stated that the Almighty could and would forgive, indeed it may be doubted whether they, who most longed for reconciliation, would have ventured on the seeking it; whether the tremendousness of having to address themselves to a Being, whose very nature armed Him for their utter destruction, would not have overpowered the encouragement derived from the gracious but indefinite communication.

How different is it now, when there is a daysman, a Mediator, betwixt us and God. There is no diminished representation of the divine holiness or justice. God is not made to appear less fearful in his attributes. But it is a man to whom we have to flee, a man to whom we may address ourselves, a man, with all a man's sympathy, and all a man's experience—oh, how can the sinner fear to come to the Saviour, when that Saviour can be "touched with the feeling of our infirmities," having been "tempted in all points, like as we are, yet without sin?" I do not know whether you may all appreciate the difference; but I am sure that a trembling penitent, casting about for a possibility of deliverance, will feel that it incalculably alters the case, if, after saying to him, go to God as to a father, I add, go to Him through "the man Jesus Christ" as a Mediator. Does it give him some measure of hope, that I can say to him, God is not inexorable, He can receive you, if you approach Him with due submission and humility? It may: but much of fear will mingle with his hope; and the nearer he approaches, the more will he be terrified at the brightness of the Lord. But when I come to him with another message; when I tell him of the human nature, as well as of the divine, of the Saviour, then will he be encouraged to hope and ask at once for forgiveness: there may be a sound as of that which should forbid despair, in words such as these, "The Almighty Lord is a most strong tower to all them that put their trust in Him:" but, oh, the music that goes to the heart, and makes it thrill with delight, is in language like this, "A man," "the man," "shall be as a hiding-place from the wind, and a covert from the tempest."

But let us now proceed to consider with what justice or propriety the several assertions, here made, may be applied to our Saviour, to the "man, Christ Jesus," on whom we are taught to rest every hope of acceptance. There are four assertions in the text: four similes are used to represent to us the offices of the Redeemer, or the benefits derived to us through his gracious Mediation. These assertions or similes are not indeed all different; on the contrary, there is great similarity, or even something like repetition. Thus, "a hiding-place from the wind," does not materially differ from "a covert from the tempest:" the idea is the same; and there is only that variety in the mode of expression which accords with poetic composition. Neither is "the shadow of a great rock in a weary land," altogether a different image: the idea is still that of shelter, shelter from the heat, if not from the tempest. Though it might perhaps be more correct to say that there are two great ideas embodied in the text, and that there are two figures for the illustration of each. The first idea is that of a refuge in circumstances of danger; and this is illustrated by "a hiding-place from the wind," and "a covert from the tempest." The second idea is that of refreshment under circumstances of fatigue; and this is illustrated by "rivers of water in a dry place," and "the shadow of a great rock in a weary land." We will adhere as much as possible to this division of the text, in what we have yet to advance; though there is one thing, common to three of the illustrations, which should be separately and carefully considered.

The hiding-place, the covert, and the rock, give shelter and relief, through receiving on themselves that against which they defend us. The tempest beats upon the tower, or the tree, to which the traveller runs from the fury of the elements: the fierce rays of the sun fall upon the rock, beneath which he thankfully pauses, when almost fainting from the heat. It is true indeed that the hiding-place and the rock, in affording protection, cannot be said to suffer inconvenience: they are evidently not sensible to the evil which they serve to intercept, and thus keep away from the traveller. But something similar might be urged of all imagery, which, derived from what is material and inanimate, is brought to the illustration of the offices of the Redeemer. And our business is to refine, as it were, and spiritualize the imagery, that so, if possible, we may disencumber it of what is dead and insensible, and make it burn and breathe with life and sensation. Thus, if the hiding-place and the rock do not feel the storm and the heat from which they serve to give shelter, yet, when they are given as images of Christ, we ought, as it were, to endow them with sensibility; so that, over and above the idea of evils intercepted, which they naturally furnish, we may derive that of evils endured, which is equally needful to the completeness of the figure. And when once you draw this latter idea from the similes employed in our text, when you consider that the hiding-place, the covert, and the rock, can yield shelter and protection, only through receiving on themselves what they divert or turn away from us; indeed it were a dull imagination—to speak more truly, it were a cold heart—which does not instantly recognise the appropriateness of the figure, as taken in illustration of the Lord our Redeemer. For who does not know, who, knowing it, does not confess with gratitude and awe, that Christ Jesus placed Himself, as it were, between the sinner and that eternal wrath which his sins had provoked, and, by allowing the wrath to break on Himself, kept it from rushing forwards to overwhelm the world? How was it that Christ "redeemed us from the curse of the law," except through being "made a curse for us?" How came the sword to be sheathed, which our iniquities had caused to be drawn, except through the execution of the command, "Awake, O sword, against my shepherd, and against the man that is my fellow, saith the

Lord of Hosts?" How was it brought to pass, that the sinful may escape the everlasting penalties of sin, except through God's having "bruised and put to grief" his only and well-beloved Son, except through the Son's having "borne our sins in his own body on the tree?" The power and the preciousness of the scheme of our Redemption lie mainly in this, that there was actual substitution, that Christ Jesus stood in our place, so that there descended upon Him what, but for so mighty an intervention, must for ever have been descending on ourselves. That Christ endured and obeyed in our stead, as our surety and representative; that He did not merely avert from us God's wrath, but averted by exhausting it, receiving it all in his own divine person—this it is which enables the believer to look with confidence to God as having reconciled him to Himself; for this it is, which, as proving that every demand on the sinner has been discharged to the last fraction, proves also that "there is now no condemnation to them that are in Jesus Christ."

But how ought it to melt the heart, how to excite in us emotions of ardent gratitude and love, to remember at what a cost, and through what an endurance, the Lord our Redeemer procured our deliverance! It is marvellous, as it is melancholy, that the simple statements, Christ died for us, Christ gave Himself for us, should fall, as they commonly do, on listless ears, and languid affections. One would think, to see with what coldness and indifference such statements can be heard, that Christ had redeemed us at no personal sacrifice, that He had paid our ransom in treasures which He could produce by a word, and multiply without effort. Whereas he redeemed us by sorrows such as no other human being ever felt; by an agony of which it is fearful to read; by unknown pains, by inscrutable torments of the body, by mysterious darkness and desolation of soul. Remember this, when you hear, or read, or think, of Christ Jesus as a refuge. If He be that city, figured by cities of old, to which the man-slayer might flee, when pursued by the avenger of blood, remember that He did not build the city of wood or of stone; He built it, as it were, of his own broken body, and cemented it with his own precious blood. And when you admire such passages as our text, which, with great variety of similitude set forth the Saviour as the Being to whom we must turn, if we would escape the bitter pains of everlasting death, oh, fail not to give due force to the figures, by failing to observe how they suppose Christ to have incurred what He enables us to avoid; it may soften what is yet hard in the heart, it may warm what is yet cold, to call to mind that "a man," "the man," had to receive on Himself all the terribleness of the hurricane, all the fierceness of the fire, ere that man could be "as a hiding-place from the wind, a covert from the tempest, and as the shadow of a great rock in a weary land."

But having thus shown you how the emblems, adopted in our text, exhibit Christ as enduring, in his own person, the evils from which he shields and shelters his people, we have yet to expand the two ideas of protection in danger, and refreshment in fatigue, which, as we have already explained, these emblems embody. "A hiding-place from the wind, and a covert from the tempest," if our blessed Saviour be these, then are we to consider ourselves as travellers through some wide desert, where, overtaken by a hurricane, we are in danger of being buried in the sand which rises on all sides with tumultuous swell; or as mariners on a tempestuous sea, whose bark must soon founder, if no haven be at hand. For scriptural figures, if, under one point of view, they represent to us Christ, under another must represent to us ourselves; and it is simply because there is so little feeling of our own actual condition, that there is so little appreciation of the characters under which the Saviour is described. It is almost useless to speak of "a refuge" to a man, who has no consciousness of being in any danger; a refuge must imply that there is something to flee from as well as a place to flee to; and he who does not feel that there is peril to be escaped, what ear can he have for tidings of a covert, beneath which he may be safe? The words, "I am the good Shepherd," have little beauty or interest for the man who does not yet feel himself a wandering sheep, torn with the briers and thorns of the wilderness. But, oh, how exquisitely will they sound, when once he comes to himself, when he feels that he has gone astray, and would fain, if he could, return to the fold.

It is, and it must be, the same with all the imagery of Redemption. Christ is represented by certain figures; but those figures suppose us in a particular state, and conscious of that state; otherwise it is impossible that there should be appropriateness in the figures; at least, that this appropriateness should commend itself to our feelings. Thus with the emblems, or similes, of our text—are there any of you to whom they do not seem to possess much of suitableness or force? it must be because you are not yet alive to your danger, practically not aware of the position which you occupy as transgressors of God's law. What is this position? My brethren, as the descendants of Adam, through whose disobedience death passed upon all, we were born into the world, children of wrath, and under the condemnation of God. And though, as baptized into the Christian Church, we were delivered from the guilt of original sin, and endowed with grace which might have kept us in that holy fellowship into which we had been brought, it is probably but too true of all of us, that we grew up in the practice of many known sins, that, in place of holding fast our privileges, we virtually gave ourselves to the service of Satan, or sold ourselves again under the yoke from which we had been graciously delivered. And therefore, notwithstanding the work of Redemption, notwithstanding the regeneration of baptism, is every unconverted man, every man who is not labouring to live as a Christian, exposed to the wrath of a righteous God, certain, if he die without repentance, to have to bear that wrath through Eternity. The thing wanted, is, that any man amongst you, who may be living unconcernedly in sin, should be made to feel this. I speak parables to that man, in speaking of a Saviour, till he be made to feel this. But let him once be roused to a perception of the facts of the case, and he is in utter alarm at the perils by which he sees himself surrounded. When conscience, acted on by the Spirit of God, whose instrument it is, wakes up from slumber, and forces on a man his many and multifold offences, there will be no peace for that man, till he hear of an advocate, a surety, a propitiation. For, along with the conviction of sin, there will be a sense of such holiness and justice in the invisible God, as must quite preclude hope of sin being overlooked, or allowed to pass without heavy punishment. And the awakened sinner, whatever the thoughts which he may for a moment indulge, will quickly discover that there can be no virtue in his repentance to the procuring forgiveness; inasmuch as a broken law derives no satisfaction, whether from sorrow for the past, or from obedience for the future. So that there will soon be presented to him no imagery but that of danger and death; he will see that he has arrayed against himself the attributes of God; and that he is therefore in the position of one, over whom the clouds are gathering, and round whom the winds are rising, whilst he is far away from any shelter, and may expect nothing but the being swept down by the fury of the hurricane.

Must, then, those clouds break on his devoted head? must those winds come against him in their unrestrained force? oh, now is the time for displaying the Saviour: now is the time for the exhortation, "Behold the Lamb of God which taketh away the sin of the world!" The clouds need not empty their indignation on thee, O terrified sinner. The winds need not wreck their fierceness upon thee. The wrath of God, which thine iniquities have provoked, has already been poured upon one who acted as thy surety, thy substitute. In and through the Lord Jesus Christ, who "died the just for the unjust," God can receive thee as a Father, extend to thee forgiveness, avert from thee all anger, reconcile thee with love. Flee, then, to this Saviour: hasten to Him for shelter: and oh, as you seek in Christ what shall certainly be found in Him, but found in none else, you will need no one to explain to you, though you may have heretofore but little appreciated the beauty, the power, the gloriousness of the saying, "A man," "the man," "shall be as a hiding-place from the wind, and a covert from the tempest."

But we come now, in the last place, to the second main idea embodied in the imagery of our text—that of refreshment under circumstances of fatigue. The character of Christ, which we have just been considering, is that under which He specially displays Himself at the time of a man's conversion: not, indeed, that then only is He a refuge—for what is genuine religion but a ceaseless flying from ourselves to Christ?—but that then there is peculiar appropriateness in his discovering Himself as a hiding-place; forasmuch as then there is peculiar consciousness of exposure to utter destruction. And if the first great idea in our text commend itself specially to men at the moment of awakening from spiritual torpor, the second may be taken as specially applicable whilst they afterwards pursue a Heavenward course. Not that, here again, the idea, or the imagery, is out of place, if introduced at the moment of conversion: for at such a moment the man needs refreshment as well as protection: but, on the whole, a traveller, fainting in the desert, is an apter figure of the believer, as he toils on in the way of God's commandments, than of the sinner, when first made aware of his error and danger. Who of you, if it be indeed his endeavour to follow them who "through faith and patience inherit the promises," is not often conscious of the fatigues of the way, so that, like a man oppressed with heat, and overcome of thirst, he is almost tempted to lie down at once, and give up his journey in despair?

There are so many difficulties to encounter—for woe is

unto them who think it an easy thing to save the soul—so many trials, so many temptations; the path is often so rough, and the noontide sun so fierce; that no wonder if creatures, compassed with infirmity, feel at times as if it were well nigh impossible to make further progress. Oh for fountains in this parched desert! oh for shelter from these scorching rays! And must such wishes be breathed in vain? What then is Christ? Did not the angel of the Lord open the eyes of Hagar in the wilderness, and she saw a well of water? and is any thing more needed than the opening of your eyes, and the fixing them on the Saviour, in order to your finding in Him all that you want in your faintness and exhaustion? "A man;" "The man" "shall be as rivers of water in a dry place, as the shadow of a great rock in a weary land." The beauty of this imagery would be more felt in an Eastern country, where vast deserts of sand have often to be traversed, and that too beneath the rays of a sun which it is almost death to encounter in its noontide strength. But we all know enough of the condition, in which the imagery supposes the traveller, to be able to appreciate the promise of refreshment. And is not the promise one which is made good in Christ? Through Christ, as the fruit of his passion, the result of his intercession, we obtain those supports and consolations of the Holy Ghost, which leave no wound without its balm, no sorrow without its solace. These communications of the Spirit, flowing through Christ, are verily as "rivers of water in a dry place;" he who opens to them his heart obtains "a peace which passeth all understanding," a peace which not only subsists in the midst, and even in spite of opposition, enmity, disaster, but which seems actually to be multiplied by troubles, troubles appear to arise that Christian peace may spring from them; if "a dry place" occur, it is that waters may gush forth, not in streamlets, but in rivers.

Such is the fulness which there is in Christ; oh that none of you would think of slaking the soul's thirst at any other source! "the water," saith the Redeemer, "that I shall give him, shall be in him a well of water, springing up into everlasting life." And if fierce trials invade us, if earthly comforts wither, as withered the prophet's gourd, and, like Jonah, we seem left without shelter from the intolerable heat, what have we to do but turn to the Redeemer, that great High Priest, who can be "touched with the feeling of our infirmities?" "Shadow of a great rock in a weary land," we have but to come within thy circuit, and "the sun shall not smite us by day, neither the moon by night." He who always stands, if we may use the expression, close by Christ, secures for himself that "all things work together for his good;" though, if he ever leave the Redeemer, if ever he be tempted to wander from his side, then it is with him, just as it is with the man who quits his place beneath the rock; he meets the heat in its intenseness; there is nothing to cool the air, and he has only himself to blame if he sink under the force, the unmitigated force, of the tempest.

But a rock is stationary, and we are pilgrims; we must be on the advance through the desert; and how can we be always standing beneath the rock? Ah, my brethren, do you not remember how St. Paul describes Christ, when speaking of the wanderings of Israel in the wilderness? "They drank of that spiritual rock that followed them, and that rock was Christ." The rock goes with us; it is always as a wall to us; if we ever lose its shadow, it is because we stray beyond appointed limits, into forbidden ground; not because, in our necessary progress, we are forced to leave behind what gave refreshment and shelter. The believer cannot be where duty allows of his being, and yet be where Christ is not ready to be found at his side. The sun has only to be fierce, and the rock rises where there had seemed only an interminable plain. The privileges of a believer are not those of exemption from trouble and freedom from danger; but they are those of support under all affliction, and deliverance from all peril. Would there were a greater sense amongst us of the preciousness of the Saviour! We do not prize Him, we do not love Him, the thousandth part we ought. These, our cold hearts, give Him cold returns for his marvellous benevolence. O for a more ardent devotedness! O for more of spiritual thirst, for more of the feeling of faintness as "strangers and pilgrims upon earth!" We drink too much at polluted fountains, forgetting that all our springs are in Christ. But the thirsty, the fainting—and such we ought to be, such we are by profession—will they not daily value more, yet daily mourn that they value so little, "a man," "the man," who makes Himself as "rivers of water in a dry place, as the shadow of a great rock in a weary land?"

LECTURE VII.

The Hundredfold Recompense.

MATT. xix. 29.

"And every one that hath forsaken houses, or brethren, or sisters, or father, or mother, or wife, or children, or lands, for my name's sake, shall receive an hundredfold, and shall inherit everlasting life."

THESE are the words of our blessed Redeemer; and they were called forth by an assertion and a question of St. Peter, "Behold, we have forsaken all, and followed thee; what shall we have therefore?" The Apostles had, for the most part, been taken from amongst the poor and illiterate: in a worldly point of view, they had made no very considerable sacrifice, in abandoning their boats and nets, and devoting themselves to the service of one who "had not where to lay his head." But it is well worth your observing that Christ, in no degree, depreciates the amount of the sacrifice which had been made in his cause: his answer merely bears on the remunerating power of God, on the certainty that they who, for the sake of religion, gave up any thing which they loved, should find themselves, perhaps in the present life, undoubtedly in the next, immeasurably recompensed. There was something almost of a complaining tone in the interrogation of St. Peter: he seems to magnify what had been surrendered, as though he were almost in doubt whether a thorough equivalent would ever be received. Christ immediately speaks of "a hundredfold," as if to scatter, and put to shame, the suspicion that a man could ever be eventually a loser by what he lost for God.

We wish to fasten on this reply of our Lord, as furnishing guidance for us in our endeavours to act upon men, and persuade them to give heed to religion. It will not do, constituted as men are, to enlarge to them abstractedly on the beauty of holiness, and on the satisfaction derivable from a conscience at rest. They are not to be persuaded that virtue is in any such sense its own reward, that it were better for them to be self-denying than self-indulgent, even if there were nothing to be brought into account but the amount of actual enjoyment. They feel, that, in asking them to be religious, we ask them to renounce some good, and endure some evil; and they demand, with some show of justice, that we rigidly prove to them that they shall be gainers by doing as we urge. And hence the theology which is likely to prevail with them—and certainly this is the character of the Scriptural theology—is one which insists much on "the recompense of the reward;" and which, whilst it gives no quarter to the pleasures of sin, and insists unreservedly on the not setting the heart on perishable treasures, plies them with representations of a heavenly kingdom, and dims the present by unfolding the radiance of the future.

We are assured indeed that no terms of reprobation can be too strong for the folly of the man who is deterred from religion by the sacrifices which it exacts. But our assurance is not drawn from an opinion that the sacrifices are in themselves inconsiderable; but simply from the certainty, that, even in this life, these mortifications are more than counterbalanced by the comforts of religion, and that, in the next, they will be a thousandfold recompensed. The yoke of Christ is easy, and his burden is light: but nevertheless there is a yoke, and there is a burden. And when we read of taking up the cross, and following Christ; of forsaking all that we may be his disciples; of cutting off the right hand, and plucking out the right eye, which may offend; it were not easy to deny, that "if in this life only we have hope in Christ, we are of all men most miserable." It must therefore be right that, in dealing with men, we labour to convince them how immeasurably it will be for their advantage, notwithstanding the confessed sacrifices which obedience must entail, to hearken to the call which summons them to forsake all for Christ. We shall endeavour, on the present occasion, to set before you this fact under various, but all practical, points of view. Our subject of discourse may therefore be understood without further preface; we should perhaps only hamper it, were we to propose any methodical arrangement. We are simply about to illustrate the mode of dealing adopted by our Lord, when Peter seemed disposed to make much of the sacrifices which he had made for religion—not the mode of depreciating, or undervaluing those sacrifices; but that of magnifying the remunerating power of God—"every one that hath forsaken houses, or brethren, or sisters, or father, or mother, or wife, or children, or lands, for my name's sake, shall receive an hundredfold, and shall inherit everlasting life."

Now we begin with the case of the young, who, with life just opening before them, and the attractions of the world soliciting their pursuit, are urged to the duty of remembering their Creator, and setting their affections on things that are above. We shall not deny that there is something apparently harsh and repulsive in a message which demands of those, in whom the passions are strong, and the spirits elastic with the hope that the scenes, on which they are entering, will yield unlimited pleasure, that they renounce what they are just beginning to enjoy, and forsake all with which they have just formed a friendship. We cannot expect to gain at first a favourable hearing, when we come down upon persons, who have not known the bitterness of disappointment, and to whom the objects of sense, and the delights of earth, are wearing all that beauty which is soon worn off by trial—and require of them that they "crucify the flesh with its affections and lusts," and "love not the world, neither the things that are in the world."

Indeed they are free agents, and may, if they will, decide for the world in preference to God. But we give them fair warning: it is virtually between God and Satan that you are asked to decide, between Heaven and Hell that you are invited to choose. And if, by the energy of remonstrance and warning, we prevail on the young to hesitate, ere they continue the course we denounce, then presently the thought of all which we ask them to surrender comes upon them with great power, and they feel as though it vere unreasonable to urge them to such sacrifice.

If they hearken to our admonition, they must separate themselves from associations in which they find great delight. They must probably exchange the smile and goodwill for the frown and opposition of those whom they love. They must abstain from pleasures most congenial with their tastes, and from practices which promise them advancement. They must not seek the wealth which is most sparkling, nor drink of the stream which is most inviting, nor pursue the honour which is most alluring. We put it to the young amongst you, who may not be wholly indifferent to the saving of the soul, who may have occasional misgivings as to the wisdom and safety of protracting that friendship with the world, which is declared in Scripture to be "enmity with God," we put it to you to decide whether it be not the pleasures of sin, and the treasures of earth, which you are reluctant to lose. We should have you quickly on our side, and you would enter on a religious profession, if it were not that so much which you love must be forsaken, so much, of which you are in eager pursuit, be abandoned, as unworthy your regards. And how are we to meet you when taking this position of resistance? It will be of little use that we expatiate on the unsatisfactoriness of your pleasures, and endeavour to win you from the world by proving it delusive. You will have no ear for this kind of argument. All your senses, and passions, and appetites, and hopes, protest against our reasoning: you will find delight in what we ask you to resign, and we shall make, therefore, no way by plying you with proof that it cannot yield happiness.

We do not, therefore, press upon the young, that what we ask them to surrender is not worth being kept, or what to endure not worth the being reckoned. We may have our own conviction on this matter; but we do not expect them to adopt this conviction, if it have not yet been forced on them by experience. We must try another method—Christ did not tell Peter that the boat and the net were worth but little at the most. We rather allow the extent of the sacrifice, and frankly admit that it is asking much, to ask the young to give up the allurements and pleasures of the world. But then we have a high ground to take, when we have abandoned that of the little value of what they have to lose. We have to take the ground of a recompense being in store, which shall be immeasurably more than an equivalent for all which they renounce, and all which they endure. We say to them, it is true, you must renounce cherished gratifications, and we do not suppose that you can go along with us in despising and decrying those gratifications. You must cease to seek your wealth in earthly treasure, and your honour in earthly fame; and you are not yet prepared to regard that treasure as dross, and that fame as a meteor. But in whose cause, and at whose command, are you summoned to the sacrifice? Is it for the service of one who has nothing to bestow, that we ask you to exchange the service of Satan? Is it to make friendship with a being who has nothing great, and nothing good, at his disposal, that we urge you? And are all the advantages which your nature can solicit and appreciate, on the side of that alliance which we entreat you to dissolve?

On the contrary, we address you in the name of the living God, whose is the earth, and the fulness thereof. We invite you to be reconciled to the Creator, who can supply all your wants out of his riches in Christ. We offer you the favour of a being who can impart "a peace, which passeth all understanding," a hope full of immortality, and a joy with which no stranger intermeddles. We propose to you the placing yourselves under the guardianship of Him, on whom wait the eyes of all in every district of immensity, who hath spread out the heavens, and garnished the earth, at whose right hand are pleasures for evermore, whose is the treasure which the moth cannot corrupt, and the thief cannot rifle, and whose promise it is, a promise immutable as Himself, that they who are faithful to the end shall be throned in blessedness, and receive a crown that fadeth not away. And are we then to hear of the extent of the sacrifice, and to hear nothing of the wealth and happiness secured by the sacrifice? Are we to be told of the treasures of earth, and to hear nothing of the thousand times ten thousand talents of gold, which are the inheritance of those who will break league with the world and its idols? Oh, let us speak of something besides the boat and the net. It is to your zeal for your own interests, to your love for your own-selves, to your wish for riches, to your appetite for honours, to your longing for pleasures, that we make our appeal. We address ourselves to the young, whilst yet in the spring-time of their days, and we ask them to forego no gratification, for which we do not offer a richer and more satisfying. We entreat them to abandon no pursuit, without opening before them a far nobler and more engrossing. We summon them to no act of self-denial, which is not as nothing in comparison of its reward. If we ask the surrender of the corruptible, we offer the incorruptible;

of the transient, we offer the enduring; of the visionary, we offer the substantial. We bid them withdraw affections from objects on which they have eagerly fastened; but it is that we may direct them to objects unspeakably better suited to engage them: we bid them cease to employ their powers on designs in which they are intently occupied; but it is that we may turn them upon others which are alone commensurate with their energy.

And thus it is precisely as our Lord dealt with Peter, that we would deal with the young, who may be halting between two opinions, and have a difficulty in deciding to surrender what they love. They may array before us, as we urge them to religion, the pleasures they must resign, the advantages they must forego, the connections they must dissolve, and the hardships they must endure, if they hearken to the admonition, and dare to be in earnest as to the saving of the soul. But we have only one answer to return to their every statement; and that is an answer drawn from the remunerating power of God. We tell them, that, if, with Peter and the other Apostles, they forsake all and follow the Saviour, and then propose the question, "What shall we have?" there is a glorious reply, a reply which should make them ashamed of a moment's hesitation, "Every one that hath forsaken houses, or brethren, or children, or lands, for my name's sake, shall receive a hundredfold, and shall inherit eternal life."

We go on to observe, and there cannot be many in this assembly, whose experience does not bear out the observation, that it is the apparent conflict between duty and interest, which causes us, in variety of cases, to disobey God, and withstand the pleadings of conscience. We speak of apparent conflict, because we deny altogether that interest and duty can ever be really opposed. It is but vindicating the righteousness of God's moral government, to maintain, that, whatever He has made it our interest, He has made it also our duty, to do. But whilst there can be no real conflict between interest and duty, we admit, of course, that there will be often an apparent. Indeed, the world would cease to be a scene of probation, there would no longer be any trial of obedience, were it always manifestly for our advantage, to follow the course which God's law prescribes. It is only by carrying on our calculation, and bringing the future as well as the present into the account, that we reach the conclusion, that what is duty is, in the long run, also interest. There will often be a great deal gained for the moment by disobedience, and therefore a great deal to be surrendered, if we resolve to obey. And though we can be confident, that it is merely for the moment that any thing like advantage results, even in appearance, from thwarting the dictates whether of conscience or of Revelation, yet so long as interest and duty may thus seem to lead different ways, there will necessarily be often a struggle in the mind; and it will be hard to do what is right, in the face of an apparent advantageousness in the doing what is wrong.

And what we want you again to consider, is the correct way of dealing with men, between whose interest and duty there may thus seem a conflict—whether it be not the magnifying the remunerating power of Him, in whose cause the sacrifice is made, rather than that of depreciating the sacrifice itself—the making much of future recompense, not the making little of the boat and the net. If you try the latter mode, the depreciating the required sacrifice, you are immediately opposed by the strongest feelings of our nature; and the man, whom you attack, is not only loth to surrender what he values, but indignant at finding that what is so important to himself, is held so cheap by another. But if you try the former mode, the magnifying the remunerating power of Him who has required the sacrifice, you make the attack in the channel through which our nature is most accessible, that of our own interest, and the probability is very great, that the wavering will be determined to the side of duty.

We may refer, in illustration of this, to the case of an individual who is tempted to break the Sabbath, because his trade is then likely to be specially gainful. We are not insensible to the strength of the temptation which presses on a tradesman, who finds it hard to procure a livelihood for himself and his family, and whose business will perhaps yield more profit on the Sunday, than can be wrung from it through all the rest of the week. We are quite ready, on the contrary, to regard the man who for conscience sake runs apparently the risk of bringing starvation on his family, as doing something quite as noble as the Apostles, when they forsook all at the bidding of the Redeemer. For, very possibly, it is in humble life that the greatest demands are made upon faith; and men, in obscure stations, of whom the world never hears, may have the hardest tasks to perform, and the greatest sacrifices to make, in the cause of God and religion. We will not lavish all our applause and admiration on such as stand foremost in the ranks of Christianity, and whose names are conspicuous amongst the champions who have done and suffered much, in defending truth and maintaining constancy. We will not confine the honours of martyrdom to those who have gone up bravely to the scaffold, and unflinchingly sealed their confession with their blood. If we can find an individual who, for conscience sake, is exposing himself and his children to starvation; who, rather than to do what he knows to be wrong, boldly shuts up the avenues of subsistence—why, we affirm of this individual, that he displays all the staunchness of the martyr; and we would not more give our reverence and esteem to the intrepid confessor, who holds fast the profession of his faith amid the battlings of persecution, than to the poor shopkeeper, who is resolute in observing the Sabbath, when, if less conscientious, he might ward off penury from his little ones.

We make a great mistake, when we confine eminence in religious exploit to public scenes, and turbid times: it is in the loneliness of the domestic circle, and in the discharge of the most commonplace duty, that faith often fights its hardest battles, and wins its finest triumphs. And thus are we far enough from depreciating the trial which that man is called to undergo, the chief part of whose gains is made by Sunday traffic, and on whom conscience is pressing the obligation that he keep holy the Sabbath. We have rather, as we before said, a great sympathy with this man; we feel that he is summoned to an effort, which is scarcely to be estimated by such as are placed in comparative affluence. And we could not go into his shop, to remonstrate with him on the duty of abstaining from all business on the Sunday, without a painful consciousness, that we were about to urge on him a sacrifice, such as we had never perhaps ourselves been required to make, and to prescribe to him a task, for which, in like circumstances, we might prove quite incompetent.

But, nevertheless, the duty is clear, and it is not the difficulty of discharging it which can excuse its neglect. With what argument then shall we address the man, who cannot keep the Sabbath, except at a vast risk of bringing starvation on his household? We find him perhaps disturbed in mind, forced to own to himself that his conduct is wrong, but deterred, by the threatened and seemingly inevitable consequence, from boldly acting on his conviction, and closing his doors on his Sunday customers. Now we should like to read to this man, as he leans on his counter, and tells us of a young family, and of a scanty pittance derived mainly from the traffic of the Sunday—we should like to read to him the account how Christ dealt with Peter, when disposed to dwell on sacrifices made in his cause. We take high ground. We tell him that the Being who delivered the law of the Sabbath, as He can and will punish its infraction, so He can and will reward its observance. We tell him, that, so sure as the Bible is truth, unto them that "seek first the kingdom of God and his righteousness," shall all else that is needful be added. We are certain, that, in determining at all hazards to obey the Lord, he puts himself under the immediate protection of Him, respecting whom it is declared, "The young lions do lack and suffer hunger; but they that seek the Lord shall not want any good thing." We can affirm, without a jot of hesitation, that, in resolving to follow duty, without consulting interest, he engages on his side the succours of that Providence, which can give bread in the desert, and secures to himself that blessing which emphatically maketh rich. Are we then to be deterred from urging on the man that he keep holy the Sabbath, by the greatness of the surrender involved in obedience? Are we to be fearful of enjoining the duty, in all its strictness and sacredness, as though we were not certified that the Lord of the Sabbath is the Lord also of the Creation; and that, having at his disposal whatever exists in the universe, He hath made an everlasting covenant with his every true worshipper, "I will never leave thee, nor forsake thee?" Oh, the waverer between duty and interest may point out to us how the sustenance of his household apparently depends on the traffic which we entreat him to renounce, and he may speak pathetically of the penury which threatens to come in like an armed man, if he listen to our advice—but we have only one thing to say against all this dwelling on present advantage; and that one thing is not in depreciation of the boat and the net—but simply what our Lord said to Peter, "Every one that hath forsaken houses, or brethren, or sisters, or children, or lands, for my name's sake, shall receive an hundredfold, and shall inherit everlasting life."

Now you will all have observed for yourselves that, in thus examining the case of a man, whose interest seems to demand the profanation of the Sunday, we have advanced truths quite as applicable in many other instances. There is no passage of Scripture more worthy than our text, to be carried with them, by the man of business amongst you, into the scenes of their ordinary occupation. If David could say, "Thy word have I hid in mine heart, that I might not sin against thee," thus implying that Scripture should be taken with us as a safeguard against evil, we are sure that no text of Scripture can be better suited than the one now before us, for the talisman of the merchant, as he prosecutes the enterprises of commerce.

We may believe that every condition of life has its peculiar temptations, so that, whatever our circumstances and employments, there will be a full share of moral difficulties and dangers. But, undoubtedly, in some instances, the temptations are more marked and apparent than in others, and no man can be unaware of those which attach specially to mercantile life. There is no exhibition, which we reckon more fraught with moral beauty and greatness, than that of commerce, when prosecuted honourably and conscientiously. We see mixed up with the dealings of commerce the grandest purposes of God towards our fallen creation. It has been made for the advantage of the whole world that there should be a perpetual interchange of property. Every country might have been its own storehouse of every necessary and every comfort: there might have been nothing to be found, whether for use or adornment, in the whole circuit of the globe, which was not equally and profusely furnished in each separate province. But had there been, as there might have been, this uniformity of produce, it is evident that nations would have had little cause for intercourse; and that, each possessing all it could need within its own confines, they would comparatively have walled themselves off the one from the other. As it is, one land producing one thing and another another, the several parts of the human family are brought into association: commerce knits together the ends of the earth, and may therefore justly be pronounced the great propagator of Christianity. Therefore is it that we have great delight in the movements of commerce. We view in them far more than manifestations of the restlessness of cupidity, and the cravings of luxury. And when the ocean is before us, dotted with vessels, which are hastening to every quarter of the earth, or returning with the produce of far-off islands or continents, we look on a nobler spectacle than that of human ingenuity and hardihood, triumphing over the elements, that wealth may be accumulated, or appetite pampered: we are beholding the instrumentality through which God hath ordained that the sections of the human family should be kept bound together; and the preparation which He hath made for the diffusion of Christianity, when it shall please Him to give the word, and great shall be the company of preachers.

And we would go yet further in our encomiums upon commerce. We have an admiration the very highest for that merchantman, whose conduct proves him a man of sterling piety. We have so great a sense of the temptations to which commercial men must be exposed, that we regard those, whose religion can flourish in the atmosphere of business, as men in whom the spiritual life must have gained extraordinary vigour. Hence the engagements of commerce, as there is great risk of their hindering a man in his providing for Eternity, so, if pursued in a spirit of watchfulness and prayer, they may be subservient to his advance in godliness, and enable him to reach a high point in Christian attainment. There may be much in the occupations of merchandise which tends to the keeping down a man's religion: but this only calls for a greater measure of vigilance, and greater intenseness in supplication: and if commerce bring these along with it, we know no reason why the frequenter of the wharf and the mart should not far outstrip in righteousness the inmate of the study, and gain an eminence in spirituality, which shall be higher in proportion to his greater dangers and greater difficulties.

Thus, with every feeling awake to the necessary perils of commercial life, we can, nevertheless, regard the scenes of business as a stage on which may be won the richest of the recompenses proposed by Christianity; and we can therefore look upon a merchant, as we would upon a combatant, to whom is appointed a post of honour, because of danger; and who, if exposed to more risk, may be animated with more hope.

But whilst we do not hesitate to deliver these sentiments in reference to commerce, we must be plain with you in speaking of the perils which necessarily attend its prosecution. The likelihood is extreme, that men will become so engrossed with secular occupations, as to neglect, either partially or altogether, the concerns of another life; and there is at least a possibility, if we may not call it a probability, that, tempted with the prospect of advantage, they will engage in speculations which are not strictly honourable, and stoop to some species of underhand dealing. And when we recommend our text as a kind of talisman, it is specially against dangers such as these. It may be that there are individuals amongst you, with whom the pressure of business is an excuse for the slight attention which they give to the salvation of the soul. We can readily believe your time so engrossed, that religious duties seem unavoidably neglected. But we are certain that it ought not to be thus engrossed, for we are certain that God allows every man leisure enough for the escaping Hell, and the gaining Heaven. And therefore we contend that, as accountable creatures, you are unspeakably blameworthy in giving yourselves thus exclusively to secular engagements. If it be matter of fact, that business does not leave time enough for religion, you are bound, at whatever worldly cost, to circumscribe your business within narrower limits, and bestow the redeemed hours on the high concerns of Eternity. And you may meet us here with some such question as that proposed by St. Peter, if we give up all this, the boat and the net, "what shall we have therefore?" You may tell us that what we enjoin as duty, can only be done with great loss; and that, if you attempt to withdraw yourselves at all from the world, and to follow, with a less incessant industry, the occupation of your profession, it must be at an immense sacrifice of substance and prospect. Sirs, if you cannot be religious, but through bankruptcy, let not your name in the gazette scare you from inscribing it in the Lamb's Book of Life. You cannot be losers, by resolving not to lose the soul. We come down upon you with the truth of the inexhaustibleness of God. It is the proprietor of the wealth of both worlds, of the gold and diamond of earth, of the magnificence and blessedness of Heaven, in whose service we entreat you to break off your alliance with those who live as though they were never to die. And why speak of risk, when run for Him who cannot fail his servants? Why speak of loss, when sustained in his cause, who "openeth his hand, and filleth all things living with plenteousness?" Oh, you may say to us, you require the surrender of a great deal; we hardly know how to make the venture: "what shall we have therefore?" but you should be nerved to boldness in determining to make religion the prime concern, when you have heard these words of our Lord, "Every one that hath forsaken houses, or brethren, or children, or lands, for my name's sake, shall receive an hundredfold, and shall inherit eternal life!"

We need scarcely add, that our text should be a preservative, not only to those who may be tempted so to engross themselves with business as to leave no time for religion, but to others who may be solicited to turn aside, be it ever so little, from rectitude and integrity. If we have passed a high encomium upon commerce, of course it has been upon commerce as prosecuted with the strictest honour and conscientiousness, and not as deformed by any thing approaching to evasion or overreaching. The transaction which, though not punishable by law, may be convicted of meanness, or proved inconsistent with a high sense of honour, is as unbecoming to a Christian as what is actually dishonest. What the world calls a shabby thing, the Christian should call a sinful thing. The morality of the Gospel is vastly more delicate and sensitive than the nicest principle of what men call honour; if it make the fighting a duel sinful, it makes the giving an offence sinful; it requires us to consult in every thing the glory of God, and is, therefore, as abhorrent from trick and underhand dealing, as from robbery and extortion. If, therefore, men be placed in such circumstances, that they may make a profitable speculation, and amass much present wealth, if they will but swerve a little from just and honourable conduct, we require them to remember that the God, whom they profess to serve, is a God by whom actions are weighed, whose balances are so nice that they will detect fraud in what is mean, and expose as iniquitous all that is disreputable.

And if the swerving from what is upright in trade promise a man advantages which he is loath to forego, let him dwell on the word "hundredfold" in our text, and strengthen himself in rectitude by thoughts of the divine fulness and power. Thy God is the God who hath said by his Prophet to those who made their religion secondary to their money, "Ye looked for much, and lo, it came to little; and when ye brought it home, I did blow upon it." He is the God of whom Solomon declares, "By the fear of the Lord are riches, honour, and life." Therefore, why speak complainingly of the boat and the net which have to be left, when every one who leaves any thing for Christ shall receive a hundredfold, and inherit eternal life? Whenever, then, you are tempted to do wrong, for the sake of a present advantage, bring to mind what we have insisted on throughout our discourse, the remunerating power of God. If we would resist evil, our thoughts should be much upon Heaven. If we lived in the expectation of glory and immortality, at what a great disadvantage would the objects of sense, and the things of the world, make their attack. We should not waver for present gain, if we were counting up the "treasure in the heavens which faileth not, where no thief approacheth, neither moth corrupteth." And therefore would we have you animate yourselves for the moral warfare, by considering what great wealth is promised to the faithful. Is the gold seducing you? are the precious stones dazzling you? Then think of that city, whose street is pure gold, and whose every gate is one pearl. Is earthly fame alluring you? Then think of that throne which the righteous are to ascend, of the crown they are to wear, of the sceptre they are to wield. Are worldly pleasures tempting you? Then think of pleasures so deep and ever flowing, that they are spoken of as a river, of joys so unmeasured, that he who partakes of them will be abundantly satisfied. Oh, thus—whenever inclined to ask, as if in doubt and hesitation, "What shall we have therefore?"—take our text as an answer with which to repel the tempter, "Every man that hath forsaken houses or lands for my sake, shall receive an hundredfold, and inherit eternal life!"

LECTURE VIII.

The Life more than Meat.

MATT. vi. 25.

"Is not the life more than meat, and the body than raiment?"

THERE is a simple but a very strong argument contained in this question; and it can hardly fail, we think, to be for your advantage that we should examine and explain it. Our blessed Lord and Saviour is reproving the faithlessness of his disciples, who were anxious in regard of the supply of the daily necessaries of life. "Take no thought," He saith, "for your life, what ye shall eat, or what ye shall drink; nor yet for your body, what ye shall put on." And why were they not to take thought? was there not some measure of uncertainty as to their obtaining sufficiency of what they needed? and if so, on what principle were they to dismiss all anxiety? Our text gives the answer to these questions. From whom had life proceeded? by whose hands had the body been wrought? Surely God, and God alone, was to be regarded as the Author of their being: He had called them into existence: from Him had come that structure which was so "fearfully and wonderfully made." Well, then, if God had given life, was He likely to withhold the means by which life might be sustained? if his hands had made and fashioned the body, would He be neglectful of his curious work, and leave it without raiment? He had already given the greater good, would He then refuse the less? "Is not the life more than meat, and the body than raiment?"

You see now the drift of the question. The argument is, that, having given the costlier thing, God must be ready to bestow the less precious; meat was inferior to life, raiment to the body; surely then, by giving the life and the body, God had pledged Himself to the giving also the food and the raiment; and why then should there be mistrust, why anxiety as to the supply of daily wants? Ah, my brethren, there is indeed fine practical logic in this: if God's love towards us have prompted Him to the bestowing on us a great good, ought we not to infer from that bestowment his readiness to bestow on us every lesser good? St. Paul throws the same argument into its highest form, when he says, "He that spared not his own Son, but delivered Him up for us all, how shall He not with Him also freely give us all things?" You will readily perceive that this is precisely the same argument. God, in giving us his Son, has bestowed the highest possible gift; we may be sure then that the love, which would not withhold this greatest of all boons, will prompt to the conferring whatsoever of lesser good would be really for our advantage. Indeed, we might throw our text into the closest resemblance to this saying of St. Paul: Christ Himself is our life; He gave his own body, his flesh, for the life of the world—who then can doubt that God will bestow on us such good things as we need? they cannot be beyond his love, inasmuch as they must be inferior to what his love has already conferred, "Is not the life more than meat, and the body than raiment?"

But we cannot bring out the argument in all its force and extent, unless we first enlarge on the fact, that, in giving us life, that life which is in his Son, the Lord Jesus Christ, God hath displayed the greatest possible love, inasmuch as the gift involved the greatest possible sacrifice. If this shall once be established, if it shall be evident that the love, which could consent to the giving up of Christ, can have nothing more costly to surrender, nothing more tremendous to encounter, then, indeed, we are on a vantage-ground from which to resist every form of unbelief; we shall have right to stand beneath the cross, and say to all doubts, anxieties, and fears, "Is not the life more than meat, and the body than raiment?"

Now there is perhaps no history in the Bible, with which we are all more familiar than with that of Abraham offering up Isaac. We become acquainted with it whilst children; and the facts cling tenaciously to us when we have grown into men. And not only are we acquainted with the narrative; we are all more or less aware of the typical character of the transaction: we have no difficulty in recognising in Isaac a figure of our blessed Redeemer, but suppose that, as the lad bears the wood, and submits unresistingly to the being laid on the altar, he represents the Lord Jesus Christ, carrying his own cross, and meekly giving Himself as a sacrifice for the sins of the world.

But if the son of Abraham thus serves as a type of the Son of God, is there any thing typical about Abraham himself? may we presume to think, may we think without impropriety, or irreverence, that the earthly Father, in the feelings which must have agitated him, as he surrendered his well-beloved Son, may be looked at as representing, however partially and dimly, the heavenly Father when He gave up Christ to ignominy and death? We should proceed with great caution when we thus inquire into the possible extension of the type. But at the same time we are not to allow the fear of ascribing human feelings to God, to keep us from endeavouring to obtain as correct an idea as our imperfections will admit of the movements and workings of the everlasting mind. No doubt, it were to forget what God is, how deeply, how sublimely imperturbable, to suppose that the first person in the Trinity, when giving up the second to death, felt as Abraham must have felt, when stretching forth the knife to slay Isaac. But are we therefore to think that the Father felt nothing? are we to suppose that it cost the Father nothing to give his Son for our Redemption? This were manifestly preposterous. What would become of the well-known text, "God so loved the world that he gave his Only-begotten Son," if there were not a great sacrifice made by the Father in giving the Son, as well as by the Son in giving Himself? We do not then say that the Father, when bruising and putting to grief the Son, felt exactly as Abraham felt when offering up Isaac. But, probably, we come nearer the truth than in any other way, by taking the earthly parent as a faint and remote image of the heavenly. We may still be immeasurably distant from the actual feeling of the divine mind, and we must be careful not to think that this mind could have been agitated and torn as must have been the human. But, at all events, let us be sure that God did feel, that He was sorely pained, and mysteriously stricken—however defective, or even inappropriate, such language may be—when He gave Christ to be a sacrifice for the sins of the world. The apparent impropriety of ascribing pain to God should only make us believe that it was something immeasurably more painful than what we call pain which Deity endured.

And we should wish it strongly impressed upon you, that the Father, as well as the Son, had an immense part to do in the work of your Redemption. We have very little fear of Christians overlooking what was done for them by the second person in the Trinity—it was done by Him in the form of a man visibly and palpably; and even the most indifferent can scarce shut their eyes to the agony and bloody sweat, the passion and the cross. But we have the greatest fear of your comparatively overlooking what has been done for you by the first person, and by the third, and of your thus acknowledging three persons in the essence of Godhead, whilst you practically acknowledge but one in the work of Redemption. And of these two persons, the first and the third, it is the first which you are most likely to forget, inasmuch as the third, the Holy Ghost, is still busied, though invisibly, on your behalf; and his operations on your minds must serve occasionally to admonish you as to his existence, and the debt which you owe Him. But the first person, because He had apparently nothing to do in your Redemption, because He remained in the magnificence of his uncreated glory, whilst the second came down to suffer in our nature, and the third to sanctify that nature; this first person is likely to be regarded by you with wholly different feelings from those with which you regard the second or the third, with a far lower sense of gratitude, of veneration, of obligation. We caution you against this. If Abraham had slain Isaac for your benefit, and Isaac had consented to be thus slain, would you not have felt that your debt to Abraham was of just the same amount as your debt to Isaac? that it must have cost the Father as much to give the Son, as it cost the Son to give Himself? Apply without hesitation, but with the deepest reverence, the very same principle to the Godhead; and when you say how shall we ever repay the untold love of the Son who spared not Himself, say also how shall we ever repay the equally untold love of the Father who "spared not his own Son," but gave Him up for the life of the world.

For you must further remember, in order to the laying a broad foundation for our argument, that Christ was God's Son in no figurative or metaphorical sense: there is no power in the Scriptural reasoning to which we have referred, if you suppose Christ to have been a creature: its strength wholly lies in his having been one with the Creator, from everlasting and to everlasting, co-equal and co-eternal. But, acknowledging this, into what a depth, what a mystery, do we immediately plunge, when we would ponder that exceeding great love of God which was manifested in his sending his own Son as our Saviour. We might have supposed that sin would have so alienated God from us, that, on the moment of apostacy, we should have become objects of nothing but his righteous hatred and indignation. This would seem to have been the case when angels transgressed. We read of nothing to show that loftier beings than ourselves, which kept not their first estate, have enjoyed any visitations of love. They become, as it would appear, immediately and hopelessly, outcast wanderers on a sea of tribulation, with no single star of mercy discernible through the clouds which hung fearfully above. But it was different with man. He too had cast Himself on a sea of tribulation; and over him was woven a firmament of clouds; but, so far from having been left to buffet hopelessly with the storm, and to look up despairingly to unmitigated blackness, God gave him notices from the first, of a covert from the tempest, and painted on the dark masses, which appeared charged with destruction, a bow whose bright stripes were prophetic of deliverance. It is beyond us to give reasons for a difference so vast in the divine dealings with angels and with men. We acknowledge it as a mystery, profound, unfathomable, that, whilst love for the higher rank of being seems to have been destroyed by rebellion, love for the lower survived that rebellion, yea, prompted God to give his own Son for our rescue.

But there is no need that we should be able to explain a truth, in order to our believing it, and drawing from it consolation. God's ways indeed are not our ways, neither are his thoughts our thoughts: but we may adore where we cannot fathom; we may rejoice where we also marvel. God was not willing that man should perish, though man had altogether pulled down ruin on himself, and not a tongue could have been raised in complaint of injustice, had the race been abandoned to the wretchedness which it had wilfully incurred. But how will God succour the race? how, pledged as He is by his nature, as well as by his law, to punish every sin, will He maintain his own attributes, and yet not destroy the guilty? Ah, here was the question for which finite wisdom could afford no solution; but of which we now wish you specially to observe, that, when solved, it presented a difficulty which no finite love could have ever overcome. Infinite wisdom devised a plan through which God might be just and yet the justifier of sinners. But this plan required that a person of the ever-blessed Trinity should assume human nature, and make expiation in that nature, for sins done therein by countless generations. And then came the question, Will divine love consent to this plan? Will that love show itself so great as to proceed with the purpose of Redemption, when such a decision has been reached as to who alone can be the Redeemer? Yes, God "spared not his own Son, but delivered Him up for us all." No lesser sacrifice would have saved us; and God loved us so well that He would save us at any sacrifice, except that indeed of his own attributes or perfections. Wonderful love! what else is the thousandth part as wonderful? unless it be that the human heart can be proof against this love, and that men can give scorn and contempt in return for God's giving his only and well-beloved Son! I think that this wonder, but this alone, is more surprising. There may be one exhibition which surpasses in its strangeness that of God's not sparing his Son; but it can only be that of man's rejecting the gift. Yes, obdurate sinner, if such an one there be in the present assembly, angels looked wonderingly on, when a person of the Godhead assumed thy nature to bear thy sins; but they look, it may be, more wonderingly still upon thee, who canst resist such a Saviour, or set at naught such a sacrifice.

But if the displayed love do nothing in regard of the obdurate sinner, but prove him wonderful in his obduracy, and therefore deserving of signal condemnation, what effect ought it to produce on such as repent of their sins, and desire in all things to yield themselves to God? Surely a most encouraging and animating effect. God, the timid disciple will say, is indeed surpassingly great; there cannot be the good which it is not in his power to bestow, nor the evil which it is not in his power to remove. If therefore I might only venture to think that God is favourably disposed towards me, I might indeed exclaim with the Apostle, "Who can be against me?" But, "iniquities prevail against me," "my sins are more in number than the hairs of my head:" I dare not then look up to this wonderful Being: that He is amazing in power and wisdom, is every where traced on the visible universe: but I know also that He is of purer eyes than to look upon iniquity; and how then can I, a transgressor from my youth, be comforted by thoughts of his unmeasured supremacy? Indeed, it is true that you require other intelligence than can be gathered from the visible system of things, with all its majesty, and grandeur, and harmony! We must take you therefore to Calvary; we shall find encouragement for you there, beneath a darkened heaven, and on a trembling earth, if you cannot gather it from a firmament strewed with innumerable worlds, and a landscape rich in every beauty. Standing beneath the cross, every fear ought to vanish. God is there revealed in a character which must satisfy you, if any thing can, that He loves you, and is ready to impart to you every possible blessing. We wish to make you feel, that, as a redeemed creature, you have God on your side. But it is nothing that we say to you, "God spake, and it was done; He commanded, and it stood fast." It is nothing that we say, look on the worlds which He hath formed, think of the tribes upon tribes which He hath animated, consider the thousand times ten thousand evidences of his being Lord of the Universe, "glorious in holiness, fearful in praises, doing wonders." This does not meet your case; you rather shrink from a Being so refulgently awful. But when we tell you that God so loved you as to give his Son for you; when we point to the expiring Saviour, and tell you that He dies that you may live, life, your present life, your future life, being all drawn from his deep wounds, then what is to hinder you, surrounded though you may be by every form of want, and fear, and anxiety,—what is to hinder you from a confident reliance on the love of God as adequate to your every need, a reliance which will find expression in the triumphant question, "Is not the life more than meat, and the body than raiment?"

Now, in thus laying a foundation on which to expand the argument involved in our text, we have already in a measure set forth that argument itself. Our object has been, by dwelling on the love of God as manifested in his giving his own Son for our Redemption, to show you that we have already received from God the greatest gift which even God Himself could bestow. We declare it impossible for even imagination to suggest any thing greater which could be done for us by God, than was done when He surrendered, for our sakes, the Lord Jesus Christ to ignominy and death. And since the love which could prompt God to give us this greatest gift must be sufficient to move Him to bestow any lesser, you have only, in our text, to consider life as resulting from the sacrifice of Christ, and you may scatter every doubt as to the supply of daily wants, by the emphatic question, "Is not the life more than meat, and the body than raiment?"

You must all, we think, be alive to the strength of this simple reasoning. I cannot gaze on the Redeemer of human kind, wearing the form of a servant, though I know him all the while for the everlasting God; I cannot behold Him travelling in the greatness of his strength, and nevertheless "a man of sorrows and acquainted with grief," without feeling that the love, which could prompt on my behalf so stupendous a substitution, must be verily a love which can withhold from me nothing which would be for my good. It is not that every thing will be bestowed which my heart may desire; but it is that nothing will be denied which my happiness may need. I have an assurance which nothing can shake, nothing, at least, short of an absolute demonstration that Christianity, after all, is but a "cunningly-devised fable,"—an assurance that I am the object of a love, which I cannot overdraw by any want, or any wish, seeing that whatsoever I can ask must come short of what I have received. I know not where doubts, fears, anxieties, would be, if Christians lived more habitually beneath the shadow of the cross. Christians are too much accustomed to take their estimate of divine love from temporal appointments; whereas, the sacrifice of Christ should be always their measure. Not that divine love does not appear gloriously great, when judged by its common and daily manifestations. O cold hearts, which glow not as love provides for our wants, gives health and abundance, and gladdens us with the sweet charities of home. But these manifestations may be interrupted: sickness and want may be upon us: death may break up our circle, and disappointment mar our hopes: whither then am I to turn for assurance of Divine love, if my measurement of it have been derived from what I have lost? But measure by the cross of Christ, and I know, I feel, the love infinite, though I may be an outcast, worn with pain, deserted by friends, hunted by calamity,—as well as though my path were over flowers, and every present good were placed within my reach. It must be in love that things are denied me: it must be in love that things are taken from me: He who gave his Son for me cannot be unwilling, must be desirous, to give me also whatsoever would advantage me; and, therefore, whilst I can point to the cross, and say with Thomas, "My Lord and my God," I ought to be able to defy penury, smile at affliction, trample upon death, confident that the Almighty loves me with an everlasting love.

Would that you might all learn to make this use of the sacrifice of Christ. We want those of you who are believers in Christ, to turn, if you will allow us the expression, the atonement to daily account. We would not have you regard it as less awful, but we would have you employ it more frequently,—not reserving it as a high mystery of faith, to be contemplated only in moments of pure and seraphic abstraction, but carrying it with you as a practical thing, just as the mariner would carry his compass and chart. There is not a care by which you are harassed, which the atonement might not lighten, if not disperse: there is not an evil with which you are threatened, from which the atonement might not take all menacing aspect: there is not a loss with which you are visited, the void left by which the atonement might not fill. Glorious, universal, inexhaustible truth! the cross opens to us Heaven, and, at the same time, irradiates earth: it secures us every present good, as well as every future: it fills the ages of eternity with blessedness, and the moments of time with assurance: it dries tears, hushes griefs, soothes anxieties, whilst it pardons sins, subdues corruptions, proffers glories. I marvel not that St. Paul should exclaim, "God forbid that I should glory, save in the cross of our Lord Jesus Christ." Oh, whilst we look upon the bleeding Lamb, and feel that through his death we have life, we may also feel that no want shall be unsupplied, no sorrow unsanctified, no real good withheld; for we can ask in a tone of confidence, in a tone of triumph, "Is not the life more than meat, and the body than raiment?"

But now it is necessary to guard against any misapprehension or abuse of the doctrine which we have derived from our text. We have endeavoured to show you that the love of God, as evidenced by the gift of his Son, must necessarily be so great that the true believer may be confident that nothing will be withheld from him, the receiving which would be eventually for his good. Our argument has been, that, in giving the greater good, God shows a love which must move Him to the bestowing any lesser: having given life, He must be ready to give food, food being inferior to life: having given the body, He must be ready to give raiment, raiment being inferior to the body: having given his Son, He must be ready to give all things, there being nothing which can be comparable with that mighty bestowment.

But though the Divine love towards men be thus wonderful, thus immeasurable, there is nothing in it to encourage transgressors, who persist in transgression. There is no ground for saying, Surely God loves man too well to permit his destruction: He will never cast into hell beings whom He has redeemed at so stupendous a cost. There might have been some ground for saying this, had God published a free pardon, without requiring an expiation. But, as we have constantly to remind you, God's hatred of sin was just as strongly displayed as his love of men, in the gift of his own Son; so that the atonement, if irresistible in its testimony that every repentant sinner may be saved, gives equally decisive witness, that every impenitent sinner must be lost.

And we wish you to observe, that, though nothing can be larger than what a Christian may take as the measure of God's love, when the life in our text is identified with that life which is "hid with God in Christ," still the passage is so worded as to encourage none but those who are true believers in the Saviour. We admit that, although it is of life in the ordinary sense that Christ speaks in our text, yet the argument itself cannot stop short at this: it must be extended so as to take in life in that large, that magnificent sense which belongs to it when Christ is spoken of as the "Life of the world." But though, when thus extended, the one gift, the gift of his own Son, proves God's readiness to bestow every other, it does not prove his readiness to bestow good on any but those to whom his Son is emphatically life. If Christ is your life, then you have full right, from the argument of our text, to consider God as pledged to the withholding from you no good thing: but if Christ be not your life—and He is not the life of those of you who are still "dead in trespasses and sins," living in iniquity, in contempt of religion, in neglect of the soul—then, as yet, you have practically nothing to do with the question, "Is not the life more than meat?" the life is more than meat; but till you have the life, you are not in a position to draw the inference as to the meat: with Christ, every thing is pledged to you; without Christ, nothing.

And it is worth your observing how accurately, as thus explained and limited, our text corresponds with that saying of St. Paul, to which we have, all along, been supposing it parallel. "He that spared not his own Son, but delivered Him up for us all, how shall He not with Him also freely give us all things?" "With Him also," observe that. It is a joint gift, so to speak, to which God has pledged Himself through the scheme of Redemption—the gift of all things with Christ, but of nothing without Christ. If you will take Christ, you may be sure of every thing besides; but if you refuse Christ, there is no promise, no pledge—no, not even in the love which prompted God not to spare his own Son—that any blessing whatsoever shall fall to your portion. And whilst this secures our text against any but the most wilful abuse, leaving men inexcusable if they find in the atonement any ground for expecting that God will not finally punish the unbelieving, it ought also to furnish a rule as to what may be lawfully the objects of a Christian's desires, and the subjects of his prayers. May I wish for this or that thing? may I ask for this or that thing? These questions may be answered by another—is the thing one with which Christ may be joined? is there any incongruity between it and Christ, so that I could not ask Christ and it in one breath? The promise is, that God will give us all things "with Christ;" that where He has given the life, He will not withhold the meat; but such a promise excludes, by its very terms, whatsoever is not in harmony with Christ, whatsoever does not accord with his being our "life," "in whom we live and move and have our being." Tell me that all things are promised or pledged; and I might wish, I might ask, for riches, and pleasures, and honours; but tell me that all things are promised "with Christ" as "my life," and I shall be ashamed to entreat what would not combine well with Christ.

Shall I ask wealth? nay, there may indeed be no reason why wealth and Christ should not go together: but when I think that the Redeemer had not where to lay his head, I feel as though it were like insulting his poverty, to ask that he and riches may unite in my portion. Shall I pray for distinction? nay, again, it may very well happen that Christ and earthly honours fall to the same possessor: but we speak now of what a Christian may desire, of what he may pray for, rather than of what his God may allot: and I think the aspiration for distinction will be stopped, and the prayer for it choked, by the remembrance that what is promised is promised with Christ, and that human fame is a strange ingredient to compound with the lowly Redeemer.

And if, from observing how the Christian's desires should be chastened, and his prayers regulated, by the promise of the "meat" being only to those who have the "life," you regard it as a part of the promise, part of the covenanted blessing, that, with every thing which the believer has, he is also to have Christ, whose breast does not kindle, whose heart does not leap? God gives nothing to his people, with which he does not, at the same time, give Christ. Christ being the life, all else that He gives is made to maintain and cherish life in us. He may give riches; but He gives Christ with the riches; so that, sanctified by the Redeemer, they shall be employed to his glory. He may give sources of earthly happiness; but He gives Christ with those sources, Christ to make them doubly sweet, and yet to prevent their drawing off the affections from heavenly joys. He may give trouble: but, sorrow and sighing, will ye not flee before such a promise? He gives Christ with the trouble, Christ to enlighten darkness, Christ to hush disquietude, Christ to say to the fearful spirit, as He said to the terrified disciples, "It is I, be not afraid." The Christian should find nothing precious in which he does not find Christ, nor any thing disastrous in which he does. And Christ with every thing is his covenanted portion—O noble heritage! what is beautiful in itself becoming immeasurably more beautiful by and through the accompaniment, and what is disastrous losing all its power to injure. Is not such a heritage beyond human hope, as it evidently and incalculably is beyond human desert? Nay, not so,—does it appear to you far to transcend what man might dare to expect, that God should freely give him all things with Christ? It may, if you judge Divine love from what is traced by burning worlds on the firmament, or written in the loveliness and abundance which mantle the earth. But not if you judge from the cross; not, if you estimate from the scheme of Redemption. All things may be ours with Christ; all things are ours with Christ: unbelief itself may well shrink from the reason which we urge—are not all things in the power of Him who "spared not his own Son, but delivered Him up for us all? having given us his Son, what else can He be willing to withhold? for tell us, ye of little faith, "Is not the life more than meat, and the body than raiment?"

There is little that can need to be added, even were our time not just exhausted. We would only guard you for a moment against a possible misapprehension of our foregoing argument. Remember what that argument has been,—that a greater gift is a pledge for every lesser; life for food, the body for raiment, Christ for all things. But this in no degree takes away the freeness of the gift: by giving the one, God has not bound Himself, in such way or sense, to the giving the other, as that we are not indebted for it to his unmerited bounty. The gift of Christ as our life, does indeed both ensure and include every other; but, as it was of God's free grace that we have Christ, it is of God's free grace that we have whatever flows from or is incorporated with this "all in all" to the believer.

We should be jealous, with a holy jealousy, of any interference with the doctrine of grace. God gives not in return for any thing which we have done, not in expectation of any thing which we may do: God gives freely, out of his own wonderful, incomprehensible goodness. We had no claim upon Him before we were redeemed: neither have we any claim upon Him now that we have been redeemed: it was purely of grace, that He sent his Son to die for us: and it is purely of grace, that He follows up that gift with "all things that pertain unto life and godliness." O that we may never lose sight of this. We are so prone to pride, that we require to have plain words made plainer—"gift" made "free gift"—else shall we be intruding something of our own, and imagining that, at some point or another, God becomes our debtor rather than our benefactor. From first to last, we draw upon his bounty—the life, the meat; the body, the raiment; all are free gifts.

Let us serve Him with all diligence; let us consecrate to Him our time, our substance, our strength; still, at last, eternal life will be his gift, his free gift, through Jesus Christ our Lord. "Where is boasting then? it is excluded." But, where is gratitude? alas! often excluded too. O God, it is a new mercy, to be sensible of mercies. We receive every thing from Thee,—enable us to trace every thing to thy grace, that we may use every thing to thy glory. This is but asking what may sustain the life in us: it is to crush that life, to forget its Author. And if we ask humbly for grace, that we may own, and cherish, Christ "formed in us," it will not, it cannot be denied—our Lord Himself is our warrant, in his pregnant and emphatic question, "Is not the life more than meat, and the body than raiment?"

LECTURE IX.

Isaiah's Vision.

JOHN xii. 39–41.

"Therefore they could not believe, because that Esaias said again, He hath blinded their eyes, and hardened their heart; that they should not see with their eyes, nor understand with their heart, and be converted, and I should heal them. These things said Esaias, when he saw his glory, and spake of Him."

WHEN Esaias saw whose glory? when he spake of whom? There can be no debate upon this; for the Evangelist is here undoubtedly referring to Christ: he is relating the unbelief of the Jews, notwithstanding the many miracles which Jesus had wrought; and therefore it is the Lord Jesus Christ whose glory Esaias had seen, and of whom this Prophet had spoken. And to what particular occasion does the Evangelist refer? When had Esaias seen Christ's glory? when had he spoken of Christ? This is determined by the words which St. John quotes, describing the judicial blindness which was to settle on the Jews. But when was it that Esaias had spoken of God's blinding their eyes, and hardening their hearts? You have heard in the first lesson of this morning's service, the lesson which contains the account of a marvellous vision vouchsafed to Isaiah; and wishing to discourse to you on that vision, we take our text as furnishing the clue to its right interpretation, inasmuch as it shows, what we might not else have been able to prove, that the personage therein introduced, with so much of sublime and magnificent accompaniment, is none other than the ever-blessed Redeemer, the "Man of sorrows," but, at the same time, the "King of kings, and Lord of lords." It was Christ, whom the Prophet saw seated on a throne which could be none other than that of absolute Deity, before whom seraphim veiled their faces, and in regard of whom they called the one to the other, "Holy, holy, holy, is the Lord of Hosts; the whole earth is full of his glory."

For this was the vision. The Lord was on his throne: his train filled the Temple: the seraphim stood around, each with six wings—burning creatures; for such the name signifies—with two of these wings each seraph covered his face; wherefore, but in token, and in adoration, of the awful majesty of Christ? "With twain He covered his feet;" wherefore, but to teach us that we may not always think to trace the course of God's dealings? The feet of his ministers are covered as well as winged; yea, covered by their wings, so that their very motion may be concealment. "And with twain he did fly;" wherefore, but to show us the alacrity with which angelic beings give themselves to the executing the purposes of their Maker? You read that the train of the Lord filled the whole Temple, just as, according to the song of the seraphim, was the whole earth to become "full of his glory." Who are we that we kindle not at the thought of the universal dominion of Christ? When the Pharisees would have had our Lord rebuke his disciples because they shouted his praises, "He answered, and said unto them, I tell you that, if these should hold their peace, the stones would immediately cry out." And as though both to incite and reproach us through inanimate things, the chorus of the seraphim, heard perhaps coldly by ourselves, produced commotion in the magnificent sanctuary: the wood, if not the stone, answered to the call, and seemed to breathe out response in mysterious cloud; for we read, "And the posts of the door moved at the voice of Him that cried, and the house was filled with smoke."

And what effect was produced on Isaiah, when he thus saw the glory of the Redeemer? We cannot wonder that he was confounded by such an unearthly manifestation, that the splendours of the occupant of the throne, the voices of the seraphim, the shakings of the Temple, all combined to the overwhelming him with dread. You have the effect thus described: "Then said I, Woe is me! for I am undone, because I am a man of unclean lips, and I dwell in the midst of a people of unclean lips; for mine eyes have seen the King, the Lord of Hosts." The Prophet, however, was not left in this his dread and perplexity. You next read, "Then flew one of the seraphim unto me, having a live coal in his hand, which he had taken with the tongs from off the altar; and he laid it upon my mouth, and said, Lo, this hath touched thy lips, and thine iniquity is taken away, and thy sin purged."

We think that there is very interesting and instructive subject-matter of discourse, both in the deportment or conduct of Isaiah, and the emblematical action which was then wrought upon him. We invite you to the careful consideration of both of these, brought before us as they have been by the lesson of the day. Come, then, and let us examine the perturbed exclamations of the Prophet, and the mode which God took to re-assure his servant, on that memorable occasion when, according to the Evangelist John, Esaias saw the glory of Christ, and spake of Him to the world.

And was then the Prophet confounded and overcome? Ah, my brethren, how affecting a testimony is given to the corruption and alienation of our nature, by the fact that a manifestation of the Divine glory could produce in us nothing but dread and confusion. Not one of us will for a moment imagine that less terror would be excited in himself by the throne, and the voice, and the smoke, than was displayed by Isaiah. Put the case. Gathered as we are within the house of the Lord, we may suppose the house suddenly filled with manifestations of that presence which is not indeed the less actual, because not proved by any visible tokens: we may imagine the Divinity, who is undoubtedly in the midst of us, though not so as to be perceptible by our senses, forcing Himself, as it were, on every eye, and every ear, by an unearthly spectacle and unearthly sounds. We do not speak of a manifestation of God as taking vengeance; but only of a manifestation of glory and greatness, stripped so far as such a manifestation could be, of every thing necessarily appalling—a manifestation of the pomp and splendour of heavenly places and heavenly beings; a manifestation of Christ in his essential dignities, surrounded by ministering spirits who celebrate his holiness.

It might be, that, on a sudden, a brightness, such as was not of this earth, pervaded the house of the Lord:

the radiant form of the Son of Man, throned on the fire and the cloud, might be visible to every eye; whilst seraphim went to and fro, mysteriously beautiful, weaving a high song of triumph and celebration. And what effect would be wrought on the whole of this assembly? Not merely on those who are still at enmity with God, and living in actual contempt of his authority, but on others who may be regarded as righteous, whose endeavour it is to keep the commandments of their Creator and Redeemer? We need not hesitate to say that the effect would be universally the same as on Isaiah. If all utterance were not taken away by terror, every tongue, the tongue of the righteous, and the tongue of the unrighteous, would fearfully exclaim, "Woe is me, for I am undone:" in place of any thing like delight in the glorious manifestation, and desire for its continuance, there would, at the best, be a sense of uneasiness and dread, a kind of feeling analogous to that which prompted the Gergesenes to beseech the Redeemer to depart out of their coasts; and it would be considered as a relief, every one would be more at his ease, when all traces of the burning display had disappeared, and there were no longer the figures of seraphim before our eyes, nor their anthems in our ears.

But how is this? Wherefore comes it that there should be such shrinking from contact with the invisible world? a shrinking of which every one must be conscious, forasmuch as the dread of what is called an apparition may be declared universal, and the stoutest, if they thought themselves confronted by a spirit, the inhabitant of another state of being, would experience a fear and a recoil such as an army of living men, however threatening their attitude, might fail to excite. Ah, my brethren, you cannot require that we should go at any length into answering these questions. You can answer them for yourselves. Your own hearts, your own consciences, furnish the reply. It is nothing but the corruption, the alienation, of our nature, which makes us averse from immediate contact with spiritual intelligences. Man is far gone from original righteousness: even those, who have been renewed through the operations of God's Spirit, retain so many traces of the fall, indwelling sin is still in such measure unsubdued, that there is want of thorough congeniality between themselves and beings of unspotted holiness; and this want of congeniality will produce a sense of uneasiness, whenever they are forced into unusual intercourse. Were we an assembly of unfallen creatures, waiting for a season when we should be admitted into intimate and eternal communion with God, it would be to us a foretaste of blessedness, to have the Lord amongst us on his throne, and the angelic throng made visible in their beauty: far from imitating Peter, when he exclaimed, overpowered by the miracle, "Depart from me, O Lord," we should copy him in his rapture on the Mount of Transfiguration; we should long to build tabernacles, that we might detain the shining visitants, and never again lose so delightful a companionship.

But, alas, sinfulness has been so ingrained into our nature, that it must be eradicated by death, before we can bear Heaven. We cannot feel at home with God, and with Christ, and with Angels, until the earthly house of this tabernacle be resolved, that both soul and body may be purged from all remainders of corruption. But is not this amongst the most melancholy and convincing of proofs, that it is not the exaggeration of a morbid theology, which declares the human heart to be "deceitful above all things, and desperately wicked?" It tells, we think, almost more against our fallen nature, that a good man should shrink from God, than that a bad man should league with Satan. And you might, when wishing to give evidence that we have indeed gone astray, like lost sheep, from God, point out such an instance as that of Saul in the cave of the sorceress, asking whether, as there went on the unhallowed incantations, and the form of an old man came up shrouded in a mantle, and the appalled monarch, from whom the Lord had departed, so that He answered him neither by dreams, nor by Urim, nor by prophets, sought to disquiet the dead, and wring from them secrets, there was not furnished a terrible demonstration of the disruption which sin hath made between man and holiness—but indeed there is another scene which is yet more affecting in its testimony—not the cave of the sorceress, but the Temple of Jehovah—that Temple, not crowded with wild figures, that have risen beneath the circlings of the wand of the magician, and not echoing the muttered spells of necromancy; but filled with the train of the Lord, and resounding with the melodies of angels; and Isaiah, in the midst of the gorgeous manifestation—Isaiah, chosen of God as the Prophet to his people—Isaiah, smiting on his breast, like one in utter despair, exclaiming, "Woe is me, for I am undone," though, all the while, according to our text, it is Christ, the Redeemer, of whom he beholds the glory, and Christ, the Redeemer, of whom he speaks.

But we have not yet touched on the reasons which Isaiah gives for being sorely confounded at beholding the glories of Christ. We have only considered the general truth, that a manifestation of the Divine glory will always be overwhelming to men in their present condition, and we have used this truth as a testimony to the depravity and alienation of our nature. It must be observed, however, that it was on a special account that Isaiah pronounced himself "undone," and this special account must not be passed over without examination. "I am a man of unclean lips, and I dwell in the midst of a people of unclean lips; for mine eyes have seen the King, the Lord of Hosts." Himself a man of unclean lips, how was he to speak, as he ought to speak, in the name of that Being in whose presence he stood, and whose purities were so dazzling as to be fearful? The people, moreover, amongst whom he was to minister, were a people of unclean lips: he was sent to require from them that they should worship God in spirit and in truth; but how were they to obey with tongues so defiled? Thus it would seem that, in looking on the glories of God, Isaiah became penetrated with the sense of having unworthily borne the office of Prophet: never before had he felt, as now that the Lord discovered his Majesty, what awful and ill-performed duties were his—he a Prophet of unclean lips, and ministering amongst a people of unclean lips. It was the glory of the Lord which threw light upon this: he had never seen his sin in all its enormity, till he saw it irradiated by the shinings of God's presence.

And, my brethren, if you will consider for a moment, you will have little difficulty in understanding why the sight of the King, the Lord of Hosts, should have moved Isaiah to so piteous an exclamation. It is the effect which a manifestation of the Divine purity must produce in every one who endeavours to act up to his vows as a minister of Christ. Whilst he is actually engaged in the business of his calling, plying the ungodly with the threatenings of the Word, and striving to build up the righteous in the faith of the Redeemer, it is possible enough that he may see but little with which to reproach himself: he cannot, indeed, fail to be conscious that he comes far short of what a pastor should be—but to come short is human; and, with all his defects, he is perhaps proposed as a pattern by his fellow-labourers in the ministry. The mere excitement and bustle of duty will perhaps do much towards preventing his discovering his manifold imperfections; and even when he sets himself patiently to the hard work of self-examination, there are so many cross-lights, the medium through which every thing is viewed is so deceitful and distorting, that he will be almost sure to err in his conclusions: he cannot think too meanly of himself, but alas, alas, how easy not to think meanly enough.

But, oh, if he had but one glimpse of the glories of Heaven; if, for one moment, he were environed with the splendours of that Being, who "clothed Himself with light as with a garment," and whose "eyes are as a flame of fire;" what confusion of face, what self-abasement, what terror must ensue! Have I dared to speak in the name of a God thus awfully resplendent? I, who am myself shapen in iniquity, and who cannot abide the searchings of this terrible brightness—have I presumed to teach others, wicked, depraved as myself, how to worship and serve so fearful, because so holy, a Being? indeed, indeed, upon earth, whilst I knew God only by the ear, I appeared earnest, devout, faithful; but in Heaven, now that mine eye seeth Him, I am worse than an unprofitable servant: I seem to have placed myself before an altar, the fire kindled upon which must consume the polluted creature who has ventured to draw near, and undertake so tremendous an office. Yes, my brethren, it could not be but that a sight of the Lord upon his throne, with the seraphim standing round him in their brightness, would force the most sincere and diligent of pastors to break into such an exclamation as that of Isaiah. It is not necessarily that he can accuse himself of actual inattention to the duties of his calling. It is not that he can say that he has failed to warn, with all fidelity, the hardened transgressor, or that he has kept back the rich promises which God, in his graciousness, has breathed to the repentant. But it is, that, habituated to human standards, and earthly measures, he has but dim conceptions of the burning majesty of the Being whose messages he has undertaken to deliver. In proportion as those conceptions are strengthened and cleared, he will necessarily be more and more struck with his own unfitness for so high a ministration, and more and more conscious that it has been so discharged as to entail upon him, in justice, nothing but wrath. Give him, then, the conceptions which an actual view of Heaven would generate, and who shall tell us how overwhelming will be his sense of deficiency and danger?

I may stand here now, and publish the everlasting Gospel, offering in the name of Him who died upon Calvary, pardon to every sinner who will confess and forsake sin. And whilst there are none around me—none, that is, visibly—but creatures of the same race and sinfulness with myself, there may be in me all the aspect of faithfulness and zeal; I may, perhaps, feel, whilst I throw all mine earnestness into an energetic remonstrance and appeal, as though I had no cause for self-reproach, but must, at all events, be clear from the blood of those whom I have been commissioned to address. But imagine the preacher arrested in the midst of his discourse by such a manifestation as was vouchsafed to the Prophet—the sanctuary becoming mysteriously illuminated; the Redeemer displaying Himself, not as the Man of Sorrows, but in all the radiance which He wears at the right hand of the Father; the angelic hosts dazzlingly beautiful, yet showing how unworthy is the highest of creatures to do service to God, by veiling their faces with their wings—and I am sure that the preacher would be instantly struck dumb—not merely, and not mainly, because a supernatural exhibition will always produce terror; but because that exhibition, being one of the glories of the Mediator, must equally be one of the infirmities, the deficiencies, the transgressions, of his ministers; and the preacher, if he found a tongue at all, would find it only to exclaim, "Woe is me! for I am undone; because I am a man of unclean lips, and I dwell in the midst of a people of unclean lips"—thus taking as his own the very things which Esaias said, when he saw Christ's "glory, and spake of Him."

But now let us consider the symbolical action of which the Prophet was made the subject, and the comforting words with which he was addressed. He had, you observe, confessed his sin, and that too in terms which sufficiently showed that the heart went along with the lip in the touching acknowledgment. And though there had not then been the full revelation of the plan devised by God for human forgiveness, the connexion between confession and pardon had all along been declared; so that, under the Jewish dispensation, as well as under the Christian, to acknowledge iniquity was to have interest in promises which pledged its remission. It was, therefore, in consistence with the general course of Divine dealings, that the Prophet's confession should be followed by an assurance of the Almighty's forgiveness. It was further, a sort of anticipation, or revelation of the privileges belonging to believers in Christ, that one of the seraphim should be employed in conveying to Isaiah the assurance of pardon: we know that angels are "all ministering spirits, sent forth to minister unto them that shall be heirs of salvation;" and it might have helped to teach the Prophet this comforting truth, that there came a messenger from that burning throng, on which he had hardly dared to look, to tell him that his iniquity was taken away.

But with what was the seraph armed? through what instrumentality did the glorious spirit convey, as it were, pardon to the terrified Prophet? You read that the seraph had "a live coal in his hand, which he had taken with the tongs from off the altar:" with this coal he touched the lips whose uncleanness Isaiah had bewailed; and, having done this, he pronounced that the sin, committed or confessed, was now also purged. And we are evidently to understand that the purifying virtue was in this live coal: the action was not only symbolical or significative;

it was operative and efficacious; for the angel makes the taking away of iniquity to follow on the application of the coal, just as an effect follows on a cause—"Lo, this hath touched thy lips, and thine iniquity is taken away, and thy sin purged."

But what was there, what could there be, in a coal taken from the altar of burnt-offering at the entrance to the Temple, to make it prevalent to the forgiveness of the Prophet's transgression? The altar, indeed, was that on which the fire, divinely kindled at the first, blazed perpetually, as though to image the inextinguishable lustres of God: but how could sin be pardoned through the mere application of fire, though celestial in origin, and burning night and day as burn the seraphim that stand before the Lord? We need hardly observe to you, that there could have been no virtue naturally in the coal; that the whole virtue must have been derived from some fire, or some burnt-offering, to which the coal bore a typical relation. And no one living in Christian times, and blessed with Christian privileges, can doubt for a moment what this typical relation was. We have already shown you, from our text, that the vision was a vision of Christ; that the Lord on Whom the Prophet gazed, "sitting upon a throne high and lifted up," was none other than the second Person in the Trinity, Who had covenanted, that in the fullness of time He would assume our nature, and take away sin by the sacrifice of Himself. And if this were a vision of Christ in his glory, rather than of Christ in his humiliation, a vision more fitted to instruct Isaiah as to the exaltation of the Mediator, than to show him how He would be the "propitiation for our sins," you are yet to observe that the scenery of the vision was laid in the Temple, that Temple, all whose furniture, and whose every rite, was emblematical of the suretyship and the oblation of Christ. The fire was still burning on the altar, though the Lord was on his throne, clad in that glory which was to be gained through extinguishing the sacrificial flames, extinguishing them by the one oblation of Himself. And therefore might it justly be said that the Temple, thus lit up, and thus crowded with brilliant forms, presented to the Prophet a complete parable of Redemption: from the altar of burnt-offering, whose fires went not out though celestial shinings flooded the Sanctuary, might he learn that the Divinity, in the person of the Mediator, would not rescue the humanity from the flames of God's wrath against sin: from the throne, with all the attendant gorgeousness, might he be instructed, that when the work of suffering was complete, there would be given to the Saviour "a name above every name," and that Saviour should sit "in heavenly places," "the Head over all things to the Church."

O blessed and comforting truth, that, in his office of Intercessor, Christ still preserves the character of a sacrifice. Well for us, that the train of his glory, whilst filling the Temple, leaves the flame still bright upon the brazen altar. Continually offending, we need a propitiation continually offered: and verily we have it, forasmuch as, though crucified but once, and the one death sufficing for the life of the world, Christ Jesus appears in heavenly places "a Lamb as it had been slain," and intercedes on our behalf by pleading the merits of the blood shed on Calvary. There needed nothing beyond the mere touch ing of the lips of the Prophet—those who, when Christ was upon earth, touched even the hem of his garment, were immediately made whole of whatsoever disease they had; and now that Christ is in Heaven, they who believe upon his Name, and by that belief bring themselves, as it were, into contact with his sacrifice, obtain at once the remission of sins, and may hear celestial voices assuring them of pardon.

But then it is as a "live coal" that Christ acts, when apprehended and appropriated by faith. He was to "baptize with the Holy Ghost and with fire." The spirit of burning is in the communications of Himself—a spirit to consume our dross, to refine us even as silver is refined, that we may be a worthy offering to his Father in Heaven. He was verily the "live coal," in that He was ardent with zeal for God, and with love for man; in that He was jealous for both, with a jealousy such as we read of in the Book of the Canticles, "the coals thereof are coals of fire, which hath a most vehement flame." But He is still the "live coal," wheresoever He is the Saviour. He will, He must, burn out the corruptions of our nature, where He sets the seal of forgiveness. That seal is a thing of fire: the impress which it leaves is an impress of purity; but purity is to be wrought in creatures like ourselves, only through cauterizing processes; and, therefore, think not to be stamped as pardoned, except as sanctified through flame. Never yet has the seraph been commissioned to fly towards you with an assurance of forgiveness, if you have not found in religion a purifying energy, if the word of the Lord have never been to you, what it is called in the Prophecies of Jeremiah, "a fire," a fire to burn up the chaff and the stubble; if the Redeemer's death have not been felt by you as a prevalent motive to the mortifying the flesh; if you have not been constrained, by his sacrifice, to present yourselves living sacrifices unto God. But if indeed you can feel that a sanctifying work is going on within you; that, as though some devouring energy had been mysteriously introduced, and were powerfully, though painfully, eating away the pride, and the malice, and the lustfulness of nature, you are daily becoming more and more fitted for the habitation of a God who cannot dwell with iniquity—then it may never have happened to you to behold the Lord upon his throne; never may you have been surrounded with manifestations of heavenly glory; never may you have seen one of those bright and beautiful creatures, "the ministers of God that do his pleasure," hastening towards you with the means and tokens of forgiveness—but be of good cheer; the live coal has touched you, otherwise never would there have been these signs of spiritual renewal; and the man, who is growing in holiness, has to the full as much evidence of his pardon, as though the winged seraph had flown towards him with the live coal from the altar, and pronounced audibly the animating words, "Lo, this hath touched thy lips, and thine iniquity is taken away, and thy sin purged"—even as was done to the Prophet, when, in the language of our text, Esaias saw Christ's glory, and spake of Him to the Jews.

But we must recur to that portion of our discourse in which we dwelt on a manifestation of Divine glory, as adapted to produce in us confusion and dread; for there is an important practical lesson derivable from this fact, on which we did not touch, but which ought not to be overlooked. You can hardly be unaware, that, when inspired writers would animate Christians to diligence in their calling, they dwell especially on the second advent of Christ, overlooking, as it were, the grave, and directing thought to the Resurrection, rather than to death. When anxious to urge men to the forsaking of iniquity, or the running with patience the race set before them, they do not so much remind them of their possible nearness to the grave, or of the certainty, that, ere many years have elapsed, they must depart out of life—they rather bid them anticipate the day of wonder and of terror, when the Lord Jesus shall be revealed in flaming fire from Heaven, when "He shall come to be glorified in his saints, and admired in all them that believe."

And there is nothing in this conduct of the inspired writers, but what may be explained and vindicated upon principles, of whose accuracy you are all competent judges. There is certainly very little effect wrought by the most touching delineations of the uncertainty of life. For the moment indeed the effect is apparently great: a kind of painful spell is thrown over an audience, and the most indifferent amongst them seemed awed into attention, when the preacher makes appeal to the shroud and the coffin, and, asserting the progress of some desolating sickness, and the frequency of funerals which darken the streets, entreats men to give heed to religion, on the principle that probably death is almost at their doors. But, whatever the aspect of attention which allusions to sickness and the grave will produce in assemblies, there is commonly made but little permanent impression; and therefore it is not upon death that inspired writers dwell, when seeking to produce moral vigilance and endeavour. They strive tc bring men to contemplate the day, not when they shall be stretched on the bed of languishing, or bound up for burial, but when they shall stand before the Son of man in his glory, and have every secret exposed by the brightness of his presence. And this is wise, seeing that it is the view of the glory of God which excites in Isaiah the consciousness of his own sinfulness, and of the wrath thence deserved.

I do not, therefore, ask you to go with me to the churchyard, that there, amid the graves of all ages and ranks, you may learn how frail you are, and study the necessity of preparing to meet God. But I would have you go with me in thought to the tremendous scene of judgment. And you are not to regard yourselves as mere spectators of the mighty assize: you form part of that interminable throng which presses forward to the bar: every one of you is there; and in the awful volume which stands before the Judge, is registered indelibly every sin committed during residence on earth. What think you of your condition? What think you of your prospect of acquittal? You may have been wont to compare yourselves with others; and because the comparison seemed to tell in your favour, you may have hoped for acceptance with the Judge of quick and dead. Where is the hope now? As you behold the dazzling purities of this Judge, do you feel that He will be content with any such virtues as you once were able to regard with complacency? You may have imagined that much would pass unobserved, that, occupied with ordering all the affairs of immensity, God would not note the every action of creatures insignificant as yourselves! Where is the delusion now? Can it endure before that eye, the lightest glance of which is piercing with Omniscience? do you feel as if there might be concealment, now that the Universe is lit up by the brightness of the countenance of the Judge? You may have supposed that God would not make good his threatenings, that he would be more compassionate than his word had announced, allowing sinners to escape from the penalties, who had here lived in despite to the precepts, of his law. Where is the supposition now? Holds it good amid all this tremendous heraldry of wrath? or, as you look upon the Lord, and mark the prints of the wounds inflicted because of God's utter determination of punishing sin, do you feel that there is a likelihood of uncovenanted mercy, of the Divine word being broken that you may be delivered?

No, no—if you were before the throne, if the glory, the burning glory, of the Judge encompassed you, if the ten thousand times ten thousand ministering spirits, that shall attend the Son of man, were glancing to and fro, ready not only to gather the wheat into the garner, but to bind the tares in bundles for the burning, all self-deceit would be at an end, all hypocrisy self-exposed, all false confidence overthrown; and if you had not made covenant with the Judge as your Mediator, the piercing cry of each of you would be, "Woe is me, for I am undone; mine eyes have seen the King, the Lord of Hosts." And therefore would we be earnest in directing your thoughts to Christ's second Advent, rather than to death. Meditate much on the Advent; and in proportion as you anticipate the spectacle of the Lord upon his throne, high and lifted up, you will be likely, with Isaiah, to feel your uncleanness, and, confessing it, to obtain its being taken away. Oh, that we might all seek to be reconciled unto God, whilst it is yet the fire which purifies, not that which consumes, which burns upon the altar. Whilst seraphim are yet ministering spirits, whilst we have not yet armed against ourselves the whole company of unfallen angels, let us turn unto the Lord with full purpose of heart. There is no reason why any amongst us should treasure up wrath against the day of wrath. Though there be such a thing as judicial blindness—for it was of this, that, according to our text, Esaias spake when he had seen the wondrous vision—" He hath blinded their eyes, and hardened their heart; that they should not see with their eyes, and understand with their heart, and be converted, and I should heal them"—O fearful fate, when in just judgment for protracted impenitence, God gives men up, and withdraws from them his Spirit—still we have no cause to believe this of any of you. The throne of Judgment is not yet ascended: the coal in the seraph's hand is that which purges away our dross: Oh, God is indeed a consuming fire; but let us fall before the cross of his Son, " the Lamb of God which taketh away the sin of the world," and we shall only be refined, " made meet for the inheritance of the saints in light."

LECTURE X.

St. John the Baptist.

NUMB. xi. 29.

"And Moses said unto him, Enviest thou for my sake? would God that all the Lord's people were prophets, and that the Lord would put his spirit upon them!"

WHEN the great lawgiver Moses found the management of the whole congregation of Israel a burden heavier than he could bear, he was directed by God to select seventy elders of the people, and to bring them up with him to the Tabernacle; God declaring that He would take of the Spirit which was upon Moses, and put it on those elders, that they might divide with him the charge of public affairs. Seventy were accordingly selected; but two of them remained, probably through some accident, in the camp, whilst the others set themselves round about the Tabernacle. The Spirit of the Lord came down according to promise; but it fell, not only on the sixty and eight who were at the Tabernacle, but also on Eldad and Medad, the two who had remained in the camp, so that all the seventy simultaneously prophesied.

It seems to have been counted a very surprising thing that men should prophesy in the camp; it would have been nothing had Eldad and Medad prophesied in the Tabernacle; but such occurrences was not looked for elsewhere; and therefore we read, "There ran a young man, and told Moses, and said, Eldad and Medad do prophesy in the camp." On hearing this, Joshua, the son of Nun, the servant of Moses, immediately exclaimed, "My lord Moses, forbid them." And what feeling was foremost in Joshua's mind, that he was so prompt in desiring that Prophets might be forbidden to prophesy? Why, he was jealous for the honour of Moses, whom he counted supreme in the camp, whatever he might be in the Tabernacle. That men should prophesy in the camp, seemed therefore to Joshua an invasion of the province of Moses. Hence the sudden exclamation of Joshua—it was the exclamation of jealousy. That we do not wrong him in putting this interpretation on his words, is evident from the noble answer of Moses, an answer which at the same time exhibited the magnanimity of the lawgiver, and exposed the feelings which had dictated the speech of his servant. You have the answer in our text, "And Moses said unto him, Enviest thou for my sake? would God that all the Lord's people were Prophets, and that the Lord would put his Spirit upon them." Moses had no share in the narrow feeling which Joshua had displayed, the feeling of envy and jealousy; he had no wish to engross to himself the distinctions of Heaven, but, on the contrary, would have greatly rejoiced, had all the congregation been richly endowed from above, though he himself might then have ceased to be conspicuous in Israel. And we consider that the lawgiver, when thus firmly reproving Joshua for envying for his sake, was worthy of being intensely admired, and earnestly imitated; for that in thus showing himself above all littleness of mind, content to be nothing, so that God might be magnified, and his cause advanced, he reached a point of moral heroism, ay, loftier than that at which he had stood, when, in the exercise of superhuman power, he bade darkness cover the land of the Egyptian, or the waters of the Red Sea divide before Israel.

Now we are not about to expatiate at any length on the magnanimity which was thus displayed by Moses. We have adduced the instance in order to show you how direct a parallel may be found in the history of the forerunner of our Lord, John the Baptist, to whose commemoration the Church dedicates this day. So soon as our Saviour had entered on his ministry, the great office of John was virtually at an end. It appears however that he still continued to baptize, and thus to prepare men for the disclosures of that fuller Revelation with which Christ was charged. In this way, the ministry of our Lord, and that of his forerunner, were, for a while, discharged together, though, inasmuch as Christ worked miracles, and John did not, there were quickly, as might have been expected, more attendants on the preaching of the Redeemer, than on that of the Baptist. This appears to have excited evil feelings in some of John's disciples, who, like Joshua, jealous for the honour of their master, thought that Jesus, by baptizing, entrenched on his province, and unwarrantably drew away his followers. You see how soon the spirit of partisanship showed itself in the Christian Church. No marvel if men afterwards said, "I am of Paul, and I of Apollos;" no marvel if, in later times, men have lost sight of the perpetual ministry of the great High Priest, in their zeal to exalt some favourite pastor; since even the success of our Lord was viewed with jealousy by the disciples of John.

You read, "They came unto John, and said unto him, Rabbi, He that was with thee beyond Jordan, to whom thou barest witness, behold, the same baptizeth, and all men come to Him." There is an implied censure upon John, as though, by bearing witness in favour of Jesus, he had unnecessarily exposed himself to the being thought less of and forsaken. But the Baptist himself had no share in these unholy and mean feelings. He immediately answered and said, "A man can receive nothing except it be given him from Heaven." His commission had proceeded from God: its nature, extent, and duration, had been settled by Divine appointment; was it then for him to repine that nothing higher had been assigned? was it not rather for him to be thankful that so much had been vouchsafed? And however galling it might be to his followers thus to see their master eclipsed, to John himself it was matter of great gladness, that He, whom he had heralded, was drawing all men towards Him. His heart was in his office; and nothing could rejoice him more than to see that not in vain had he come as "the voice of one crying in the wilderness;" but that public attention had been excited, and was now fastening itself where he wished it to centre. "He that hath the bride," he goes on to say, "is the bridegroom." It was not for me to draw round me a Church: I am not He who is to bring sinners into a close and endearing relationship to Himself, giving Himself for them, and making them one, through mystic union with Himself. "But the friend of the bridegroom, which standeth and heareth him, rejoiceth greatly because of the bridegroom's voice: this my joy therefore is fulfilled." As though he had said to his envious followers, Think not that it is any source of regret to me, that men are leaving my discipleship, and flocking to that of Christ. I came not as the bridegroom, but only as the bridegroom's friend, to bid the bride prepare herself for the coming of her Lord. What then can be matter of joy to me, if not to hear the voice of the bridegroom, proving that I was not a false messenger; and to see that the bride is ready to receive Him, so that not in vain did I give notice of his approach? "This my joy therefore is fulfilled;" the tidings which you bring me satisfy my most ardent longings; and in place of being depressed, I greatly exult.

And then the Baptist took occasion to assure his disciples, that what had moved their jealousy and displeasure was but the beginning, the first display, of a growing superiority to which no bounds could be set. They were not to imagine that there could be any alteration in the relative positions of Jesus and John, or that John would ever take that priority, which, in strange forgetfulness of his own sayings, they seemed to wish him to possess; on the contrary, he wished them distinctly to understand that being only of the earth, a mere man like one of themselves, he must decline in importance, and at length shrink altogether into insignificance. Whereas Christ, as having come from above, and therefore being above all, possessing a Divine nature as well as a human, and consequently liable to no decay, would go on discharging his high office, and enlarging his sway, according to the prediction of

Isaiah, "Of the increase of his government and peace there shall be no end, upon the throne of David and upon his Kingdom." And all this, this gradual fading away of himself, and this continued exaltation of Christ, the Baptist gathered into one powerful and comprehensive sentence, saying of our blessed Lord, "He must increase, but I must decrease." And what we have to ask of you is, whether he, who could thus correct the jealousy of his followers, who could show a perfect indifference in regard of himself and his position, so that his Lord and Master might but be honoured and exalted, did not display precisely the same nobleness of mind as is indicated in our text? whether the Baptist, whom the Church this day commemorates, did not, in saying of Christ, "He must increase, but I must decrease," rival Moses, the great type of the Redeemer Himself, when he finely exclaimed, "Enviest thou, for my sake? would God that all the Lord's people were Prophets, and that the Lord would put his Spirit upon them?"

But now let us consider more distinctly how character was here put to the proof, or in what it was that either Moses or John deserve imitation. The truth is, that it is natural to all of us to envy the growing reputation of others, and to be jealous when it seems likely to trench on our own. We may speak, and very justly, of the littleness of mind which is displayed by the envious and jealous; but nevertheless this littleness of mind belongs naturally to most, if not all of us; and he wins a fine triumph, or displays great command over himself, who can be content with inferiority, provided the cause of God and of truth be advanced. This is the precise case in which both

Moses and John showed greatness of soul; and though it be the case in which we have most reason to look for a forgetfulness of self, experience shows that the expectation is but too often disappointed. In other cases, we can hardly wonder that men should be mortified by the superiority of their rivals, and that they should look with dislike and bitterness upon those who eclipse them in the respects in which they most wish to shine. The courtier who has been long toiling to stand high in the favour of his sovereign, and who perceives that a younger candidate, who has but just entered the field, is fast outstripping him, so that the probability is, that he will soon be widely distanced,—we cannot marvel if he regard the youthful competitor with irritated feelings, in place of generously rejoicing in his rapid success. It would be a very fine instance of magnanimity, if this courtier were to cede gracefully the place to his rival, and to offer him, with marks of sincerity which could not be mistaken, his congratulations on the having passed him in the race. But we hardly look for such magnanimity—the occasion, if we may venture to say so, scarcely warrants it—the whole business is of so worldly, so ignoble a character, that the high principles of religion can scarcely be supposed brought into exercise; and yet the loftiness of spirit is such as these principles alone can be considered adequate to produce or sustain.

The case, however, is widely different when it is in the service of God, and not of an earthly king, that the two men engage. Here, by the very nature of the service, the grand thing aimed at is the glory of God, and not personal distinction or aggrandizement; and there is therefore ground for expecting, that if this glory be promoted, there will be gladness of heart in all Christians, whoever the agent who has been specially honoured. But, alas for the infirmity of human nature, there is no room for questioning that even Christians can be jealous of each other, and feel it a sore trial when they are distanced and eclipsed in being instrumental in promoting Christianity. I can imagine to myself a missionary settlement, where a devoted servant of God has striven for many years with idolatry, but has made but little way in winning Heathens to the faith. Here and there he can point to a convert from superstition; but, for the most part, he seems to have laboured in vain; and he is often forced to exclaim with the Prophet, "Who hath believed our report, and to whom hath the arm of the Lord been revealed?" And then there arrives in that missionary settlement another and a younger preacher of truth; and God has endowed him with higher powers, and honours him with greater success; so that there is a rapid demolition of the whole system of Heathenism, savages renouncing by hordes ancestral superstition, forming themselves into peaceful communities, and embracing with delight the religion of Christ. Now it is very easy to say that the elder missionary ought to feel nothing but exultation and thankfulness, as he marks the glorious results which follow the labours of the younger. The object which he had nearest his heart, was the conversion of Pagans; and what shall he do but rejoice in the accomplishment of this object, though effected through the instrumentality of another? And we do not say that the elder missionary would have other feelings than those which he is thus bound, by his own profession, to entertain. But, nevertheless, there will have been a great deal to try that missionary: and we can hardly doubt, forasmuch as his being a Christian will not have destroyed his being a man, that his breast must have been the scene of no inconsiderable struggle, and that there must have been earnest prayer and a vehement resistance to natural feelings, ere he could bring himself to survey with complacency the distinguished honour which God put on another.

We are far enough from regarding it as a matter of course, that the veteran in the missionary work would feel contented and pleased at seeing that work, which had gone on slowly with himself, suddenly progressing with amazing rapidity when undertaken by a younger labourer,—on the contrary, arguing from the known tendencies of our nature, we suppose that he must have had a hard battle with himself, before he could really rejoice in the sudden advance of Christianity; and we should regard him, as having won, through the assistance of Divine grace, a noble victory over some of the strongest cravings of the heart, when he frankly bade the stripling God speed, and rejoiced as he saw the idols falling prostrate before him.

And here we have very nearly the case of Moses and John, though we will confine ourselves to that of John, as brought before us by the services of the day. You are to remember that John had filled a most distinguished place as the forerunner of Christ. Prophets had spoken of him long ages back; an angel had announced his birth; and miracle, suspended for centuries, had again been wrought to fix attention on the child. And when he had grown up, and entered on his ministry, the whole nation of the Jews was agitated by his preaching, so that multitudes of every class flocked to him in the wilderness, "and were baptized of him in Jordan, confessing their sins." Was it nothing to John, regarded as a man of like passions with ourselves, to become of no importance, after having occupied so eminent a station? or would it have cost one of us no great effort, if called to such a post as had been assigned to the Baptist, to shrink into comparative privacy, and leave the scene clear for one mightier than himself? There is no better way of estimating a display of magnanimity than by making the circumstances as much as possible our own, and then examining what effort it would require to imitate the conduct which we cannot but admire. And if we have not overstated the case of the missionary, we may safely declare that any one of ourselves would find few trials harder than that of seeing himself wholly eclipsed; and that he might bring himself with less difficulty to almost any duty, rather than to that of rejoicing that another was made useful whilst he was passed by.

Never then, as we said of Moses, never was the Baptist more glorious, never did he more exhibit greatness of soul, than when he not only disclaimed all share in the petty jealousy shown by his followers, but proved that he exulted in being nothing in comparison of Christ. In the absence of all feeling of rivalry or disappointment; in the thorough willingness to be just what God pleased, eminent or forgotten, according as his purposes might require; in the honest joy that One greater than himself had assumed the office of a teacher of the people,—in these have we finer proof than in all the rest of his history, that the Baptist had subdued himself, and thus gained the hardest, as well as the most important, of all moral victories. And

I can admire John the Baptist, as he lives a severe life in the desert, "his raiment of camel's hair, and a leathern girdle about his loins," mortifying the flesh, and thus exhibiting to others that rigid self-denial which he enjoined as a preacher of repentance. I can admire him, as he boldly reproves vice in the great, daring even the terrors of a prison, rather than leave unrebuked the crimes of the profligate Herod. But, oh! never does he appear to me so transcendently great, never so free from the dross of human passion and infirmity, as when I see him surrounded by his followers, who have come, with jealous and angry feelings, to tell him how the world was flocking after Jesus, and hear him exclaiming, in a fine burst of pleasure and of gratitude, "He must increase, but I must decrease;" thus emulating the great lawgiver of Israel, who was not so noble, when he showed mastery over the proud enemies of his people, as when he showed mastery over himself, saying to Joshua, jealous that others should share his great gifts, "Enviest thou for my sake? would God that all the Lord's people were Prophets, and that the Lord would put his Spirit upon them."

But now having thus shown you how admirable was the Baptist in thus copying the lawgiver Moses, we would speak on the peculiar appropriateness of his being, though the forerunner of Christ, compared with Moses, inasmuch as John belonged strictly neither to the legal nor the Christian dispensation, but stood between the two. The time was not come for the full manifestation of God's purpose of mercy; and therefore, though the Baptist might urge to the abandoning vice, and the following after righteousness, he could not wield those weapons which are "mighty through God to the casting down of strong-holds:" he could not animate by the promises of the Gospel, nor show, by pointing to the cross, how all the terrors of Hell could be poured upon sin, whilst all the glories of Heaven were opened to sinners. And probably this peculiarity of his position, as standing between Moses and Christ, may have had to do with the words which he employed, when so beautifully imitating the one, and doing homage to the other. He well knew that he had not taught the great truths which were to be revealed under the new dispensation. He well knew that his baptism had been but introductory; that the mortification of the flesh, and the performance of moral duties to which he had urged, could not secure men from the wrath denounced against their sins; and that, consequently, unless he were to be followed by one charged with a clearer Revelation of mercy, his mission would be fruitless, and leave the world where it found it, under sentence of death.

And therefore was it far enough from his wish, that he should not be displaced, and surpassed in the office of a teacher from God. It would have been no pleasure to him to know, that he had communicated all the intelligence which God intended to give, in regard of his purposes towards our fallen race; and that He, whom he had been sent to announce, would teach no higher lessons, and unfold no better hopes. On the contrary, it was his gladness to feel that his own ministrations were but as the twilight which is lost in the full blaze of day, and that, when the Sun of righteousness, to whom he had served as the morning star, should pour his rich beams on the world, he himself must decline, and at length vanish out of sight. Could it then have been with any emotion of regret that he received the intelligence brought him by his disciples, intelligence that Jesus was gathering multitudes around Him, amazing them by his miracles, and not less by his doctrines? It was only that for which he had longed, that which was required to prove his own commission Divine, and to make it of any worth. What, he seems to say to his followers, are ye indeed envious for my sake? would ye have had me unsurpassed in the office of a teacher? Think ye that the baptism with which I have baptized, and the repentance which I have preached, are sufficient for the moral wants of a world lying in wickedness? The austerities which, by my practice, I have recommended; the duties which, by my teaching, I have inculcated—think ye that these alone will avert wrath, and save a soul from death? No, these must depart: these, like the shadows and ceremonies of the law, must be swept away, as preparatory indeed, and quite important in their place, but, nevertheless, insufficient, and therefore only temporary. My theological system has been imperfect: it has wanted explicitness on the points most important to the weak and the sinful; and what then can await it but the being forgotten and set aside, when God shall speak to the world by the mouth of his Son?

I behold—thus it is St. John seems to speak—the progress of the Gospel. I mark, with prophetic eye, the rolling away of all that has been preliminary: the sacrificial rites of the Temple are abolished: the penance and the fasting, these are pronounced ineffectual: and every doctrine gives place to that of which Christ Jesus shall be at once the teacher and the theme. I behold this doctrine abolishing the idols. I behold it purifying the heart, till, at length, all other systems are destroyed, and the globe, in its every department, worships the one God, through the "one Mediator between God and man." Yes, this is the vision which passes before me, as I direct my gaze to future times, the vision of all that has been introductory in the Divine dealings with man shrinking from the scene, that the message of reconciliation, which Christ will publish, may pass throughout the world, every where opposing falsehood, and every where at length triumphant. Prophets are silent; for "the spirit of prophecy is the testimony of Jesus;" and, Jesus having come, there is no need of further witness. Types are abolished; they did but prefigure Christ; and what purpose can they answer, when He, whom they represented, hath shown Himself to the world? And whilst the law and the Prophets thus resign to Christ the office of teacher, whilst Moses and Elias bow before Him, confessing their part fulfilled, and rejoicing that a greater hath descended to reveal the invisible God —am I to repine that my commission must terminate? am I to think it matter of complaint that the forerunner, with his imperfect theology, must give place to the Redeemer, with his full, and glorious, and overwhleming tidings?

Yes, into such shape as this may we throw the Baptist's answer to his envious disciples. Moses, far removed from the promised Messiah, could only breathe a wish for a general outpouring of God's Spirit on the Church. But John, though only the forerunner of the Christ, caught clearer views of the Gospel dispensation; he, therefore, could speak triumphantly of the progress of Christianity, as sweeping away all former dispensations, and could repress envy by the noble acknowledgment, "He must increase, but I must decrease," whilst Moses could only breathe the earnest wish, "Would God that all the Lord's people were Prophets, and that the Lord would put his Spirit upon them."

But by setting apart this day for the commemoration of John the Baptist, the Church designs to excite us to imitation of one so illustrious in office, and so admirable in character. Let us take then his acknowledgment as to Christ, "He must increase, but I must decrease," and see whether it ought not to express our own feelings, if we be firm and sincere in the Christian religion. It can scarcely be needful for us to tell you—and yet so prone are men to forget elementary truth, that you may require to be reminded—that the Gospel is a system constructed on purpose to abase the sinner, and exalt the Saviour. The system may be declared based upon the truth, that we are not sufficient of ourselves to think or do any thing as of ourselves; but that there have been fastened upon us, as the entailments of our first parents' sin, a moral helplessness, and a moral perversity, which must prevent our doing aught which can be acceptable to God, and ensure our doing much by which He will be sorely displeased.

And until a man is persuaded of this, the foundation truth, as we may call it, of Christianity, there is no hope of bringing him to close thankfully with the proffers of the Gospel: he will see nothing of the beauty, and feel nothing of the appropriateness of those proffers: like remedies offered to a man who is not conscious of sickness, they will appear of little worth, just because they do not meet any felt want or exigence. Hence it is, that, in all our strivings with the conscience, in all our endeavours to win over the unconverted, whether we find them on sick beds, or in the courts of the Lord's house, our great effort is given to the inculcating the doctrine of human disability; for if God enables us to bring a man to feel that he can do nothing for himself, he will be just in the attitude to hear with eagerness, and to receive with thankfulness, tidings of a Mediator who has done every thing for him. And thus it is virtually our endeavour to gain a cordial acknowledgment of the Baptist's confession: or rather, this confession involves a principle for which we strive, at the very outset, to procure admission into the theology of the man, whom we long to see walking in a heavenward path. We want to bring him to a consciousness, that he must think little of himself, and highly of Christ; and we should know that he had indeed passed the strait gate, and entered on the narrow path, if there were even an incipient persuasion in his mind, that Christ must increase, and that he must decrease.

Let each of you, who may be counting himself a converted man, bring his case to this criterion: let him examine, with all diligence and all faithfulness, whether it is his experience, to seem less and less in his owne yes, and to feel more and more the sufficiency of the Saviour. It is appointed by God; nay, we might say, it results from the very nature of the case—that the glories of Christ are discerned in the same degree as our own vileness and depravity. The more we feel how undeserving, how helpless we are, the more shall we admire the exceeding love of God, and cry out, in amazement as well as gratitude, "What is man that thou art mindful of him, and the son of man that thou visitest him?" The more we perceive the hatefulness of sin, and the immenseness of the wrath which it provokes, the greater will be our sense of the virtues of Christ's death, through which pardon has been placed within reach. In proportion as we feel how utterly unable we are to keep the law in a solitary tittle we shall look with awe and veneration on one "found in fashion as a man," "who did no sin, neither was guile found in his mouth." The greater our consciousness of a defilement, which must unfit us for those pure mansions where God displays his brightness, the more intense will be our estimate of those expiatory and sanctifying influences, through which we can be presented without spot or wrinkle, or any such thing. Who knows the worth of the Mediator, like he who feels, in every recess of his soul, that he has destroyed himself, thrown himself to an immeasurable distance from God and from happiness, and that there he must have eternally remained, had no Intercessor come to "seek and save that which was lost?"

In short, to whom will Christ Jesus be so nearly "all in all," as to the man who is most nearly emptied of self? "He must increase, but I must decrease"—it is what every true Christian will desire to be able to say, with more and more of the gladness and confidence of the Baptist. "I must decrease"—I must be more humbled under a sense of sin; I must have yet lower thoughts of my own moral powers, and deeper views of my vileness as an alien from God. But "He must increase." The fulness which there is in Christ must be more and more perceived: the sufficiency of his sacrifice, the cleansing power of his blood, the prevalence of his intercession, these must be increasingly recognised and confided in: though He cannot become greater in Himself, He must become greater in my esteem; and with a warmer love, and a stronger faith, must I daily proclaim Him "Chief among ten thousand, and altogether lovely."

And does there yet remain no other sense in which the Baptist's words may be applied? are there no tongues but our own on which they are appropriate? The words were prophetic: they echoed, as we before said, the prediction of Isaiah, "Of the increase of his government there shall be no end." And the whole of this creation seems to us to catch the sentiment, and to be vocal with its utterance. The sun, coming forth as a bridegroom from his chamber, proclaims, "He must increase, but I must decrease"—these Heavens are to be rolled up as a scroll; and the New Jerusalem is to have no need of the sun, "for the glory of God will lighten it, and the Lamb will be the light thereof." Moon and stars take up the proclamation: there is to be no night in that city; and therefore must they wholly vanish, quenched in the effulgence of Him who will for ever scatter all darkness. And what sound is that which comes rolling as from ten thousand times ten thousand voices? It is the utterance of "every creature which is in Heaven, and on the earth, and under the earth, and such as are in the sea," pronouncing, "Worthy is the Lamb that was slain, to receive power, and riches, and wisdom, and strength, and honour, and glory, and blessing." Then all orders of intelligence, Angel and Archangel, principality and power, are bowing before the Mediator, extolling Him whilst they abase themselves; and what then is that mighty chorus which John the Evangelist heard, but the echo of those words which John the Baptist uttered, "He must increase, but we must decrease?"

Yes, King of kings, "thou must reign, until thou hast put all enemies under thy feet." Every other dominion is to decline, that the vision, vouchsafed to Daniel, may be accomplished, and thy dominion be established as an everlasting dominion, thy royalty be extended over all the creatures of God. Here indeed we are launched on an ocean without a shore. There may be, throughout eternity, fresh manifestations of Deity; and if every manifestation add, as it must, to the dignity and lustre of Him, "in whom dwelleth all the fulness of the Godhead bodily," we can set no bounds to the increase of Christ. And though we ourselves shall be ever on the advance, reaching successively greater heights in knowledge and in happiness, yet may our Redeemer so exceed every creature in the growth in all that is glorious, that every creature, when brought into comparison with Him, shall seem to diminish, rather than expand. Still therefore may it be, that, in the midst of the unimagined progress or march of eternity, we shall have to speak of ourselves as decreasing, and of Christ alone as increasing. He will be continually separated from us by such broader and broader districts of magnificence, notwithstanding our own growing majesties, that we shall continually think less and less of ourselves, and more and more of Him. To extol Him will still be duty: but that duty will be happiness; though we must die, and enter into possession of the heavenly inheritance, before we can even conjecture with what emotions, contemplating how Christ outshines every creature, so that the most glorious veils his face, we shall seize the golden harps, and sweep them to the strain, "He must increase, but we must decrease." The Spirit of God can alone fit us for this blessedness—with Moses, then, let us pray on behalf of others and ourselves, "Would God that all the Lord's people were Prophets, and that the Lord would put his Spirit upon them!"

LECTURE XI.

Building the Tombs of the Prophets.

LUKE xi. 47, 48.

"Woe unto you! for ye build the sepulchres of the Prophets, and your fathers killed them. Truly ye bear witness that ye allow the deeds of your fathers; for they indeed killed them, and ye build their sepulchres."

AND wherefore this woe? Was it not rather commendable than blameworthy, that the Jews showed reverence for the prophets whom their fathers had slain? They seemed hereby but to testify that their fathers had done wrong, that the Prophets were God's messengers, who ought to have been differently received—what could there be to condemn in this? Our fathers killed Ridley, and Hooper, and Latimer, noble men, who were contending for the faith once delivered to the saints. We erect a martyrs' memorial: we build the sepulchres for these slain witnesses for truth: and is it necessarily a woe which we hereby incur? God forbid: we reproach indeed our fathers, we publish their guilt, when we rear a stately pile in honour of these martyred men: but if we love and reverence the cause for which the blood was shed, we are doing, we may believe, what is acceptable to God.

But the Jews, whilst honouring the Prophets, and reproaching their fathers, were flattering themselves that they could never have done the like: they said, as we learn from St. Matthew, "If we had been in the days of our fathers, we would not have been partakers with them in the blood of the Prophets!" Would they not indeed? were they not at the very moment thirsting for the blood of Christ, and contriving his destruction? Alas for the fatal facility with which those who are quick in discerning the faults of others, can blind themselves to their own! It is amongst the most memorable of the sayings of our Lord, "Why beholdest thou the mote that is in thy brother's eye, but considerest not the beam that is in thine own eye?" The improving our own character, and therefore the correcting our own faults, should evidently be our chief purpose or object; and the knowledge that we may be keen-sighted as to the errors of others, and, all the while, blind to our own, should produce circumspection and inquisitiveness in respect of ourselves, making us cautious as to the condemning a neighbour, or concluding that we should act differently under similar circumstances.

Here was the fault of the Jews. They were the descendants of men who had persecuted and slain the Prophets of God. But they themselves were ready to do the very same: they were plotting the death of the greatest Prophet, the greatest in all the signs or evidences of a Prophet, that had ever arisen in their land. And, nevertheless, they could see well enough how wrong their fathers had been, and could join in showing honour to the righteous persons whom they had treated so ill: but it does not seem to have struck them, that they were closely treading in their steps, and were about to imitate, or rather, far surpass, what they so loudly condemned. They reared the gorgeous monument, and ostentatiously adorned the graves of those who had lost their lives in the cause of God and of truth—thus publicly evidencing their sense of the innocence of the martyrs, and of the guiltiness of those who had put them to death. Thus far there might have been sincerity; their fathers had done foully; and though it might not well become children to expose and upbraid the faults of their ancestors, the flagitiousness was so great that much might have been forgiven to a just and righteous indignation. But they went on to compare themselves with their fathers, and to argue from the comparison, that, had it been in their days that the Prophets had arisen, they would never have been treated in so injurious a manner. Alas for their ignorance of themselves! they were plotting to put a Prophet to death, whilst building the tombs of those Prophets whom their fathers had slain.

But is there no lesson here for ourselves? We, on our part, are ready enough to condemn the Jews, wondering at their blindness, and execrating their sin: but may we not, like the Jews, be doing the very thing which we denounce, so that, at one and the same moment, we both copy and condemn? Let us not too hastily conclude that there may be no parallel amongst ourselves to that which we are so ready to wonder at and reprove: human nature is always the same; and if the manifestations of its corruption be somewhat different at different times, you have only to look a little below the surface, and you may find the difference wholly superficial. Come then with us, that we may search and see whether there be nothing in our own day of execrating in others the very sin which may be charged on ourselves; whether, in short, whilst we are the bitter enemies of Christ and his Apostles, we may not, like the Jews, be flattering ourselves that we could never have taken part in the cruel persecutions of earlier days, and thus giving cause for the reproachful saying, "Truly ye bear witness that ye allow the deeds of your fathers; for they indeed killed them, and ye build their sepulchres."

Now, let us first fix attention on the singular fact, that what is admired in the dead, may be execrated in the living. There was no essential difference between the preaching of Christ, which excited the fierce anger of the Jews, and that of the Prophets which had similarly displeased and irritated their fathers. In both cases the preaching was that of the necessity of repentance, and of the certainty of vengeance, if not averted through the forsaking of sin. And the Jews, in the time of our Lord, could profess a high admiration of the preachers who had pressed these truths on their fathers, though, all the while, they were full of indignation against those who laboured to press them on themselves. They reared the stately monument in honour of intrepid men, who had published, in a former age, the very message and doctrine which they were resolved at all hazards to silence in their own. And thus did they honour the memory of the dead for the very thing which made them hate and persecute the living—as though God compelled justice to be done to the righteous, and wrung from their adversaries a testimony in their favour.

The same takes place in our own day and generation. Call to mind the names of martyrs, and confessors, and preachers, who, whilst they lived, drew on themselves almost universal detestation, by their zeal in the publication of truth, and the exposure of error. Gather opinions as to these martyrs, confessors, and preachers, and you will obtain well nigh an unqualified verdict, pronouncing them amongst the worthiest of men, ornaments to their own age, and examples to every succeeding. Open a subscription for some testimonial to their honour; and money will flow in for the building their tombs and garnishing their sepulchres, just as though there were a general anxiety to evince a sense of their worth, and of the injustice of their contemporaries. But now go on to examine what the principles were which these dead worthies upheld, what the doctrines which they published, what the practices which they denounced. And do you think you will find that these principles are in general repute, these doctrines generally esteemed, these practices generally shunned? Oh, not so. The principles are still those which excite opposition, the doctrines are disliked, the practices are cherished. If you could bring up from the grave the minister whose uncompromising discharge of his sacred office drew upon him hatred and persecution, but to whom posterity gives its approval; and if he were to engage once more in the duties of the ministry; do you suppose that he would be generally esteemed and admired, even as though there had passed a great change over the spirit of the times, and truth, which had been hateful, had now become acceptable? Not so; the opposition of the cross has not ceased: it is neither local nor temporary: it may be less openly shown at one time than at another: but the feeling of dislike to the Gospel is the feeling of human nature, the produce of the heart, and asking nothing but its corruption in order to its growth. And the minister, whom we suppose to return to the scene of his labours, and whose memory is so cherished and hallowed, would again have opposition to encounter, opposition which, if it assumed not as determined an attitude, would evidence as radical a dislike as when some century back he had striven to impress truth on a scornful generation.

For you do not observe that it is yet the high road to the approbation and affection of men, to tell them of their faults, and to preach to them, that if they would be wise, they must become fools. On the contrary, there is no denying that the peculiar truths of the Gospel are heard with dislike and aversion, and that he, who gives himself to their full and unflinching publication, must lay his account for no small share of prejudice, misrepresentation, and opposition. What right, then, can there be to think that if the dead were brought back, the dead whose memories it may be the fashion to honour, and whose sepulchres to adorn, they would receive a different treatment, and find themselves listened to with approval, though that approval is withheld from those who are labouring to walk in their steps? With human nature just what it was, and the Gospel just what it was, I have no reason to suppose that the persecution of the present day would not have been the persecution of a former, and the persecution of a former the persecution of the present, had the living been the dead, and the dead the living. The man who now dislikes the truth, and who shows his dislike by contempt or ridicule of the teachers of truth, would, for any thing that I can see to the contrary, have shown his dislike by violence and injury, had he lived when such modes were commonly resorted to by the supporters of error. The dislike is the producing cause of opposition; and this being the same, the only difference will be in the form which the opposition assumes; and the form will be determined by the habits and customs of the times. I can find no ground whatever for thinking that the individual who is thoroughly opposed to Evangelical doctrine, but who as thoroughly repudiates the attempt to put it down by open persecution, would have had a word to say against the killing men for their religion, had he lived when it was usual to hurry the faithful to the stake and the scaffold. There is no difference as to the actuating principle between him and those who took a bloody course in order to rid themselves of tenets which they utterly disliked. And if the actuating principle displayed itself, in the one instance, in fierce cruelty, whilst, in the other, its only manifestations are ridicule and contempt, the difference is to be ascribed to an altered state of society, and to the general diffusion of more tolerant sentiment, rather than to any such inherent difference in men as would forbid our supposing that he who persecutes by a frown, might have persecuted with the sword. Oh, let no one think that he could never have joined with the men of an earlier day in resisting truth by violence and bloodshed. If he resist truth now by such modes as the temper of the age will permit, he has the best possible reason for concluding, that, had he lived when other and harsher modes were allowed, he would equally have acted up to the spirit of the times. There is quite sufficient evidence in the honour rendered to the dead, but withheld from the living, to induce a persuasion that the tombs may be built, and the sepulchres garnished, by those who would have joined in slaying their occupants.

I want to know how it comes to pass, that there is so great and general an admiration of martyrs, and confessors, and other bold champions of Protestantism, even whilst the doctrines of Protestantism may be but little regarded. I want to know how it comes to pass, that the names of men who, in their own day, were made "the offscouring of all things," are now held in universal respect, though the tenets which they laboured to enforce, and the enforcing of which exposed them to scorn, are as much as ever the objects of a deep-rooted dislike. I should have expected, from the veneration in which our martyrs are held, that the principles which they died to maintain, would be every where cherished with devoted affection. I should have expected, from observing the justice which posterity renders to faithful ministers, whose faithfulness made them through life the victims of malice and contempt, that the pure unadulterated Gospel would be prized as the best boon that God hath given to man. But the expectation is disappointed: those who will venerate the martyrs, may have no love for the truths which their martyrdom sealed; and many who hallow the memory of an Evangelical teacher, may turn with loathing from simple Evangelical doctrine.

And it is by the feelings entertained towards the things taught, and not by those expressed towards the dead who were their teachers, that we are to judge whether men would have joined in persecuting the Prophets. I care nothing for the stately mausoleum. I have no faith in the laboured panegyric. I am not to be persuaded, because sculpture and painting may devote themselves to the representing the magnanimous dead, or poetry consecrate its richest melodies to the story of their deeds and their wrongs. If the truth, for which the dead died, be not beloved by the living, there is no evidence that the living would not have aided in their destruction. If the doctrines which brought such obloquy on the departed do not now secure respect for their faithful publishers and upholders, what are the encomiums passed on the departed, but so many hypocritical sayings, which, if not expressly designed to deceive, prove that those who utter them are deceiving themselves? And judge ye whether when men are tried by their attachment to truth, and their zeal in maintaining it, by the favour which its proclamation conciliates for the living, and not by the applause which it secures to the dead, they can be acquitted of all likelihood that they would have joined in persecution, had they lived in the days when the righteous were slain. Oh, we have in abundance the building of the tombs, and the garnishing of the sepulchres? But whose tombs and whose sepulchres? The tombs of men who laid down their lives in support of doctrines, which are either secretly disliked, or openly denounced, by the builders: the sepulchres of preachers who would not keep back statements that are still sure to provoke the enmity of the garnishers. And what then are we to do but charge with hypocrisy, as Christ charged the Jews, the men who, overlooking the evidence which their own hearts might furnish, would condemn in others what they only want temptation and opportunity to commit? what but address them in the language of our text, as we see them honouring in the dead what they repudiate in the living, "Woe unto you! ye build the sepulchres of the Prophets, and your fathers killed them. Truly ye bear witness that ye allow the deeds of your fathers; for they indeed killed them, and ye build their sepulchres."

But we may identify our own case yet more closely with that of the Jews. There is perhaps no more common feeling than that of amazement and indignation at the treatment which our Lord received from his countrymen. If ever there moved upon the earth the being who seemed likely to disarm all enmity, and attract towards himself universal affection, that being, undoubtedly, was Jesus of Nazareth. He had, so evidently, no object but that of benefiting others, and he gave such evidences of ability to compass this object, that we might have supposed that all classes would have eagerly welcomed him as a Prophet and deliverer. And the apparent improbability of the rejection of Christ may easily induce a persuasion that, had we been in the days of the Jews, we could never have shared in their crime. But how ought such passages as our text to stagger us, showing us, as they do, that the Jews equally flattered themselves that they were incapable of the sin of putting a great Prophet to death. We make no doubt, that, had we been contemporary with Christ, had we beheld his miracles and listened to his preaching, we should never have been of the number of those who sought his destruction. But what is this persuasion but the very persuasion of the Jews, who sat in judgment on their fathers, as slayers of the Prophets, and determined that they could never have joined them in their crime;

and this too at the moment when they thirsted for Christ's blood, and bent themselves to compass his death? If there were not our text in the Bible, I might almost have thought that no other people but the Jews could have perpetrated the deed from which the sun drew back, and at which the earth trembled. But when I find that even the Jews could fancy themselves unable to do as their fathers had done, I look with apprehension on any verdict of self-acquittal, and almost take it in evidence of a depravity adequate to the crime. It may be, that, as I look on the Scribes and Pharisees plotting the destruction of Jesus, I feel that I could never have joined the guilty conclave, or that I should have joined it only to give my protest against the desperate wickedness. It may be that, as I beheld the infuriated multitude insulting the Redeemer, and demanding his crucifixion, I feel that I should at least have shrunk away in horror, if I had not had the courage to stand forward in defence of persecuted goodness. It may seem to me almost impossible that I should have conspired against Christ, that I should have helped to weave the crown of thorns, and to drive the nails into his hands and his feet. But am I so unlike the Jew, is there any such radical difference between myself and the Jew, that I am warranted in believing that his wickedness could never have been mine? Ah, there is at least one point of similarity between us; and this ought to make me fearful of hastily concluding that there cannot be more. And what is this point? why, that the Jew and myself are equally ready to plead too much goodness to allow of joining in killing a Prophet. My way of judging and declining was precisely his, the reference to a crime which others committed, and the determining against the possibility of any participation.

And where there is the same assurance of inability to perpetrate a sin, there is probably the same ability. Let us trust to no verdict of acquittal which we may be disposed to pass on ourselves, after listening to that which the murderers of Christ so complacently uttered. If I wish to make out to you the possibility that, had you lived in the days when Messiah was on earth, you would have joined in heaping on him ignominy, and compassing his death, it may be in vain, as I have already said, that I lead you to the Hall of Judgment, and to Calvary, and there show you the spotless Redeemer given up to the will of his enemies. I well know with what indignation you will repel the supposition that you could ever have taken part in persecuting so benevolent and righteous a being. Well, I will not argue with you, where there is so much to stir the passions, and to make the blood boil. But I am sure it ought to make you suspicious of your confidence, and afraid that you vastly overrate your own virtue, when can show you these very Jews repelling, with the same indignation as yourselves, the supposition that they could ever join in a deed of cruelty and wrong, pronouncing with the same complacency as yourselves on the impossibility of their slaying the righteous. Ah, be bold if you will, whilst you only hear the Jews exclaiming, "Crucify him, crucify him," "not this man, but Barabbas;" but will it not stagger you to look upon these Jews, engaged in rearing costly memorials to the martyrs of another day, engaged in this work as a sort of evidence that they abhorred the putting those martyrs to death, and could never have taken part in so atrocious a deed, and thus drawing on themselves the denunciation of our text, "Woe unto you! truly ye bear witness that ye allow the deeds of your fathers: for they indeed killed them, and ye build their sepulchres?"

But even yet, we have not succeeded in giving to our text that thorough personal application of which we believe it susceptible. There is no more singular instance on record than this of the Jews, of the power which there is in men of deceiving themselves, of discerning clearly enough the faults of another, whilst altogether blind to those faults in themselves. But we wish to see whether we may not transfer the whole passage to our own day and generation, or assert the repetition amongst ourselves of what was said or done by the profligate Jews. There is no difficulty in tracing the parallel, if you keep out of sight the hostility of the Jews to the greatest Prophet that the world ever saw. The parallel is then established, if the men of our own day be ready to build the tombs of the Prophets, and boldly to maintain, that, had they lived when blood was being shed, their hands should never have been stained. And beyond question, they are ready enough for this, if you put the Jews for the fathers, and Christ for the slain Prophet. There is abundance of outward honour to the founders of Christianity, abundance of what we may call the building the tomb, and the garnishing the sepulchre; and men have but little hesitation in execrating the crime of the Jews, as a crime far outdoing their own power of commission. So far therefore we may safely take the text, and give it as descriptive of what occurs amongst ourselves. But may we also denounce the woe which it contains? That woe is evidently denounced on account of the hypocrisy of those whose actions are described, on account of their conspiring against the living Christ, whilst joining to do honour to the murdered Prophets.

And is there any thing parallel to this amongst ourselves? Indeed there is: for it is very easy to be indignant against those who put Jesus to death, and all the while to overlook our own share in the guilty transaction. It is very easy to give up to universal execration the Roman and the Jew, and to be unmindful of the causes which brought round the Crucifixion. It is very easy to take the narrative of Christ's sufferings, just as you would the narrative of some doleful occurrence that happened in a remote age, and which has little more than its sadness to give it interest with your feelings. But who slew the Lamb of God? who drove the nails? who reared the cross? Not the Roman and the Jew. These were but agents and instruments. Christ died for the sins of the world: the sins of the world were really his murderers, though they used the Roman and the Jew as his executioners. And no man regards the death of Christ under a just point of view, who does not charge himself with a share in the perpetration. He who does not make himself one of the murderers can scarcely have faith in the propitiation. It is easy to condemn the Jews for murdering Christ, precisely as we condemn our own fathers for murdering Charles I. In both cases we may condemn, without feeling that we had personally any thing to do with the crime; and the condemnation may be the severer, from the complacency with which we regard our own innocence.

But there is all the difference between the cases of the Jews murdering Christ, and of our fathers murdering Charles I. It is quite true that we are ourselves innocent of the latter crime; but it is just as true that we are ourselves guilty of the former. And there is no safety for a man until he become self-convicted of this guiltiness. I must feel myself the shedder of the blood by which I am cleansed, the slayer of the Mediator by whom I am saved. He died for his murderers, and the benefits of his death are available to those only who know themselves his murderers. And, whilst men are pleasing themselves with the thought that they could never have joined in killing a Prophet, may they not be actually engaged in hostility to Christ, yea, actually employed in effecting his Crucifixion? If not, what means St. Paul when he speaks of some who "crucify the Son of God afresh, and put Him to an open shame?" what means Christ Himself, when saying to the enemy of his Church, "Saul, Saul, why persecutest thou me?" There may yet, there may now, be such a thing as piercing the Son of God, heaping on Him ignominy, and nailing Him to the tree. It is virtually done whenever, notwithstanding his amazing interference, and the provision made at so incalculable a price for human deliverance, men turn away from the Redeemer, refusing to accept the mercy which He proffers, because they will not quit the sins which He abhors. It is virtually done by every wilful act of rebellion, by unbelief, by pride, by hardness of heart, by resistance to the strivings of the Spirit, by disobedience to the precepts of the Gospel. The wilful transgressor does all which he can do towards rendering necessary a second Crucifixion: he commits more and more of that which crucified Christ; and therefore, so far as his own guiltiness is concerned, may literally be charged with crucifying Him again.

And, over and above this, you are to consider that Christ is continually coming to the impenitent and obdurate, in and through the ordinances of religion, presenting Himself to them as their Redeemer, and beseeching them to receive Him, as they would hope to escape eternal destruction. But they treat Him with contempt. He calls, but they refuse: He stretches out his hand, but they will not regard. And what is all this, if not the repetition of the Jewish denial and rejection of Christ? If, in the exercise of my office as a minister of Christ, and speaking in the name of Christ, I propose to the self-righteous that they renounce their own righteousness as nothing worth, and trust for their acceptance to the righteousness of the Mediator; and if they proudly refuse, determining that they will take the imperfect and polluted, in preference to the glorious and spotless; I should like to know what this practically is, if it be not the shouting with the Jews, "Not this man, but Barabbas." If again, in the exercise of the same office, and speaking in the same name, I come down upon the sensual and the profligate, and conjure them that, without a moment's delay, they break loose from practices which must issue in death, showing them the Saviour, and entreating them not to persist in that which he abhors; and if they turn away from the entreaty, anxious only to get rid of the molestation, and to be left undisturbed in their impiety—I should like to know what this practically is, if it be not the raising the cry, "Crucify him, crucify him!" I say not, that, exalted as He is to a throne of light, and invested with all power in Heaven and earth, Christ can any longer be smitten and wounded as when, in the days of his humiliation, He gave his back to the smiters, and his cheeks to them that plucked off the hair. But the question is not what Christ may yet feel; it is only what man may yet do. There may be all the intention and all the criminality on our part, whilst there is an incapacity of suffering upon his. So that under every point of view, it is but a just, though a fearful accusation, that which arraigns all wilful transgressors as crucifiers of Christ. And nevertheless these wilful transgressors bear the Christian name, and may even do much to advance the Christian cause. Yes, whilst living in disobedience to Christ, and therefore in the practical rejection of Him as the deliverer from sin, there are numbers who will show Him all outward respect, even helping to build churches, and establish missions, that his Gospel may be spread far and wide. Ah, then, have we not at last made out thoroughly the parallel, and shown that our text may be brought down without the change of a letter to our own day and generation? "Woe unto you, hypocrites!" Woe unto you, men who with no hatred of sin, and therefore no love of Christ, call yourselves Christians, and even take part in the promotion of Christianity! Ye are building the tombs of the Prophets, ye are garnishing the sepulchres of the righteous. But ye are, all the while, of the number of those who are bent on the rejection and crucifixion of the Christ. Rear churches if you will, as the Jews reared the stately mausoleum in honour of the dead whom their fathers had slain. But know ye that, so long as ye do not give the heart to the Saviour, ye crucify Him afresh, and must be ranked with his murderers. And you may execrate the wickedness of the Jews: you may flatter yourselves that you, for your part, could never have joined in persecuting Christ, seeing that you are ready to bow at his name, and to yield respect to his religion. But all this only brings you more accurately under the woe of our text; all this only identifies you more thoroughly with the men who, whilst bent on the destruction of Christ, could join in doing honour to the memory of the martyred dead, and thus give cause for its being said of them, reproachfully and indignantly said, "Truly ye allow the deeds of your fathers: for they indeed killed the Prophets, and ye build their sepulchres."

Now there is yet another and an important point of view under which, in conclusion, we wish to place our text. The Jews may have believed and boasted themselves incapable of taking part in the killing a Prophet, little suspecting that they needed only the being placed in the same circumstances as their fathers, in order to their imitating their crimes. And this is but the illustration of a general truth, that, whilst men are not tempted to a sin, they cannot judge whether or not they would commit it if they were. With singular propriety are we instructed to pray, "Lead us not into temptation;" for only temptation may be needed to our perpetrating the worst crimes that disgrace human nature. They say that the earth contains varieties of seed: and that, according to concurrent circumstances, is there one production at one time, and another at another. And this I am sure is the case with the heart, "out of which," according to Christ, "proceed evil thoughts, murders, adulteries, fornications, thefts, false witness, blasphemies." The seeds of all these iniquities are deposited in the heart; and a certain state, so to speak, of the moral atmosphere, or a certain combination of exciting causes, is all that is required to develop them in the practice.

It does therefore but argue great ignorance of ourselves, to suppose that this or that sin is too bad for us to commit. And the persuasion that we could not commit it, is but an evidence of the likelihood of our being betrayed into the commission; for it shows a measure of self-confidence, as well as of ignorance, which God may be expected to punish by withdrawing his grace—and if that be withdrawn, where is human virtue? We are bound, as believers in Revelation, to believe that nothing of evil is beyond our power, and nothing of good within it, if we be left to ourselves, and are not acted on by an influence from above. And our only security against becoming perpetrators of crimes, at whose very mention we perhaps shudder, lies in such a consciousness of our own depravity as leads to a prayerful, continual dependence on the preventing and restraining grace of God. "Is thy servant a dog that he should do this?" was the exclamation of Hazael to the Prophet, when told of the crimes which he would live to commit. He did not feel himself bad enough for the perpetration, and therefore was no sooner on the throne than the perpetration came. If, on the contrary, he had said, Thy servant is naturally bad enough for this; but, whilst I distrust myself, I will look up to God to withhold me from such crimes; it may be that he would never have committed the atrocities which now darken his name. The Jews could build the tombs of the Prophets, and garnish the sepulchres of the righteous, proudly thinking, whilst they recorded the sin of their fathers, that themselves were too pure to reject and ill-use a messenger of God. And therefore when the messenger arose in their land, they did worse than their fathers, and cast him out of the vineyard, and slew him. It may be that if, on the contrary, whilst they reared the monument, and pronounced a just judgment on their ancestors, they had confessed the heart to be "deceitful above all things and desperately wicked," and had added to the confession prayer for strength against temptation, they would never have been left to commit the vast enormity, for which they yet labour under the malediction of Heaven.

Let us be warned, men and brethren, by instances like these. We have only to be confident in ourselves, and there is no wickedness which we may not ultimately commit. Remember David, and "let him that thinketh he standeth take heed lest he fall." I do not say that we are not to build the tombs of the Prophets. I do not say, that is, that we are not to mark our sense, and signify our abhorrence, of the sins of our fellow-men, whether our ancestors, or our contemporaries. It was not in this that the Scribes and the Pharisees were wrong: crime is to be reprobated, and the more public the reprobation the better. But we are to be careful that we do not acquit ourselves, whilst condemning others. The sin was the sin of men; and what men have done, men may do. Build then the tomb, garnish the sepulchre: but, all the while, say, "O Lord, we have the same evil heart as our fathers: restrain thou then us by the power of thy Spirit; otherwise shall we, in like manner, bequeath to our children tombs to build and sepulchres to garnish."

LECTURE XII.

Manifestation of the Sons of God.

ROMANS viii. 19.

"For the earnest expectation of the creature waiteth for the manifestation of the sons of God.

IN this and the following verses, St. Paul gives a remarkable description of the present state of the visible creation. He represents it as in the agonies of travail, and as intently expecting the manifestation of the sons of God. The creature itself, he tells us, has been made subject to vanity—referring, we may believe, to that universal prostitution of the works and gifts of God, which, in different degrees, has subsisted ever since the fall. There is scarcely the object, whether in the animate or the inanimate creation, which has not been abused by man to the purposes of vanity. Indeed, whatsoever God hath made has been worshipped as God; so that idolatry, which is emphatically vanity, has turned the universe into its storehouse of deities. But there shall come an end to this subjection of the creature; and, as though the material system were conscious alike of its thraldom and its deliverance, St. Paul represents it as groaning, and yet anticipating a glorious emancipation. "The whole creation groaneth and travaileth in pain together until now. The creature itself also shall be delivered from the bondage of corruption into the glorious liberty of the children of God."

We learn, from the bold imagery thus used by the Apostle, that times of refreshing have to break on this oppressed and disordered creation; and that, when righteousness shall receive its final and public approval, the world itself will spring into liberty, and walk the heavens in renovated beauty. It was the world, with all its tenantry, that Christ redeemed from the bondage of corruption; though, as yet, there has been no open assertion of a conquest which included whatever was affected by human apostacy. And we are taught, by many portions of Scripture, as well as by that which is now under notice, that the application of Redemption shall be finally co-extensive with the consequences of the fall, so that whatever withered beneath the curse will bloom again through the influence of the Atonement. For a long season indeed evil is permitted to retain its dominion; and therefore may the creation be depicted as groaning and travailing in pain. But a day is determined, on which Christ will appear to assert his victory, and exterminate pollution; and therefore it is said that the creature is "subjected in hope."

St. Paul then goes on to declare, that a sense of burden, not to be overcome by the certainty of deliverance, was not confined to the inanimate, or irrational creation. It was not merely the visible world, with its profaned and misused productions, which groaned and heaved beneath the pressure imposed by transgression. "Ourselves also," saith the Apostle, "which have the first-fruits of the Spirit, even we ourselves groan within ourselves." Was it to be thought that the creation suffered thus acutely, because there were no beginnings of relief, no foretastes of the yet distant rest? Nay, argues the Apostle, we have the first-fruits of the Spirit, and yet take part with the creation in signs of pain and distress. And thus the greatness of the oppression is strikingly displayed—to know deliverance certain, and yet to groan; to receive earnests of peace, and still to be in agony. We forget the groans of the inanimate system, and of irrational or irreligious creatures, when we hear those of believers in Christ. Shall not they who feel themselves redeemed, who already enjoy the foretastes of everlasting bless, be free from that suffering which seems the heritage of the fallen? Shall not they, at least, find such present gladness and rest, that they will not be engaged, like the creatures around them, in longing for a promised deliverance? The Apostle answers these questions decidedly in the negative. "Not only they, but ourselves also, which have the first-fruits of the Spirit, even we ourselves groan within ourselves, waiting for the adoption, to wit, the redemption of our body." You will observe what it was for which the true Christian waited and longed—"the redemption of the body"—for this will help us to understand "the manifestation of the sons of God," which is mentioned in our text. They are evidently, if not the same thing, yet things which should occur at the same time: the redemption of the body, that is, its final resurrection, is to constitute, or to occur with, the manifestation of the sons of God. The sons of God are to be manifested, gloriously owned and displayed in the face of the universe, when the grave shall give up its deposit, and soul and body be admitted into Heaven. Here will be a point deserving very close attention—an interest, an importance, is attached to the resurrection of the body, which may place that great article of our faith under a new point of view. At the same time, you should carefully observe, that, by pursuing the context of the passage on which we discourse, we have found that "the earnest expectation of the creature," an expectation which is indicated by tokens of agony and distress, is shared by true believers; for they too are described as "groaning within themselves." Let us follow out the trains of thought which are hereby suggested—here is the whole creation, the true Christian as well as every other being, groaning in pain: here is the resurrection, or redemption, of the body represented as the thing longed for in this universal distress: when we have carefully looked into all these facts, we may, by God's help, understand something of the force of the remarkable saying, "The earnest expectation of the creature waiteth for the manifestation of the sons of God."

Now, we would first observe that no passages of Scripture can be more valuable to the Christian than those which open to him the experience of the most eminent saints. If he can prove that the conflicts in which he is involved, and the sorrows by which he is oppressed, are just those which engaged and weighed down God's people of old, he has no right to think his own condition strange, nor to use his experience as an argument against his security. There are many who distress themselves with suspicions that they are not true believers, because they feel their love of God to be cold, and they are painfully conscious that corruption is still mighty within them. We do not say that the languor of spiritual affections, and the strength of indwelling sin, ought to be other than occasions of grief and humiliation. But no one can, on these accounts, be warranted in concluding himself an unrenewed man, who remembers the pathetic exclamation of St. Paul, "O wretched man that I am! who shall deliver me from the body of this death?" If my grounds of complaint be the same with those of an Apostle, they cannot, at the most, be grounds of despair. And in this mainly lies the worth of Christian biography. The registered experience of men, whose piety admits not a question, may be compared with our own; and when we find that David, or Paul, had to wrestle with an evil heart of unbelief, and that they passed, like ourselves, through seasons of great spiritual darkness and depression, we are taught that the not being perfect is no proof of our not being safe; but that there may be much to produce contrition, which yet ought not to shake confidence. "Why art thou cast down, O my soul, and why art thou disquieted within me?"—in these words of the Psalmist, there is as much material of comfort as in the triumphant exclamation, "The Lord is my light and my salvation, whom then shall I fear? the Lord is the strength of my life, of whom shall I be afraid?" It is a great thing to know that David felt disquietude of soul. It identifies him, as it were, with ourselves, and forbids our inferring danger from depression. And we think the Book of Psalms most precious on this very account—namely, that he who is mourning for sin, and cast down under a sense of failures in duty, coldness in love, and proneness to offend, may find therein words which describe precisely his case and experience; and yet, whilst he makes the words his own, feel sure that he, who penned them, passed at death into glory.

We say nothing to excuse, or extenuate, the faults of Christians. For our most dangerous fault is perhaps the making light of our faults. But, certainly, when a man is anxious in respect to the soul, when it is his earnest desire to accept the salvation which is offered through Christ; and when the reasons, which make him fear that he is not a true believer, are drawn from deficiencies which he laments, and dispositions which he abhors; it is a legitimate source of consolation, that men, who lived nearest to God, had exactly the same reasons for suspecting their sincerity. Had David always spoken exultingly and confidently, the Psalms would have been disheartening writings, as proving that their author knew nothing of spiritual anxieties. But when we find him deploring his sinfulness, complaining of darkness of soul, and expressing fears that God had forgotten to be gracious, there is encouragement in the Psalmist's disquietude: my trials, after all, were his: they are, then, no evidences that I am not walking the pathway of life: and he, whose continued triumph would have dispirited me, cheers and strengthens by his occasional melancholy.

It is thus also with the writings of St. Paul. The seventh chapter, for example, of the Epistle to the Romans is invaluable on the very account which has just been indicated. It describes that conflict between the carnal principle and the principle of grace, of which the breast of every renewed man is the scene. This conflict it is, with its toils and alternations, which furnishes the downcast Christian with arguments against himself. The constantly recurring question is, if I were indeed a true believer, would there be in my heart these struggles, too often victories, of natural corruption? Now, it is a sound, though not always a practically convincing, answer to this question, that the very struggles are indications of sincerity. It is the renewed heart alone in which there is a conflict. But when this answer fails to satisfy, let the inquirer listen to St. Paul, declaring of himself, "The good that I would I do not: but the evil which I would not, that I do:" and though he will not think less of sin, because finding that it has often mastered an Apostle, it is strange if he be not assured and comforted by seeing his own experience portrayed in that of one so eminent in holiness.

The same remarks are applicable to the words of our text, when made to include, as the context shows that they do, the true believer in Christ. The whole creation which, with so much earnestness, and in so much disquietude, waited "for the manifestation of the sons of God," included the regenerate and the renewed, as well as the irrational and inanimate; for, saith St. Paul, even "we ourselves, which have the first-fruits of the Spirit, groan within ourselves." Now, we cannot doubt that such a man as St. Paul enjoyed no common measure of spiritual consolation. An Apostle, who had been caught up to the third Heaven, and who had "heard unspeakable words," must have known, perhaps more than any other, of the joys laid up for the saints. Indeed he here says, "We, who have the first-fruits of the Spirit." He does not say, a portion of the first-fruits: but, as though to mark a possession as large as was attainable upon earth, "We, who have the first-fruits of the Spirit." Whatever earnests and foretastes of future blessedness are ever accorded to believers, these, it would seem, were enjoyed by St. Paul; and yet St. Paul had acute mental suffering. He shared in the groans of the anxious and expectant creation—"Even we ourselves groan within ourselves." So that we can have no right, as we are often disposed, to expect perpetual peace and sunshine of spirit, or to infer that we are not advancing towards Heaven, because our expectations of its joys overpower not our griefs. It appears that the most devoted believer may groan heavily in himself; nay, that the internal anguish may quite consist with the reception of the richest earnests in Heaven. And therefore, in place of writing bitter things against ourselves, because the promised blessedness does not make us insensible to present distress, we ought to be content, if, with the holy Apostle, we can anticipate Paradise, whilst weighed down by the burthens of the flesh.

We believe of many Christians, that they distress them selves with the thought, that the hope of Heaven cannot have its due influence, unless it make them superior to the afflictions of life. If, they will argue, our thoughts were rightly fixed on everlasting glories, and we did indeed anticipate what God hath prepared for his people, present causes of distress would be unable to agitate, and we should already enjoy an unbroken happiness. But it is evident that such was not the case with St. Paul—what ground have you, then, to conclude that it should be with you? St. Paul groaned in himself, though he had the first-fruits of the Spirit; therefore, let no one suppose that, because often oppressed and wearied in mind, he is either not approaching the possession of Heaven, or not duly swayed by its motives. It is thus that our text sets itself against a frequent occasion of despondency. We indeed thoroughly acknowledge, and earnestly maintain, that the hope and anticipation of Heaven will greatly animate the Christian during his sojourn upon earth. "For I reckon that the sufferings of this present time are not worthy to be compared with the glory which shall be revealed in us." But when we expect to turn earth into Heaven, to make such use of what is promised that it shall almost annihilate what is present; and when we think it matter of self-reproach, that we are not so elevated by the majesty of what is proposed as our portion, as to soar above all sorrow and anxiety; it is well that we hearken to one whose faith we cannot think to rival, nor whose rapture to reach, and hear St. Paul, after he had made creation vocal, and the universal utterance an utterance of distress, using language which proves that he included himself in this assertion of anxiety and weariness, "For the earnest expectation of the creature waiteth for the manifestation of the sons of God."

But there is much more in these words than an implied answer to doubts produced by fixing some wrong standard of spiritual attainment. That there may be the hope and the foretaste of Heaven, even where there is great spiritual suffering—this is satisfactorily established by the declaration of St. Paul. But how it comes to pass that these may co-exist—why, with all the evidences of being a true believer, there may be groaning in ourselves—these are points which deserve serious inquiry. Then again, when the earnest expectation of the creature—the creature including the true believer—has been shown to be consistent with vital religion, the question will occur, Why should this expectation be fixed on "the manifestation of the sons of God," or, on—for we have seen from the context that this is the same thing—the redemption, or resurrection, of the body? We will strive to embrace these several matters within the remainder of our discourse.

And, first, as to how a truly religious man, in whom the Spirit of God is actively working, can yet have share in that disquieted longing which the Apostle here ascribes to the whole of this creation. You might perhaps have thought, that, where the Spirit was evidently engaged in renewing a man, exciting in him the love of God and of holiness, and continually increasing his conformity to the image of Christ, the heart would do nothing but exult, as having proof of direct interest in the promises of the Gospel. But let it only be remembered that what is done towards mastering corruption, serves but to show how much remains undone, and you will immediately perceive that what proves us true followers of Christ may yet minister to sadness. We need not demonstrate this to those who know any thing of spiritual experience. They will at once admit that they discover daily more of the wickedness of the heart, and of the power of corruption; so that to grow in grace is to grow in the sense of their own great depravity. Where is the Christian, however long, and however steadfastly, he may have pressed towards Heaven, who appears to himself to have advanced towards perfection?—rather, where is the Christian whose estimate of himself is not one which asserts him further off than ever from the scriptural standard? It is not that he goes back. Nay, it is not that he fails to go forward but it is spiritual improvement, to be more and more conscious of natural depravity. One great, if not the chief, work of grace is the teaching us ourselves; and every lesson is a new demonstration of indwelling evil. Oh, he can have taken but few lessons in that most intricate, yet interesting, of subjects, his own heart, who has not learnt to say with the Prophet, "It is deceitful above all things—who can know it?" And you will all admit that this must be painful: the believer may well join his groans to those of the whole creation, if every day's experience do but add to his sense of the power of indwelling sin.

Yes, but, unquestionably, there are often vouchsafed to believers in Christ anticipations of that happiness with which the future comes charged. It is far enough from the dream of enthusiasm, that the distant world will occasionally throw open its gates, and allow those who are fighting the good fight of faith to animate themselves by glimpses of its splendours. Often, when the mind muses on the saint's rest, in the privacies of a holy solitude, and in the retirements of communion with God and his Son, the promised glories will come out, as it were, from the shadowy distance, and time, with its trials, give place to eternity with its majesties. Then it is that a "peace which passeth all understanding," pervades the mind; and faith, nerved by the promises of the Word, brings into the soul a gladness which has nothing of earthly element. In seasons such as these, the obtained view of Heaven is so clear and elevating, that, whilst privileged with the vision, the Christian rises superior to every fear and anxiety: he seems to himself to have finished his conflict, trampled death under foot, and to be already mingling with the happy throng who rejoice in the presence of God and of the Lamb. And shall a man, thus privileged, be disquieted? Shall he join his groans to those of the creation? Yes, indeed. For it were a strange thought. that a glimpse of Heaven will make him less alive to the afflictions of earth. Shall the having gazed, though but for an instant, on what is pure, and peaceable, and bright, diminish his sensibility to the pollution and turmoil of the scene in which he still dwells? Shall he, when he returns from his lofty flight, and comes down from his splendid excursion, to engage once more in the business of probation, and be again occupied with keeping under the body, and disciplining unruly passions—shall he, think you, feel less than before the irksomeness of the combat with corruption, or be more at home in the wilderness through which his path lies? Oh, it is not the view of Heaven which will lighten the burden laid on us by our sinfulness. I had almost said, it will increase that burden. Indeed, it is not possible that a believer should have gazed on the fair spreadings of the saint's home, and contemplated, however distantly, what God hath prepared for him as a member of his Son, and not have strengthened in the feeling, that Heaven is worth all his strivings, and in the resolve, that he will wrestle for its happiness. But I cannot think that he will be more at ease than before in a world which will only seem drearier by contrast. I cannot think that the having listened to the harpings of angels will make the storm and the discord sound less offensively. I cannot think that because he has tasted the fresh waters of the river of life, he will find less bitterness in the wormwood which sin will yet infuse into his cup. I cannot think that, with the earnests in possession, he will be other than more intense in his longings for the perfect fruition. And therefore do I believe that, the richer his anticipations Heaven, the deeper will be his cry, "O that I had the wings of a dove! for then would I flee away and be at rest." So that an Apostle, and that Apostle St. Paul, who had actually trodden the firmament, and seen what saints enjoy, and heard what seraphs sing, was of all others the most likely to feel the pressure of spiritual anxieties, and to sigh for deliverance; and who then shall wonder at his using language which shows that he included himself, and other true believers, in his description of a groaning and waiting creation, "The earnest expectation of the creature waiteth for the manifestation of the sons of God?"

"The manifestation of the sons of God"—we have already shown you that the manifestation is that which shall be made at the general resurrection, when true believers, "the sons of God," shall receive their glorified bodies, and take visible possession of the kingdom prepared from before the foundation of the world. The Apostle, indeed, knew himself to be a son of God. But he had not yet been declared such in the face of the universe, nor visibly enrolled in the heavenly household. There was yet to come the public acknowledgment by God of the saints as his children, and their glorious investiture with the dignities which appertain to such relationship. For this adoption the Apostle longed; yea, for this adoption, this manifestation, it was that the whole creation, groaning in its every department, looked with the intensest expectation. And this adoption, or this manifestation, is identified with the redemption of the body. The body was redeemed by Christ as well as the soul: but, for wise purposes, the application of this redemption is so deferred that death still claims the body as its prey. It was redeemed, inasmuch as its resurrection was made sure; but we still wait for the redemption, inasmuch as it hath yet to mingle with the dust. Then will be emphatically the redemption of our body, when, appearing visibly as the Conqueror of death and of Hell, and sending forth into the sepulchres the energies of his victory, Christ shall surround Himself with the saints of every generation, a countless army, wakened by his summons, and swelling his triumph. Sown in dishonour, but raised in glory; sown in weakness, but raised in power; sown a natural body, but raised a spiritual body—this is redemption, is it not? Oh, to be no more liable to pain; no longer a weak and failing thing; no longer the subject of death, no longer the organ of sin—transformed into an auxiliary of the soul in all the high business of glorifying God; every faculty, and every sense, an engine for the executing the will of the Lord, and gathering in new material of happiness—is not this the redemption of the body?

And if redemption of the body, is it not moreover "the manifestation of the sons of God?" The believer is indeed already a child of God; but it is in the spirit rather than in the flesh, that he bears the impress of sonship. The soul presents tokens of a heavenly parentage; but it is yet true of the body, that there is a law in its members, warring against the law of the mind. But at the Resurrection, the fallen creature shall be visibly admitted into God's family, when, body and soul both purged from every trace, and emancipated from every consequence, of guilt—yea, both more nobly endowed than had the birth-right never been forfeited—man wears every feature of the lost image of God, and the son is known by likeness to the Father. And though we doubt not that the spirits of good men, inhabiting that separate state, in which the righteous expect the consummation of all things, enjoy much which can be enjoyed by none but children of God, yet do we believe their happiness incomplete, and that they eagerly long for that "manifestation" of which our text speaks. They listen for the trump of resurrection, the jubilee trump to them, as well as to this oppressed and groaning creation. They know that, at the peal of that trump, the stamp of sonship, already graven splendidly on themselves, will be communicated to every atom of that dust which constituted the tabernacles that enclosed them on earth; and that suddenly (the spirit rushing into its rebuilded home) there will be presented to the universe man, the fallen thing, the dissolved thing, radiant as the offspring of God: and that, hailed by this universe as in every lineament a child of the Most High, his manifestation will take place amid the plaudits, and consign him to a blessedness exceeding that of angels.

Great honour is thus put upon the body. We stand by the lifeless form from which the soul hath just departed; but our thoughts are with the soaring spirit, and not with the tenement which lies before us in its coldness and its stillness. We strive—though it is vain that we labour to attend the arrowy and inscrutable flight—to follow the soul into the presence of its Maker; and there we imagine it robed in light, and rich in happiness; but the body is regarded with melancholy, and almost with disgust; and we make the sad preparations for its funeral; and we seem to count it altogether lost when coffined and sepulchred. If we would console those who are mourning under bereavement, we speak of the blessed estate of the emancipated spirit: our discourse turns exclusively on the soul; and scarce a solitary word is given to the body which has been left to corruption. It was not thus with St. Paul. Death had entered the Thessalonian families, and the Apostle desired to speak peace to the mourners. The words, which he employed, were undoubtedly intended to serve as a model of consolatory discourse; for he concludes by saying, "Wherefore comfort one another with these words." But what were these words? Not words on the happiness of the separate state, its deep and rapturous repose. They were words of a resurrection. I hear in them the shout of the descending Mediator, the voice of the Archangel, the trump of God. The Apostle makes no reference to the soul: he speaks only of the body: and that the grave shall be emptied, that the saints, found alive at the coming of the Lord, shall not "prevent them that are asleep," but that "the dead in Christ shall rise first"—these are the topics by which he would animate the Thessalonians to the sorrowing not as others which have no hope. Why did he fetch the material of his consolation from the resurrection of the body? Because it was death which had brought sorrow into these families: if, then, he would comfort them, let him show them death vanquished and destroyed. Many hopes and many joys had gone down into the grave: let him then irradiate that grave, and strip it of its terrors. I know not why a churchyard should excite none but melancholy thoughts; nor why, if we are to be cheered under bereavement, our meditation must be wholly on the disembodied spirit. We have heard of the redemption of the body. With that redemption stands associated whatever is magnificent and transporting in our everlasting portion. The quickening of the buried dust will be "the manifestation of the sons of God." Shall we not, then, look on the receptacle of the dead with other emotions than those stirred by the gloom and silence of its chambers? Shall we not regard it as the future scene of the Mediator's triumphs; the spot on which shall be effected the full and final regeneration of humanity; and from which, amid the convulsions of approaching judgment, shall issue, in confessed and blazing majesty, the sons and daughters of the Lord Almighty? Shall we give nothing but our tears to the funeral procession, as though we knew not that there is borne along, in this sad solemnity, dust which will engage the watchfulness of God, dust for which a Redeemer died, and which, though it have its season of slumber and dishonour, is yet so reserved for glorious allotment, that the soul, as it rejoices in the light of God's presence, longs for its resurrection, as for that which shall usher into the promised inheritance?

Hearken to the text, "The earnest expectation of the creature waiteth for the manifestation of the sons of God." It is as though the inanimate and irrational creation, burdened with the consequences of man's transgression, fixed its gaze on the sepulchres of the saints, and longed for the moment when they shall be riven by the Judgment call. Let those sepulchres open; and there will come a restitution of the beauty which sin blighted, and of the peace which it marred. With the resurrection of the righteous will be that of the departed glories and the lost gladness of our terrestrial system. Well, therefore, may creation pant for "the manifestation of the sons of God." But not only they—shall not ourselves also eagerly expect this manifestation? With a body whose passions and appetites militate against righteousness, we are painfully conscious of unfitness for membership with the pure family of Heaven; and, therefore, however we enjoy the first-fruits of the Spirit, we must "groan in ourselves." For what then shall we look and long, if not for the application of the virtues of redemption to body as well as soul? It is not death which we desire: it is resurrection: resurrection is the redemption of the body, its redemption from dishonour, its redemption from pollution. We join creation as, with outstretched neck, it watches every token that the manifestation of God's sons draws near. The coming of the Lord is that mighty event which engages, if we know our own privileges, the longings of the heart; for He comes to "change our vile body, that it may be fashioned like unto his glorious body." Yes, the groanings which, throughout long centuries, have issued from this earth, have not been unheeded: God has heard the cry of a suffering creation, and the mourning of such as feel the burden of corruption. He will come forth from his place; He will exterminate evil from his empire. The sceptre shall be restored to the rightful King; and the sons of God, gathered from our alienated tribe, be presented "without spot, or wrinkle, or any such thing."

I may not be able to imagine the scene. This starting from the dust; this re-union of body and soul; this enthronement of the Mediator in his magnificent sovereignty; this exchange of the universal lament for the universal gladness—the fir-tree coming up instead of the thorn, and instead of the brier the myrtle—I cannot picture such august occurrences. But Scripture associates them with the coming of Christ. If then—and God grant that we may all feel weary and heavy laden with the burden of sin—we are compelled to join in the groans, we will join also in the hopes of the creation. "Looking for that blessed hope, and the glorious appearing of the great God, and our Saviour Jesus Christ." The dust, I must inhabit it for a while. But, if I carry down with me to the grave the distinctive marks of a believer in Christ, hatred of sin, and desires after holiness, the grave shall be only as the womb in which I am fashioned for immortality. When Christ left the grave, the proclamation was, "Thou art my Son, this day have I begotten thee;" and if sonship followed the resurrection of the Head, adoption and manifestation shall be perfected in that of the members. I add nothing but my earnest prayer to the God of all grace, that we may all be found in Christ at his second appearing.

LECTURE XIII.

St. Paul's Determination.

1 Cor. ii. 2.

"For I determined not to know any thing among you, save Jesus Christ, and Him crucified."

And was the Apostle wrong in his determination? He speaks as if the doctrine of the cross were ample enough, comprehensive enough, for all his powers. Does this, at all, indicate that he was of a narrow and contracted mind, which could apply itself to only one topic, whilst a hundred others, perhaps nobler and loftier, lay beyond its grasp? Nay, not so; the tone of St. Paul abundantly indicates that he gloried in being thus limited to the Cross—gloried, because in comparison there was nothing else worth knowing—gloried, because this one knowledge might be said to include, or, where it did not include, to supersede every other. The tone of the Apostle is not that of a man who is apologizing for the limited character of his preaching, or its humiliating tendency; it is rather that of one who felt that the Corinthians had nothing to complain of, seeing that he had taught them the most precious, the most diffusive, the most ennobling of truths. Indeed, he had known nothing amongst them, "save Jesus Christ, and Him crucified"—but what else was there which, as sinners, it was important for them to learn? what which, if learnt, did not derive a fresh meaning, or fresh interest, from the Cross of the Redeemer?

Here, then, is our subject of discourse—the Apostle determined to know nothing save the Cross; but the Cross is the noblest study for the intellectual man, as it is the only refuge for the immortal. How different was the plan of the Apostle from that pursued by many who have undertaken the propagation of Christianity. It is recorded, we believe, of some of the Roman Catholic missionaries, that, in their endeavours to bring over the heathen to Christianity, they scrupulously kept the Crucifixion out of sight, considering that such a fact would invincibly prejudice those whom they wished to convince. And it is well known that the Moravian missionaries, men of extraordinary piety and zeal, laboured for a long time in Greenland, without, at least, giving prominence to the doctrine of the atonement, believing that it became them to clear the way, and prepare men's minds, before they advanced the truth of Christ's death—a truth so likely, as they thought, to give fatal offence even to the most degraded and barbarous. In each case the same feeling was at work—the feeling that there is something very humiliating in the Cross, and that human reason, and, yet more, human pride, must recoil from the thought of being saved by one who died as a malefactor. And you must all be aware that, whatever the error or mistake of the missionaries to whom we have referred, there is a great repugnance in men's minds to that doctrine which is virtually the essence of

Christianity, and that what St. Paul elsewhere calls "the offence of the Cross" can only cease with the thorough renewal of our nature. It must be immediately allowed that the scheme of Christianity is not one which commends itself at once to those whom it proposes to rescue.; on the contrary, it is so constructed as almost necessarily to excite opposition, because, in place of flattering any one passion, it requires the subjugation of all. But, after all, the observable thing is that Christianity is valuable and glorious on those very accounts on which, in common estimation, it must move the antipathies of its hearers. The missionary might keep back all mention of the Cross, because fearful of exciting dislike and contempt. But, all the while, he would be withholding that which gives its majesty to the system, and striving to apologize for its noblest distinction.

It is sufficiently evident, from the words of our text, that this was the opinion of the great Apostle to the Gentiles. And we reckon it of importance that we should occasionally shift the ground of debate; that, in place of admitting what may be styled the shame of the Cross, we should boldly affirm and exhibit its glory. We know not that we ought to allow that the missionaries, of whom we have spoken, acted with prudence and penetration, even supposing that they had only carnal principles for their guidance. With all our admission, that, at the first hearing, there would be something repulsive in the doctrine of Christ crucified, we believe that this doctrine has only to be fairly exhibited, and fully expanded, in order to its attracting the warmest admiration—and we can think it in the highest degree probable, even if you shut out the consideration that faithful preaching alone may expect the divine blessing, that missionaries would have made far greater way by insisting on and displaying the majesty of the Cross, than by keeping out of sight, or only partially exhibiting, what they erroneously thought so likely to displease. And it is this which, on the present occasion, we wish to make good. Give your close attention to so interesting a question. We are to set the Apostle against all those teachers who would, in any way or degree, keep back, or obscure, the doctrine of the Cross; and we are to see whether he did not display as much of wisdom as of boldness, when, in no tone of apology, but with the confidence of one who knew that he had taught what was best worth the being learned, he exclaimed to the Corinthians, "I determined not to know any thing among you, save Jesus Christ, and Him crucified."

Now, we need hardly observe to you, that, so far as Christ Jesus Himself was concerned, it is not possible to compute what may be called the humiliation or shame of the Cross. It is altogether beyond our power to form any adequate conception of the degree in which the Mediator humbled Himself, when born of a woman, and taking part of flesh and blood. It is beyond our power, because, with all our searchings, we cannot find out God, we cannot approach the confines of the Divine nature; and therefore, neither can we measure the mighty descent down which Divinity passed in assuming humanity. But, after all, the more surprising humiliation is that which seems to come more nearly within our measurement—the humiliation of the Man Christ Jesus, the humiliation to which the Mediator submitted after our nature had been assumed. In merely becoming man, or, rather, in becoming man without the taint of original sin, the eternal Word did not bring Himself under the curse: He was not accessible to death, that great penalty of transgression; neither was He heir to any of that degradation which is, literally, our birthright as the seed of the apostate. But when the Redeemer, though He had done no sin, consented to place himself in the position of sinners—when, though the violated law had no claims upon Him, He voluntarily made Himself the subject of its exactions—then was it that He marvellously and mysteriously descended—there being, if we may venture to compare things, neither of which we can measure, something less overwhelming in the fact, that "the Word was made flesh," than in the other fact, that "being found in fashion as a man, He humbled Himself, and became obedient unto death, even the death of the Cross." Here it is that the word "shame" may justly be used; for in this it was that Christ Jesus became "a curse for us." We read nothing of the shame of his becoming a man, but we do read of his dying a malefactor. Thus St. Paul declares of Him, in his Epistle to the Hebrews, "Who, for the joy that was set before Him, endured the Cross, despising the shame"—an expression which equally marks that Christ was sensible of the indignities of his death, and that He made light of them when compared with the recompense which was to follow.

And if we allow that it was a shameful thing, that it involved a humiliation which no thought can measure, that the Lord of life and glory should have hung as a malefactor between earth and heaven, with what other emotions, you may ask, but those of sorrow and self-reproach, should we contemplate the Cross? Shall we exult in the Cross?

Shall we make it matter of triumphant rejoicing, that the Son of God had to ascend such an altar, and that, stretched thereon, an ignominious spectacle, He poured out his soul unto death? Indeed, we are not so to exult as to lose those feelings of godly contrition which a sight of the Cross should always produce. The awful transactions, of which Calvary was the scene, should never be contemplated by us without a deep sense of the magnitude of the guilt which required such an expiation, and great self-abhorrence at having added to the burden which weighed down the innocent Sufferer. But, nevertheless, though of all men, perhaps, St. Paul was the least likely to forget or under rate the causes of sorrow presented by the Cross, this great Apostle, in determining to know nothing but the Cross, could adopt a tone which implied that he gloried in the Cross. And why, think you, was this? How comes it to pass that that, which, under one point of view, covers the beholder with confusion, should yet, under some other, excite feelings of exultation, as though all the shame disappeared, and there remained nothing but the magnificence of triumph? Or why, if there be so much of shame about the Cross, was the Apostle wise, when addressing himself to a refined and polished people, in determining to "know nothing but Jesus Christ, and Him crucified?"

Indeed, there is no difficulty in finding answers to these questions; the only difficulty is in the selecting those which are the more pertinent and striking. We may first observe that the great truth which the Apostle had to impress on the Corinthians was, that, in spite of their sinfulness and alienation, they were still beloved by the one true

God. And how could he better do this than by displaying the Cross? The greater the humiliation to which the Son of God submitted, the greater was the amount of Divine love towards man. We admit, what, of course, it is impossible to deny, that there was an unmeasured indignity in the death of the Cross, and that the consideration that it was for our sakes this indignity was endured, should bring us down to the dust, and fill us with penitential sorrow. But who can fail to perceive that, the greater the obstacles to our rescue, the lower the depths to which a Mediator must descend in order to lay hold on the perishing, the more intense was the manifestation of the compassions of God, of his regard to the lost, notwithstanding their apostacy? We know not whether it be lawful to speak of the possibility of our having been saved through any other arrangement. We may not be able to prove, and perhaps it hardly becomes us to investigate, what may be called the necessity for Christ's death, so that, unless Jesus had consented to die, it would not have been in God's power to open to us the kingdom of heaven. But we cannot be passing the bounds of legitimate supposition, if we imagine, for a moment, that some less costly process had sufficed, and that justice had been satisfied, without exacting from our Surety penalties so tremendous as were actually paid. And is it not too evident to ask any proof, that, in the very proportion in which you diminish the sufferings of the Mediator, you diminish, also, the exhibition of his love, and leave it a thing to be questioned, though not perhaps disproved, that God's compassions are ample enough for every case of human sinfulness and sorrow? It is the fine argument of St. Paul, an argument by which he would repress every fear and animate to confidence, "He that spared not his own Son, but delivered Him up for us all, how shall He not with Him also freely give us all things?" It is an argument which rests on the fact that nothing can be needed by us which it would cost God as much to bestow, as did that which has already been given; and which draws, as an inference from this fact, that He who has imparted the greater benefit cannot be willing to withhold the less. But you destroy the force of the argument, you take all point from the verse, if you in any degree weaken the words, "He that spared not his own Son, but delivered Him up for us all." Suppose that God had spared his own Son; suppose that the arrangements made for our redemption had not required his delivering Him up for us all; and is it not undeniable that the Apostle's reasoning is so weakened that it could not be urged in many extreme cases of guilt and destitution? There might have been room for debate whether what was required did not exceed what had already been done, and whether therefore the fact of redemption furnished groundwork of hope, or rather of assurance, that God would give what the urgency demanded.

But Redemption through the death, the death on the Cross, of a Mediator, and that Mediator the Only-begotten of the Father, leaves no place for such debate, because imagination itself can suggest nothing greater than what God hath already done, and because therefore no case can arise in which the want can be thought to exceed the munificence and mercy of God. It is then to "Christ Jesus, and Him crucified," that we make our appeal, when we would furnish such evidence of Divine love as must overbear all unbelief. We do not rest our proof on the fact that we have been redeemed, but on the fact that we have been redeemed through the bitter passion, and the ignominious death, of God's only and well-beloved Son. It is here that the proof is absolutely irrefragable. Knowing that Christ "bare our sins in his own body on the tree," we know that we are beloved with a love which no thought can measure, no unworthiness alienate, no necessities overtask. What then, as sinners alienated from God, can we want to know, if we know "Jesus Christ, and Him crucified?" In what shall we exult, in what glory, if not in this knowledge? If there be a cause of exultation, a motive for rejoicing, to a fallen creature, must it not be that he is still dear to his Maker, that notwithstanding all which he hath done to provoke Divine wrath, and make condemnation inevitable, he is regarded with unspeakable tenderness by the Almighty, watched over with a solicitude, and provided for at a cost, which could not be exceeded if he were the noblest and purest of the beings that throng the intelligent universe? Teach me this, and you teach me every thing. And this I learn from Christ crucified. I learn it indeed in a measure from the sun as he walks the firmament, and warms the earth into fertility. I learn it from the moon, as she gathers the stars into her train, and throws over creation her robe of soft light. I gather it from the various operations and provisions of nature, from the faculties of the mind, from the capacities of the soul. But if I am taught by these, the teaching after all is but imperfect and partial: they do indeed give testimony that man is not forgotten of God; but the testimony would be equally given, were there the power of receiving it, to the brute creation, to the innumerable animated tribes which are to perish at death. It is not a testimony, at least not a direct, that we are cared for as immortal beings, and can be pardoned as sinful. It is not a testimony that He who is of purer eyes than to look upon iniquity, can receive into favour even the vilest of those who have thrown off allegiance, and manifest such an exuberance of loving-kindness towards the guilty, as will not leave the worst case without hope and without succour. Show us what will give such testimony as this, and sun, and moon, and the granaries of nature, and the workings of intellect, will drop, in comparison, their office of instructor.

We show you Christ on the Cross. Are the blazings of the sun, or the milder shinings of the moon, or the processes of vegetation, or the soarings of mind, a thousandth part as demonstrative of a love in which sinners may confide, as this emblem of shame, this memento of ignominy? I gaze upon the Cross, and He who is extended there seems stretching forth the arms of his kindness, that He may embrace the world, and gather the perishing under the wing of his protection. It is no finite being who is thus suspended; though He be dying amid the revilings of his enemies, He is "from everlasting and to everlasting," as truly, as actually, God, as though throned in inaccessible splendour and summoning into existence new worlds and new orders. Then I cannot doubt the Divine love. I cannot doubt of this love, that it may justly be called inexhaustible; and that, if I will only allow myself to be its object, there is no amount of guiltiness which can exclude me from its embrace. And this it is which, as an immortal yet sinful being, I have most interest in ascertaining; this it is in which, if once ascertained, I have most cause to exult. Come then a teacher to those sunk in Heathenism, and what shall he teach? Ay, one may go and tell them of their being objects of God's providence, fed by his bounty, guided by his light, curtained by his shadow. Another may tell them of their having been made after his image, endowed with immortality, illuminated by reason. I would not be insensible to the excellence of such teaching, to the beauty of these proofs of the love of the Creator. But, feeling that these Heathen are in danger of eternal destruction, and knowing that the sacrifice made on their behalf is such as irresistibly proves that God so loves them as to do every thing to save them, except dishonour Himself, give me the teacher who would exclaim with the Apostle, "I determined not to know any thing among you, save Jesus Christ, and Him crucified."

We proceed to observe, that, although to the eye of sense there be nothing but shame about the Cross, yet a spiritual discernment perceives it to be hung with the very richest of trophies. You will remember how St. Paul speaks in his Epistle to the Colossians, in what magnificent terms he describes the achievement of the dying Redeemer: "Blotting out the handwriting of ordinances, that was against us, which was contrary to us, he took it out of the way, nailing it to his Cross; and, having spoiled principalities and powers, he made a show of them openly, triumphing over them in it;" as though he had vanquished all the enemies of God and of men, stripped them of usurped sovereignty, and fastened them, in the face of the universe, to the Cross on which Himself hung. And what was this but the matter of fact? It is necessarily to be admitted, that, in one point of view, there was shame, degradation, ignominy, in Christ's dying on the Cross: but it is equally certain, that, in another, there was honour, victory, triumph. You are all aware that such was the scheme of our Redemption, that "without shedding of blood could be no remission," and that it was made the indispensable condition of human salvation, that the Word, when "found in fashion as a man," should offer Himself as "a sacrifice for sin." And if such were the ordained arrangements for human salvation, then it follows that on the Cross was achieved the mightiest result of which this earth has ever been the scene, and that death was made the instrument of its own destruction, and of that of the great adversaries of God. We are told that through death Christ Jesus destroyed him that had the power of death, that is, the devil; and that he "made peace by the blood of his Cross." We know that, in dying, the Redeemer brake off the yoke from the neck of the human population, wrenched from Satan the sceptre which he had long wielded as the god of this world, and scattered the seeds of immortality amid the dust of the sepulchres. Might not therefore an Apostle declare that Christ Jesus spoiled principalities and powers, and made a show of them openly, triumphing over them in the Cross?

I know not whether he refers to any exhibition which was vouchsafed to higher orders of being; whether he is to be understood as affirming that there was a vivid manifestation of the triumphs of the Cross, just as though the devil and his apostate company, and death, and Hell, had all been made to pass in procession, like captives at the chariot-wheels of their conqueror, that the inhabitants of the invisible world might know how victorious had Christ been in death. But, whatever the demonstrations of conquest which may have been granted to angels, we need nothing but the eye of faith in order to our discerning on the Cross the finest trophies which a victor ever won. There, nailed with the very nails by which the feet and hands of the Redeemer were pierced, hangs the law by which all were condemned, but which has now nothing to lay to the charge of God's elect. There are impaled those principalities and powers, the originators and propagators of evil, who leagued together to effect man's destruction, but who, now that Christ has died, machinate in vain against such as have faith in the Lord our Redeemer. There is fastened death itself, that great tyrant and destroyer of humankind: for, in dying, Christ accomplished the noble prediction, "O death, I will be thy plagues; O grave, I will be thy destruction." There our sins are transfixed, having been condemned in the flesh, because borne in Christ's body on the tree, exhibited as capable of forgiveness, yet as objects of abhorrence, inasmuch as nothing shows their enormity like that which gains their pardon. And am I then to be ashamed of the Cross? It is to be ashamed of the battle-field on which has been won the noblest of victories, of the engine by which has been vanquished the fiercest of enemies. It is to be ashamed of conquest, ashamed of triumph, ashamed of deliverance. Indeed you may tell me that a result may be glorious, and yet the means, through which it is effected, degrading and ignoble. But what is called the shame is one great element in the glory. It would, comparatively, have been as nothing, that, as leader of the celestial armies, Christ should have overthrown the foes of God and of man—the splendid thing is, that He " trod the winepress alone, and that of the people there was with Him none." It would, comparatively, have been as nothing, that, putting forth all the might of Divinity, he should have shown Himself superior to every adversary—the marvellous, the amazing truth is, that he met the opposing forces as a man, a man over whom death was to have power; and that as a man, yea, a man in the agonies of dissolution, he discomfited every foe, and won every trophy. He triumphed by being apparently defeated; He vanquished, by the act of yielding to an enemy.

And therefore was his death glorious, ay, unspeakably more glorious than life, array it how you will with circumstances of honour. To have destroyed death by living, would have been wonderful: but to have destroyed it by dying, oh, this is the prodigy of prodigies, the glory of glories. This takes all signs of infirmity from the wounds of the Mediator—they were the weapons with which He conquered. This turns the crown of thorns into a diadem of splendour; for in being twined round his brow, they lost their power of injuring. This converts the sepulchre of Jesus into the avenue of Immortality; for, in entering it, He gave life to the buried, and made sure the Resurrection of whatever hath been human. And if all this may be affirmed of " Jesus Christ, and Him crucified," can I want any thing more from a teacher who visits me to guide me to God and Immortality? Must he equip himself with the learning of the schools, must he become conversant with the theories of philosophy, or must he frame apologies for what he has to tell, as though the doctrine of Christ crucified were not enough for the sinner, or as though it could not fail to excite prejudice? Nay, ye learned teachers, ye polished lecturers, ye subtile reasoners, give place to an Apostle who could thus express his fixed and earnest resolution, "I determined not to know any thing amongst you, save Jesus Christ, and Him crucified."

But we have hitherto scarcely carried our argument to the full extent of the Apostle's assertion. Not only was he determined to know amongst the Corinthians "Jesus Christ, and Him crucified," but he was determined to know nothing else. And if you consider for a moment what reason we have to believe that every blessing which we enjoy may be traced to the Cross, you will readily acknowledge that St. Paul went no further than he was bound to go as a faithful messenger of Christ. It is the doctrine of Scripture that man forfeited, through apostacy, whatever he possessed of good upon earth, as well as whatever might have been reserved for him in another state of being. And the only sufficient reason to be given, why what had been forfeited was not instantly withdrawn, seems to be that the intercession of Jesus was prevalent at the first moment of transgression, so that immediately that sin cried for vengeance, the atoning blood, not then shed, pleaded for remission. It is not enough to say that Christ, by his agony and passion, recovered for us the lost Immortality; we believe it to be just as true, that He preserved for man whatever is valuable in time, as that He regained for him whatever is glorious in Eternity. I think that we ought never to look admiringly on the magnificence of the landscape, never to gather in the harvest, never to gladden ourselves with the charities of home, never to trace the workings of intellect, without as distinct a feeling of obligation to Christ, as when we hear how the soul may be saved through his blood and his righteousness. I can say to the man of science, thine intellect was saved for thee by the Cross. I can say to the father of a family, the endearments of home were rescued by the Cross. I can say to the admirer of nature, the glorious things in the mighty panorama retained their places through the erection of the Cross. I can say to the ruler of an empire, the subordination of different classes, the working of society, the energies of government, are all owing to the Cross.

And when the mind passes to the consideration of spiritual benefits, where can you find one not connected with "Jesus Christ, and Him crucified?" The pardon of sin—it can be granted, because an expiation has been made; but that expiation was made upon the Cross. The influences of the Spirit—they can be vouchsafed, because purchased by Christ; but the purchase-money was paid upon the Cross. Death may be triumphed over—but only because Christ spoiled it of its sting, as He hung upon the Cross. Heaven may be entered—but only because, through the sacrifice of the Cross, Christ opened the kingdom to all believers. Thus, time and eternity, each is equally irradiated, each equally filled with benediction by the Cross, as though there flowed from that which, to a carnal eye, seems the emblem of shame, whatever is precious to man as a sojourner on earth, whatever is needed by him as the heir of immortality. What then do I need beyond the doctrine of the Cross? What is there of any worth to me in my immortal capacity which you can teach me, that is not derived from the Cross? Then how shall an instructor prepare himself for visiting the idolatrous Corinthians? Of course he takes with him the great truths of the incarnation and atonement; but is it necessary that he should add to these? must he have varieties to meet the various tastes of his audience? must he be prepared to back up these truths by other and collateral doctrines, or to illustrate them by curious analogies? Ah! no—so true is it that all we have, and all we hope for, flows to us from the Cross, so certain that every truth in which as immortal beings we are closely interested, is, in some way, derived from the Cross, that an Apostle, not because he was narrow-minded, but because he was large-minded, not because he wished to teach but little, but because he wished to teach much, could exclaim, "I determined not to know any thing amongst you, save Jesus Christ, and Him crucified."

But we have yet another remark to offer. St. Paul must have desired to teach that doctrine which was best adapted to the bringing the Corinthians to "live soberly, righteously, and godly in the world." If, therefore, he confined himself to any one doctrine, we may be sure that he considered it the most likely to be influential on the practice, on the turning sinners from the error of their ways, and making them obedient to God's law. And what doctrine is this, if not that of "Jesus Christ, and Him crucified?" In another place St. Paul describes himself as glorying in the Cross, because that by it the "world was crucified unto him, and he unto the world." What are we to understand by this twofold crucifixion? The world was to St. Paul as a crucified thing; and St. Paul was to the world as a crucified thing. They were dead one to the other. The Apostle regarded the world, with its pomp, its show, its riches, its pleasures, its honours, with no other feelings than he would have regarded a malefactor fastened to a cross, and whose condition could excite no desire for participation. Or, all that the world could offer appeared no more attractive to St. Paul than it would to a man in the act of dissolution, and who, suspended on a cross, would look down with a kind of insensibility on objects which before had been precious in his sight. Thus the world was to the Apostle as a crucified thing; or, to express the same idea somewhat differently, the Apostle was to the world as a crucified man; so that, if you put away the metaphor, the thing affirmed is, that St. Paul was completely "a new creature," with affections detached from things below and fixed on things above.

And he ascribes this change in himself to the virtues of the Cross, to "Jesus Christ, and Him crucified." And justly might he thus ascribe it. It is one of the great fruits of Christ's passion and death, that the renewing influences of the Holy Ghost are shed on us abundantly. We read, that, when the Mediator ascended up on high that He might claim the recompense of his humiliation and sufferings, He received gifts for men, yea, "even for the rebellious, that the Lord God might dwell amongst them." Without the descent of the Spirit, the work of Redemption would have been incomplete; for it is the Spirit which takes of the things of Christ, and shows them to our souls. It is the Spirit which applies, or makes available, the finished work of the Mediator; so that, though redeemed, we could not be saved unless the Spirit convinced us of sin, wrought in us repentance, and enabled us to believe in Jesus as our advocate with God. But, of course, if the Spirit could not have been bestowed, unless Christ had been crucified, we are not more indebted to the Cross for the "inheritance of the saints in light," than for that meetness for the inheritance, without which Heaven cannot be entered, nor enjoyed if it could. It is, therefore, through the Cross that we become new creatures, crucified to the world, and the world to us—because it is through the sacrifice presented on the Cross that those influences are derived to us, without which there can be nothing of moral renovation. And there is more to be said than this. Would you learn to despise the pomps and vanities of the world, to hate sin, to withstand evil lusts? Then must you be much on the mount of Crucifixion, much with Jesus in his last struggle with evil. Who would yield to a corrupt passion, who would indulge himself in unlawful gratifications, who would hearken to a base temptation, if his eye were upon Christ, "wounded for our transgressions, and bruised for our iniquities?" The sight of Jesus, pierced by and for our sins, is the great preservative against our yielding to the pleadings of a corrupt nature. One glance at the Cross would make us pause in the pursuit of a bauble, bring confusion of face at our daring to be sensual, and fill us with self-reproach that we could desire what is perishable.

The world was one of those trophies which, in his hour of apparent defeat, but actual mastery, Christ fastened to the tree on which he hung; for, in dying, he defaced and deformed the objects most admired and coveted amongst men; and the nails, with which he was pierced, are still those which must be driven into our passions and lusts, if, like Jael with Sisera, we would see the enemy stretched dead at our feet. And if we can affirm this of the Cross; and if the Apostle must have desired to publish that amongst the Corinthians, which was most likely to be effectual in bringing them out of darkness into marvellous light; can you any longer wonder at the determination announced in our text? We, too, will know nothing "save Jesus Christ, and Him crucified." By nature we are prisoners, and this teaches us how to be free. We are powerless—this teaches us how to gain strength. We are doomed to eternal misery—this teaches us how to become heirs of happiness. To whom then shall we go but to Christ upon the Cross? O Lord! it is only through Thee, Thee dying, the just for the unjust, that I can live; therefore strengthen me in the determination to know nothing but Thee, and Thee crucified.

LECTURE XIV.

The Song of Moses and the Lamb.

Rev. xv. 3

"And they sing the song of Moses the servant of God, and the song of the Lamb, saying, Great and marvellous are thy works, Lord God Almighty; just and true are thy ways, thou King of Saints."

In the first lesson of this morning's service, there has been read to you the inspired account of those marvellous events, the passage of the Israelites through the Red Sea, and the destruction of Pharaoh and all his hosts. It was on this occasion, when the Israelites saw their enemies lying dead on the sea-shore, that there was chanted that lofty song of triumph, which is designated in our text as "the song of Moses the servant of God." With the view then of associating our sermon with the services of the day, we take a text which represents as heard again, and in far different scenes, those exulting notes which floated over waves in whose depths had been whelmed the proud oppressors of God's ancient Church. Before the seven angels go forth to "pour out the vials of God's wrath upon the earth," the Evangelist, St. John, is cheered by a vision, representing the joy and triumph of the faithful followers of Christ, when their enemies shall have been overthrown, and their deliverance completed. He beholds "a sea of glass mingled with fire," and on it stand, "with the harps of God in their hands," those who have gained the victory over the beast, and his image, and his mark. As the conquerors stood on this mysterious sea, they sang that song of which our text is a part, and which is defined by St. John, as "the song of Moses and the Lamb."

Without pretending to settle what events may be thus prophetically alluded to, we may safely consider our text as belonging to a glorious season, when Christ shall have mightily interfered on behalf of his people, and swept away those who have resisted his authority. The song is a song of exultation, sung by the righteous, and called forth by judgments which have overwhelmed the wicked. And whilst this is undeniably its character, we need not be very careful to confine our observations to the occasion on which it was heard by St. John: we may safely extend them to the final estate of the Church, and consider the strains, which are swept from the harps of God, as those which shall float through the celestial Temple. This being premised, our text suggests two topics of discourse; for it gives what may be called a definition of the song which the triumphant Church sings; and it then furnishes us with the words of which that song is composed. We have, therefore, in the first place, to examine the name by which the song is described, "the song of Moses the servant of God, and the song of the Lamb:" we have then, in the second place, to consider the language employed, "Great and marvellous are thy works, Lord God Almighty; just and true are thy ways, thou King of Saints."

Now it admits no dispute, that, when the song of the triumphant Church is called, "the song of Moses the servant of God," the reference is, as we have already stated, to the chant of the Israelites and their leader, when Pharaoh and his hosts had been buried in the waters. And it is very observable, and, in some respects, almost mysterious, that it should be this song of Moses to which glorified saints will strike their harps. The song is one, not only of thanksgiving to the Lord, but of exultation over the wicked, and of rejoicing in their destruction. Hearken to its words as given in the services of the day: "The Lord is a man of war, the Lord is his name. Pharaoh's chariots and his hosts hath he cast into the sea. The depths have covered them: they sank into the bottom as a stone." We hardly know a more perplexing truth, nor one which more shows how vast a change will have passed over our feelings, when we shall have put on Immortality, than that of our acquiescing in the punishment of the wicked; yea, of our approving that punishment, and magnifying God for the vindication of his attributes. We cannot doubt the truth. We cannot question, that, as God will hereafter gain honour from the lost as well as the redeemed, those, to whom God is to be all in all through eternity, and who will therefore derive happiness from whatever contributes to his glory, will find material of thankfulness, and, consequently, of joy, in the condemnation of the reprobate, as well as in their own pardon and acceptance. But, with our present sensibilities and affections, this is quite incomprehensible. The case goes far beyond that of Moses and the Israelites, on the shore of the Red Sea. Even then there must have been the yearning of natural sympathy over the mighty company that had been buried in the waters. We do not believe, that, as the delivered tribes looked on the immense grave, and thought on the thousands over whom it had suddenly closed, they could fail to experience, amid all their rejoicing and exultation, something like anguish of feeling, a regret and sorrow that the wickedness of their enemies had rendered needful so tremendous a discomfiture. But the Egyptians were the sworn foes of the Israelites. There were between them none of the associations of kinsmanship; and as the people of the Lord beheld the waters meeting in their strength, and sepulchring their pursuers, there were none who had to think of a child or a parent, or a friend, grappling in agony with the irresistible tide. Suppose the case had been different, suppose that, in the ranks of the Egyptians, there had been many linked by close family ties with the Israelites—and who can doubt that there would have been sore hearts and weeping eyes, amongst those for whom the Lord had wrought the great deliverance; and that, as Moses led the song and Miriam the dance, some there would have been, whose voices would have faltered too much to swell the one, and whose limbs would have trembled too much to mingle in the other?

And yet we have here only the case which must necessarily be supposed, when all shall have occurred which was typified by the destruction of the Egyptians. It is not merely that those, whom wrath overtakes and consigns to perdition, will be our fellow-men, beings of the same race, and therefore linked with us by most intimate associations. This were much: for this would seem enough to seal our lips, or cause lament to mingle with our song. But it must come to pass, that, in variety of instances, there will be the division of families, so that, whilst one member is with the Israelites, another will be with the Egyptians. And this division must be thoroughly known. The parent, whose child has not followed him to Heaven, cannot fail to miss that child: the child, who has himself escaped the deluge, but whose parent has been overwhelmed by its rushings, must be aware of the absence of the one he most loved. And yet it is to the song of Moses that the golden harps will in each case be swept. "Sing ye to the Lord; for He hath triumphed gloriously: the horse and his rider hath He thrown into the sea." We must again confess, that, with our present susceptibilities and affections, it is hard to think that this can ever come to pass. If we were to decide by our feelings, we should be disposed to believe that it would introduce misery into Heaven, to allow knowledge of the misery of those who have been dear to us on earth. But, nevertheless, we can be certain that such will not be the case. Knowing, as we undeniably do, that nothing which has the least alliance with sorrow shall gain entrance into the everlasting city, we cannot doubt that the happiness of saints will be undiminished and undisturbed, though they should miss from the shining assembly those bound to them by the most endearing relations. Yea, we must carry our persuasion yet further than this. We must believe, that, with all the consciousness that some whom they tenderly loved, have earned for themselves a heritage of shame and despair, the ransomed of the Lord will feel how the Divine attributes have been magnified in the punishment awarded to the impenitent, and join in praising their Maker for the manifestation of his justice.

And this—however we may shrink and revolt from what appears so unnatural—this describes to us what is loftiest in Christian attainment; and what, therefore, may justly be looked for in our future state of being. I know that it would be Christian perfection to have God all in all; to make Him so completely the centre of the affections, or to be so lost in Deity, as to have no will but his will, and no end but his glory. And it is this which we are taught to expect, when admitted within the veil, and put into possession of the incorruptible inheritance. We are so to find our life and happiness in God, that He will be "our strength and our portion for ever." We are to enter into such communion with Him, so to derive every thing immediately from Him, and to devote every thing entirely to Him, that it will be his presence which animates us, his will which actuates, and his honour which employs. And what can better describe to us this being swallowed up in God, than the announcement that the redeemed, when the waves of fire shall have rushed in their resistlessness over the reprobate, and the Almighty shall have fearfully vindicated his insulted Sovereignty in the sight of the universe, will chant a high strain of praise, and roll through the heavenly Temple a chorus of lofty exultation? I know it strikes you as though this would be impossible. I know there is a feeling in your breasts, that, if there be one amongst the redeemed who is conscious that the voices of those whom he loved are swelling that deep wail which rises from the overwhelmed throng, he at least must be silent, whilst his companions weave the song, and add no note to the magnificent melody. But, oh, you are calculating by what man is, not by what man shall be. You fail to rise to the greatness of the thought, that God is to be "all in all" to his creatures. "God all in all"—then I shall rejoice in whatever brings honour to his name. This explains the paradox, this removes the mystery. And you might gather much of imagery together, to delineate how man shall be so devoted to God as to surrender every feeling which opposes the consecration; but nothing could outdo the vigour and vividness of the picture, which fetches its illustrations from the Red Sea's shore. You might catch the echoes of celestial minstrelsy, and give us fragments of those glorious hymns, which, floating on unearthly music, penetrate the mysterious solitudes of Deity, and fill them with celebrations of the universal Father. But if you are to tell us how the human shall be absorbed in the Divine; how the creature will have out-grown all the feebleness and selfishness of this finite estate, and live, and move, and have his being in the Creator; if you would describe those stately, yet ardent, affections which can find their counterpart objects in Deity alone, but which find them in Him unlimitedly and everlastingly—oh, then you have said as much as our capacities can grasp, nay, more than suffices to fill them in their utmost stretch, when you have simply quoted the assertion of our text. For it is not the mighty melody which swells and soars, when the heavenly hosts bow down in adoration of the Lord; and it is not the liquid poetry, wherewith they tell his beauty and his grace; it is not this which can show me the mastery won over mortal passion, and the deep, engrossing, burning love of the Almighty.

But this indeed is shown me, so that imagination itself is distanced, when you have bidden me listen to a song which is heard, clear and distinct, above the last crash of disjointed systems, and the cry of despairing multitudes; and have told me that this song is from the lips and the harps of those who have been gathered from our earth into the celestial Church; and have added, that the song is none other than that of the Israelites over the Egyptians, whom the waters had entombed, "the song of Moses, the servant of the Lord."

We proceed to observe that the song of the triumphant Church is described, not only as the song of Moses, but as that also of the Lamb. "They sang the song of Moses, the servant of God, and of the Lamb." Now we may be said to feel more at home with the song of the Lamb, than with that of Moses; for this is a song, of which, even now, we can strike some notes; whereas, we look on that of Moses with a kind of awe and dread, as though it were not suited to such minstrelsy as ours. The song of the Lamb, which the Evangelist heard, may be considered as that new song, which is given in other parts of the book of Revelation, and the burden of which is the worthiness of the Mediator. The "thousand times ten thousand, and thousands of thousands," who are round about the throne, were heard by St. John, saying with a loud voice, "Worthy is the Lamb that was slain to receive power, and riches, and wisdom, and strength, and honour, and glory, and blessing." This, or something similar to this, was the strain which mingled with that of lofty exultation, as the Church beheld its overthrown enemies. And if, therefore, the song of Moses were one which showed such subjection or refinement of human feelings, as is almost unintelligible, at least the song of the Lamb is in thorough harmony with what is now felt and chanted by believers. It is the song of grateful confession that we owe every thing to the Redeemer, and that his blood and righteousness have been the alone procuring causes of deliverance from ruin, and a title to immortality.

And there is vast beauty in the retention of the name of the Lamb in the melodies of Heaven. You might have thought, that, so soon as the conflict and the ignominy were over, all memory, or, at least, all trace of them would have been removed; and that, as the Redeemer went to and fro amid the throng of his admiring saints, there would be nothing to remind them that He had been "the man of sorrows, and acquainted with grief." But the very reverse of this is proved from the descriptions of the book of Revelation. When St. John beheld the Mediator standing in the midst of the throne, and of the four beasts, and in the midst of the elders, the aspect under which He appeared, was that of "a Lamb as it had been slain." Strange that the imagery of death should be preserved amid scenes where death cannot enter. Yet, why strange? Can we marvel that the Saviour should retain the prints of the nails, and appear, at one and the same time, as the crucified and the glorified? It was as the Lamb that He overthrew principalities and powers. It was as the Lamb that He defeated the machinations of Satan, and restored to its lost place a fallen creation. It was as the Lamb that he exhausted the curse which disobedience had provoked, and opened the graves, and bade the buried come forth. And the wounds which this Lamb received, what were they but the very weapons with which He conquered? "Through death He destroyed him that had the power of death, that is, the devil." He vanquished by dying, He triumphed by falling. O surpassingly strange, as well as surpassingly vast, a victory, in which the conquest was won through apparent defeat, and the foe subdued through yielding to his power. Death died in killing Christ, and the grave lost its sovereignty by reigning over the Lamb. Were not then the wounds of the Redeemer the arms with which He mastered the enemies of God? and what are they now but trophies of the unmeasured achievement? To appear therefore as the Lamb, "a Lamb as it had been slain," in the midst of all the magnificence of the everlasting city, is to appear as the mighty conqueror, who led captivity captive. You might array Him with the insignia of universal authority, and sweep away every mark of humiliation and pain, but if He is to stand in the assembly of the saints, manifesting Himself as the vanquisher of evil, wearing the spoils which He brought from the battle, clad in the robes of the champion of God and man, then He must appear with the mementos of Calvary, his crown the crown of thorns, though each thorn be a sparkle of the effulgence of Deity, and his sceptre his own cross, though so burning with lustre that it lights up the whole expanse of the Mediatorial kingdom.

And if it be as the Lamb that Christ is most glorious, what but the song of the Lamb shall be most on the lips of those for whom he died? If now we would sing the praises of our Lord, and pour forth our gratitude for what He hath done, we ask a hymn, which tells us of his marvellous condescension in assuming our nature, and into whose verses is woven the mysterious record of his agony and passion. At times indeed we take other strains: we celebrate our Redeemer as from everlasting and to everlasting, the Almighty One by whom the worlds were made, and "in whose hands is the soul of every living thing." But if the heart is to be thoroughly warmed, there must be redemption in the anthem. The Architect of this mighty creation—it is a noble theme, and asks a mighty melody. The substitute for sinners, the Deliverer of man from unimagined misery—this is the touching theme, and both asks and wakes the music of the soul. And it shall be the same hereafter, only in far higher degree. We doubt not there will be many and various hymns chanted in the celestial temple. Archangel to angel, cherubim to seraphim, and man to man, will roll sublime choruses, such as our speech cannot now embody, nor our thought embrace. But one hymn there will be, which shall be peculiar to men. One anthem shall be heard in which none but those who were once ready to perish will be able to join, but which their voices will never be weary of uttering. "Thou wast slain, and hast redeemed us to God by thy blood out of every kindred, and tongue, and people, and nation." It will not be from an angel's lips that this anthem will issue. The angel never knew the wretchedness of being a fallen creature, and, therefore, cannot know the thankfulness of a redeemed. But men—those who had rebelled, and been the enemies of God; those who had been on the brink of perdition, and who nevertheless have been raised to glory and immortality—men will dwell with ecstacy on the achievement of the Lamb, and weave that blessed name into their loftiest measure, and shrine it in thei. sweetest harmony. Men may join in angels' hymns; for theirs, too, will be the enraptured admiration of the Divine Majesty, and theirs the tribute of high-wrought acknowledgment, as Deity manifests his wonderfulness, and shows another height, or another depth, of that which, through eternity, will still be unsearchable. But angels can take, comparatively, no part in this song of the Lamb. Indeed, as the triumphant Church pours forth its praises, angels may, and we are told, they will, chime in with the thrilling notes, and strike to the same ascriptions their instruments of music. But the burst of gratitude, the rush of thankful confession, the devotedness of soul breathed into the swelling peal—these require a personal interest in the sacrifice of the Lamb; and those only who can say, He died for us, will be able to throw themselves, as it were, into the anthem, "Worthy the Lamb that was slain."

And thus, if it somewhat perplexed us to find that the song of Moses shall be sung by the Church; if it seemed like divesting that Church of the sympathies of humanity; we can, at least, have fellowship with the minstrelsy of Heaven, now that we hear of another song, and that the song of the Lamb. We may feel as though our hearts must be fresh strung, and our voices tuned, ere we can rise to the awful gladness of that chant which is to commemorate how the Lord hath beaten down his foes. There may be kinsmen amongst those foes, our friends, our children—and nature would now prompt us to the low and melancholy dirge, rather than to the choral ode of such as exult and are thankful. But "the Song of the Lamb"—

we seem to know that strain: they are familiar notes; and the melody with which the celestial temple rings is already echoed, though feebly and faintly, from the courts of the earthly. And the combination of song, the blending of the Song of the Lamb with the Song of Moses, this assures me that the redeemed, though freed from all that is weak and imperfect, and made equal to the angels in completeness of consecration to God, will retain the warm and yearning affections which now belong to their nature. The song that was heard on the Red Sea's shore, when the Egyptians had sunk like lead in the waters—had this alone been swept from the golden harps of saints, I might have thought that these saints had ceased to be men, and were no longer accessible to emotions by which they had been stirred whilst on earth. But when I hear further of a song of thanksgiving for mercies which are now the foremost in Christian celebration, then I learn that, though sublimely exalted, the saints are still men: their hearts are throbbing with the same gratitude as ours, and we can have companionship with them, and feel them still brothers. Yes, it might induce the suspicion that all remembrance of earth had been erased, and man nerved into a stern and strange superiority to all human feeling, to hear of his exulting in the song of Moses over the lost ones of his race; but it is like bringing him back into association with ourselves—for David could sing of mercy and judgment—to give as the full description of the glorified Church, "They sing the song of Moses, the servant of God, and the song the Lamb."

"Great and marvellous are thy works, Lord God Almighty, just and true are thy ways, Thou King of Saints."

Such is a portion of the lofty anthem. To take this anthem in its largest application, we may say that it celebrates the greatness and the justice of God, as displayed in the occurrences of the judgment day. And it is well worth your attention, that these two characteristics shall be finally declared to have distinguished the whole business of the judgment. It will be a great and marvellous work, when the tares shall have been separated from the wheat, all unrighteousness detected and exposed, the wicked banished, and the faithful exalted. The spectacle has never yet been presented to the inhabitants of this earth so fraught with the manifestations of Omnipotence as shall be that of the general judgment. What display of power can equal that which will be given by the resurrection of the dead, bone coming to bone, the assembling into the same identical bodies of particles which have been scattered to the four winds of heaven, so that the sea, and the mountain, and the desert, surrender each its portion of human elements? And if the gathering together of the buried generations, reconstructed and reanimated, be the mightiest imaginable display of God's power over matter, what shall more declare his power over mind than that laying bare of all the secrets of men's hearts, on which the last sentences shall be founded, and by which they will be justified? Then you must add the portents and signs which are to herald the Judge; the battalions of the heavenly hosts which are to line the firmament; the consternation and trembling which are to seize on all who have been enemies of Christ; the chastened gladness and confidence which those will display who feel that He who sits upon the throne died for them on the cross—in all this there will be the amazing power of God: I hear that power in the trumpet and the thunder: that power it is which is casting down the stout-hearted: I read that power in the tranquillity of the righteous: the storm and the calm alike proclaim that Omnipotence is there.

You cannot, then, wonder at the language of the anthem. You cannot fail to acknowledge, even with the little which can yet be ascertained of the solemn and tremendous things of the judgment, that, if ever confession were extorted of the almightiness of the Lord, it will be when the white throne has been set, and the books have been opened, and the dead, small and great, have received their portions for eternity. We may have none but most inadequate notions of what shall be seen and heard when God holds his great assize in the face of the universe, and gives scope to each enactment of a retributive economy. But if the company of the redeemed, of those who have been acquitted, and accepted, and appointed to a glorious inheritance, are to stand "on a sea of glass mingled with fire"—yes, "a sea of glass mingled with fire," for even the righteous will only be "scarcely saved," so that safety itself will look perilous—and if they are to take into their hands the harps of God, that they may pass with music and a song through the gates of the celestial city, I can feel that, as they behold the desolations which have been wrought, and think how the arm and the breath of the Lord have done valiantly, congregating the millions of human kind, and animating, and dividing them—and all this amid the tremblings and heavings of creation—oh, I say, I can feel that the delivered company, on their glassy and fiery sea, will entertain a sense, such as they never before had, of what Omnipotence is, and what Omnipotence can do; and that, therefore, moved by one impulse, every hand will strike the lyre, and every tongue add its peal to the chorus of our text, "Great and marvellous are Thy works, Lord God Almighty!"

But this is not the whole of the chorus—the Church affirms God's ways to be just and true, as well as his works to be great and marvellous. And this is a most important assertion, when considered as called forth by the transactions of the judgment. The judgment will include within its searchings and its sentences the heathen world as well as the Christian, men who have had none but the scantiest portion of revelation, and others who have been blessed with its fulness. And even in a Christian community there is the widest difference between the means and opportunities afforded to different men, some being only just within sound of the Gospel, and others continually plied with its messages. But all this invests with great difficulties the business of judgment. It shows that there must be various standards, one standard for the heathen, and another for the Christian; one for this heathen, or this Christian, another for that. And there is something overwhelming in the thought that the untold millions of the human population will undergo an individual scrutiny; that they will come, man by man, to the bar of their God, and each be tried by his own privileges and powers. We can hardly put from us the feeling, that, in so enormous an assize, there will be cases comparatively overlooked, for which due allowance is not made, or in which the sentence is not founded on a full estimate of the circumstances. But, whatever our doubts and suspicious beforehand, "Just and true are thy ways, thou King of Saints," is the confession, you observe, which will follow the judgment. It is a confession, we are bold to say, in which the lost will join with the redeemed. The feeling in every condemned man shall be, that, had there been none but himself to be tried, his case could not have received a more patient attention, or a more equitable decision.

And we rejoice in hearing the chorus which is chanted on the glassy and fiery sea. It tells us that God will be justified when He speaks, and clear when He judgeth. As yet I know nothing, whatever I may conjecture, as to the future and eternal condition of the heathen. I cannot tell how the subjects of wholly different dispensations are to be brought to the same bar, and tried by a Judge of whom thousands amongst them never heard as a Mediator. But I learn from the anthem of the Church, that, in being carried on and completed, the last judgment will free itself from all difficulty and all mystery. The thorough justice of the whole proceedings will commend itself at once to every observer: the condemned will be speechless, silence being their most expressive confession; the approved will weave their admiration of the equity into the same song with that of the omnipotence which their God had displayed. We can be certain, therefore, that, as the righteous go away into everlasting life, they will carry with them a triumphant assurance that the Divine dealings with our race have, all along, done honour to the Divine attributes. The great white throne will have been as a sun which hath scattered all darkness, and shed a brilliant illumination over the vast maps of providence and grace. For our own part, therefore, what have we to do but meekly to work out salvation, not perplexing ourselves with mysteries too deep for our present penetration, but only striving that we may be accepted at the judgment; knowing that then every cloud will be scattered, and that, so overpowering will have been the demonstration, on which we shall have gazed, of the invariable justice, and the immutable faithfulness, of the Lord, that, no sooner shall we have received the harps of God than we shall strike them in celebration of the equity and truth of all his ways, "Just and true are thy ways, O King of Saints."

We have supposed our text uttered immediately after the last judgment. No doubt it strictly belongs to an earlier time, when plagues, analogous, to those which desolated Egypt, shall fall upon the earth, and the great Anti-Christian power, which Pharaoh may have typified, shall be consumed by the might of the Lord. But as, at least, the text refers to a season when Christ shall have interfered on behalf of his people, and swept away those who have resisted his authority, there can be nothing wrong in extending it to the last great interference, the final discomfiture of all the hosts of unrighteousness. And the practical thing to be borne in mind, is, that even now we stand on a sea of glass mingled with fire. A sea of glass—for we have no firm footing, and, if we walk not circumspectly, are certain to fall: of glass mingled with fire; for if we fall, the surface may give way, and we are plunged into everlasting burnings. But if it be a sea, on which we shall hereafter stand, this may denote the boundlessness of our existence, the depth of our knowledge. The sea may be of glass, for the floor of heaven may serve as a mirror, reflecting the majesties of God. There may be fire mingled with the glass, to tell us, that, as fast as the mirror shows us more of God, there will be kindled within us a more intense flame of love and admiration. You must long to walk such a sea as this, to join the orchestra from which shall proceed the sublime song of Moses and the Lamb. Then let all be earnest in obeying the precepts, and appropriating by faith the merits of that Redeemer who is hereafter to be our judge. There is room for all on that mysterious sea; there are harps for all in that mighty orchestra. And, God helping, we may yet all escape the wrath to come, and when the earth and heavens flee away from the face of Him that sitteth on the throne, be found amongst those who shall exult and give thanks, and enter with melodious measures the kingdom prepared from the foundation of the world.

LECTURE XV.

The Divine Long-suffering.

2 PETER iii. 9.

"The Lord is not slack concerning his promise, as some men count slackness; but is long-suffering to us-ward, not willing that any should perish, but that all should come to repentance."

THE Apostle is here arguing against the scoffers, who, as he tells us, will arise in the last days of this creation, and who, reasoning from the unbroken course and order of nature, will perversely conclude that no such change can be approaching as that which prophecy associates with the second advent of Christ. "Where," say they, "is the promise of his coming? for since the fathers fell asleep, all things continue as they were from the beginning of the creation." It is not our purpose, on the present occasion, to go into the statements by which the Apostle refutes the infidel argument. We know well enough that the unbroken continuance of the present economy is no proof that the Lord will not come forth from his place in majesty and terror; and we have the sure word of prophecy, that "the Heavens and the earth, which are now, are reserved unto fire, against the day of judgment and perdition of ungodly men." We are satisfied with the assurance that "the Lord is not slack concerning his promise;" and we only pray that we may be of those who are looking for Christ; seeing that it is unto "them that look for Him that He shall appear the second time without sin unto salvation."

But there is a peculiarity in our text on which we wish to fasten, and which will furnish, as we think, a most interesting subject of discourse. Immediately after asserting that there is nothing with God of what men count slackness, the Apostle gives a reference to the Divine patience or long-suffering. Now, suppose I were one of these scoffers, what should I be most inclined to doubt, from observing that God's threatenings did not take effect? I suppose, the power of God. I should be inclined to say, God has threatened what He is not able to perform: hence the reason why sun, moon, and stars, will rise and set in their appointed order, why there hath come nothing of the menaced dislocation of the whole material system. The power is wanting. Well, if this were my way of arguing, would it be any answer to me to say, "The Lord is long-suffering to us-ward?" Yes, indeed it would; there is no proof of the Divine power so great as the Divine long-suffering. This, my brethren, is what we design to endeavour to establish. How beautifully does one of our Church Collects express this truth, "O God, who declarest thy Almighty power most chiefly in showing mercy and pity." And when the spies had brought back an evil report of the promised land, and Moses pleaded with God as a man would plead for his children, you may remember that he said, "And now I beseech thee, let the power of my Lord be great, according as thou hast spoken, saying, The Lord is long-suffering and of great mercy." The idea of Moses, as gathered from these words, would seem to have been, that God would then show Himself most powerful when He showed Himself most long-suffering. You are thus put in possession of the principle which we wish to establish, and from which we would illustrate the words of our text. It is simply the principle, that God's patience is the greatest possible demonstration of God's power. Let then the scoffer approach in his hardihood. He will not believe that the earth shall be burned up; that the sun shall become black as sackcloth of hair, the moon be turned into blood, and the stars fall from the Heavens; all this, he says, may have been long ago threatened, but nothing has come to pass; surely then God is not able to accomplish his word; ah, say not so, exclaims the Apostle: "The Lord is not slack concerning his promise, as some men count slackness:" and in proof that his power is not deficient, I tell you that He "is long-suffering to us-ward, not willing that any should perish, but that all should come to repentance."

Now before beginning to prove to you that the long-suffering is the great proof of the power of God, we would observe that this idea is at variance with those most commonly entertained; at least, if not at variance, a mere cursory glance will not show it in harmony. We have only to make mention of the power of God, and the thoughts are instantly far away amid the fields of immensity, busying themselves with the accumulations of the workings of Almightiness, star upon star, and system upon system. It is our ordinary method, in our endeavours to exhibit this power, to bid the mind go and travel through the wonders of materialism. We strive to fix the attention on that mysterious period, when as yet there was loneliness throughout unbounded space, and the melodies of the Creator's goings forth alone brake the silences of Eternity. We then bid the ear hearken to the utterance of a creative command, and the eye look forth on what just before had been one vast void; and as the countless company of glorious worlds start into being, we require the spectator to fall prostrate, and to worship God under the name of Omnipotent. And from the fact of creation we pass on to that of preservation. We tell you that the enormous and complicated machinery of the universe is superintended and upheld by God; that there is not a single wheel, in all the inscrutable combinations, which is not made to revolve by his pervading energies; and that the very weakest and meanest amongst those tribes of living things, whose number puts to shame all finite arithmetic, is so dependent for the existence of each moment on the Author of its being, that to suppose it overlooked or forgotten is to suppose it, on the instant, paralyzed or extinguished.

And far be it from us to imply that such a method of demonstrating the power of God is other than correct. It were well if familiarity with the wonders of the visible universe did not produce in us apathy to the impressions which they are calculated to make. If the creation around us exerted over us its legitimate influence, practical, as well as professed, infidelity would be banished from the earth; the necessary consequence on our continually recognising the might of Jehovah, in the various objects of the encompassing scenery, must be that our cities and villages would be wholly possessed by an awe-struck and God-fearing population. But it would appear to be possible, that, whilst searching through the universe for evidences of the power of God, we may pass by a more signal demonstration lying individually in ourselves. We speak not of the testimony which is undoubtedly given by the construction of our bodies, and by the surprising manner in which the material encloses the immaterial. We are indeed fearfully and wonderfully made; and if a man be not hardened against proof, it will be enough, when debate turns on the power of God, to send him to himself, and he must own Him omnipotent. But there may be an evidence which is still more overpowering; and that, too, an evidence which each may fetch from his own experience, and his own history. Towards each of us there has been the exercise of long-suffering on the part of the Almighty. Each of us has provoked the wrath of the Lord; and yet upon none of us has that wrath, as yet, come down in its fury. So that, if the great demonstration of God's power be God's long-suffering, then each amongst us may find in himself that demonstration in all its completeness. And thus it may be of all things the most possible, that, after dwelling amazedly on the stupendous achievements which God hath wrought in producing and actuating the systems of the universe; after summoning planets, and suns, and seas, and mountains to give in their tribute of acknowledgment to the might of Him who "spake and it was done, who commanded and they stood fast;" oh, we say, it is of all things the most possible, that angels may be looking down upon myself as the crowning point of proof,—and not because

I am marvellous as the compound of matter and spirit, of mortal and immortal; and not because I inherit a nature which hath been taken into absolute union with the Divine; but because I have sinned, and yet breathe; because I have defied the living God, and the earth has not cleaved, and the torrent has not rushed, and the bolt has not fallen; because I have been long-offending, and God has been long-suffering—therefore may they regard me as out and out the most perfect demonstration that the power of their Lord is great; and assign me, because spared in mine offences, a place amongst the witnesses to the Almightiness of their Maker, which they give not to the marchings of planets, nor to the gorgeousness of light, nor to their own beauty as ethereal things, and rapid, and masterful.

And we think that it will conduce to your allowing the truth of our position, as to the long-suffering of God being the great evidence of his power, if you dwell for a while on the difficulty which even the holiest of men experience in dealing with the workers of unrighteousness. We will refer, first, to a case of most common occurrence, and we think to carry the mind of every hearer along with us, whilst describing it, and drawing from it our inferences. If you walk the streets of our crowded metropolis, you meet often with exhibitions of wickedness which call up your instant indignation. It may be that some reprobate fellow-creature is fearfully blaspheming the name of your God; or that he is tyrannizing over some weaker one of his race; or that he is acting with great cruelty towards an animal. You know that you cannot hear him, or cannot see him, without feeling your passions vehemently excited; and the uppermost wish in your minds is that of being able to restrain him and punish him. In that most common instance, when you observe the ill-using of the brute creation—we suppose that you have all felt that scarce repressible anger, which leads you to desire to inflict on the man of cruelty something of the same pain which he is wantonly causing to his horse or his dog. There is nothing, we think, clearer than that it is only the want of power which prevents a summary vengeance: so that if you could follow your feelings, you would punish the offender on the spot, and account, that in so doing, you did only what was commendable. And we are not about to enter into any examination of the right or the wrong of the feeling; we simply wish to assert that such a feeling exists, and to make the existence a groundwork of argument. It appears that we have to put a great constraint on ourselves, when we behold an act of oppression; and that, after all, we swallow down our indignation, not because we determine by a moral effort to repress it, but, rather, because there are hindrances which stand in the way of our giving it vent. If these hindrances were removed, it may be doubted, whether, in one case out of a hundred, we should not directly interfere to deliver the oppressed, and chastise the oppressor. So that we should possibly find it of all things the hardest, to show ourselves long-suffering; and the effort which it would be to us, with the power in our hands, and the indignation in our breasts, to pass on and leave the savage undisturbed in his brutality, this is not to be described, and not even, perhaps, imagined.

And now let us carry up your thoughts from ourselves to God. You observe that the spectacle of the working of evil produces within us the most painful emotions, and that the immediate impulse, even of the best regulated mind, is towards the punishing, if possible, the offender. But we ask you to remember that the spectacle which thus moves the holy wrath, if we may so term it, of the creature, is present in all its aggravations to the Creator. With a hatred of sin, which outruns our conceptions, and much more our imitation, God is looking down on every misdoing by which the earth is polluted ; so that, mysterious as it may seem, He who so abhors evil that He is declared to be of purer eyes than to behold it, is present at the perpetration of each species of crime, standing by the blasphemer, whilst pouring out his curses, and by the murderer, whilst bearing down on his victim. If this fact be pondered, it must almost startle and confound us. God, who is so holy that the least moral blot on a creation would be reason enough with Him why that creation should at once be destroyed, God, so to speak, is at the side of every transgressor, when, by his transgressions, he disobeys and defies Him. And yet He strikes not. Present in the holiness which abhors sin ; present in the might which can punish sin ; and yet, as though the sinner were left at liberty to work out, unnoticed and unrecompensed, his iniquities, lo, the hater of sin, and the avenger of sin, puts no arrest on that which He abominates, and deals out no punishment against that which He denounces.

We call it an amazing fact, one that is most staggering to a finite intelligence. But why so? wherein lies its surpassing strangeness? simply, we think, in this. The Creator is brought before us, as exhibiting what we ourselves, under any the like circumstances, could scarcely exhibit—long-suffering. We just ask you to imagine a sensitive and tender-hearted man, standing by whilst some monster of his species was foully ill-treating a fellow-creature or an animal. Suppose him possessed of the most perfect ability of putting a stop to the cruelty, and awarding due punishment. The first impulse would be to exercise this ability. And if, in place of yielding to the impulse, he should reflect within himself, If I spare this guilty one awhile, if I visit not upon him on the instant his iniquity, he may possibly repent, and see the vileness of his conduct, and grow more humane; why, we do not deny that, by a great effort, the reflection might carry it over the impulse, the man might pass on, and, in the hope of a future amendment, resolve to administer no present correction. We allow that there is no actual impossibility against the exercise of such a forbearance. But we think you will all agree that a vast effort would be needed for the repressing the feelings; and that, if we were spectators of this deferring of vengeance, we should either join in an outcry at the hard-heartedness of him who displayed the long-suffering, or confess that a mastery had been won over the spirit, which might justly obtain for the achiever a lofty place amongst the heroes of mankind.

Now we readily admit that the things of God are not to be judged of by comparison with the things of men. Therefore we do not exactly say, that because long-suffering would prove great power in ourselves, it must necessarily prove great power in our Maker. But we may carry the argument from human feeling thus far, at least, if no further. We may state that nothing would show greater power in a creature, holy enough to abhor evil, and possessed of ability to punish it, than the exercise of forbearance. We may then fairly go on to assert, that, in proportion as both the holiness and ability increase, the forbearance more and more manifests the power. So that, if we are not yet in the position to infer that God shows his power most, when He shows Himself long-suffering, we may certainly perceive that there is nothing in such an inference which ought to strike us as strange, seeing it is only what we might arrive at by carrying up our inquiry through successive ranks of being. Long-suffering is power over one's self. If then it be reverent so to speak, God's long-suffering is God's power over Himself; and assuredly God's power over Himself must be greater than the power which He puts forth, when He deals with what is material and finite.

We may have all read of such instances as of a man, in the hardihood of his atheism, challenging, so to speak, the Deity to prove his existence by striking him to the earth. "If there be a God, let Him show Himself by smiting me His denier." Now, you can hardly picture to yourselves a being exercising over himself so perfect a command, that, with all the apparatus of fiery reply at his disposal, he should not answer the challenge by levelling him, who utters it, with the ground. Can you measure to me the effort, which it would be to a creature, to keep the thunder silent, and to chain up the lightning? Yet the atheist is allowed to depart unscathed; and the proof of God's existence, which would have seemed pre-eminently calculated to overspread a neighbourhood with terrible conviction, is mysteriously withheld; so that the blasphemer can insultingly refer to his own fierce appeal, as bearing witness that there is either no God, or none who concerns himself with what is done on this earth. But what lesson does the believer in a God derive from this absence of all answer to the daring appeal? We tell you that he learns God's might a hundredfold more from the unbroken silence of the firmament than he would do from the hoarse tones of vengeance rushing down to the destruction of the rebel. The atheist overthrown—this is as nothing to the exhibition of the atheist spared. It would have been as nothing that God should have launched the bolt—the prodigy, the marvel, whose height I cannot scale, whose depth I cannot fathom, it is that God should have withheld the bolt. I should have learnt God powerful over the elements, had I seen the blasphemer stretched, a blackened corpse, at my feet: I learn God powerful over Himself, when the questioner of his Deity passes on uninjured. A finite being might have struck: I think that none but an infinite could forbear. So that, if you give yourselves to the careful examination of the case, you must allow that in no voice could there have been so much Divinity as in silence. The atheist demands that God should show Himself by punishing: the Christian perceives that God shows Himself by forbearing. And if from this display of unavenged blasphemy, the believer should betake himself to argument with any scoffer, who, like those who are to deform the last days of our creation, would plead the delay in the accomplishment of threatenings in evidence of a want of the power to execute, oh, would he not feel that the best answer to a doubt as to God's power might be fetched from God's patience, and that he could say nothing better than that "God is long-suffering towards us, not willing that any should perish," when he would substantiate to the scorner the important proposition, "The Lord is not slack concerning his promise, as some men count slackness?"

But we wish to show you more precisely that, in the long-suffering of God, lies the great proof of his power. We must take care not so to dwell on God's bearing with his creatures, and leaving them unvisited in their misdoings, as to forget that the deferring of punishment has no connection with the diminishing it, that the allowing sin to go on for years unvisited, involves no pledge of the final remission of its penalties. We shall probably arrive at right apprehensions of God's long-suffering, as connected with God's other attributes, if we carefully review these two facts—first of all, that God can punish every sin, and secondly, that God can pardon every sin. It is essential to the long-suffering of God, that each of these assertions should, in the largest sense, hold good. Unless there is the power of punishing, there can be no long-suffering; for long-suffering necessarily presupposes, that a being, who might on the instant take vengeance, passes over for a while the iniquity. On the other hand, unless God can pardon every sin, what is there in his long-suffering? We can have no idea of long-suffering, except as is expressed in our text—that it is the bearing with an offender, in order that, time being given him to consider his ways, he may yet, by repentance, turn away punishment. And if, then, we can satisfactorily show that God is pre-eminently powerful, inasmuch as He is both the punisher and the pardoner of sin, we shall have established the point under debate, that God's long-suffering is the great measure of his power.

Look, then, at the punishment of sin—you will readily admit that it is proving God powerful, to prove Him superior to every creature; so that, were the whole universe banded against Him, there would be no way made in entrenching on his sovereignty. But how can we more thoroughly assure ourselves of God's superiority to every creature, than by ascertaining that over every creature which swerves from obedience, God can exercise the office of avenger? There is nothing parallel to this in the furthest carrying out of human authority. The subject may revolt from the ruler, and prosecute his treason so successfully as to wrench the crown from its rightful possessor. And it were absurd to talk of the ruler as long-suffering, unless he have the power of seizing the traitor, and do not exercise it. If, then, the whole earth were brought under the sway of a single sceptre, you could not better sketch this universal supremacy than by saying of him who held it, that long-suffering was his characteristic. For if the seat of this unlimited empire were in England, and there came tidings of revolt in Asia or America, then, if I could assign as the reason why such revolt was not instantly checked, that the monarch was long-suffering, I should certainly imply, that, if the monarch chose to put forth his might, he could immediately quell these insurrections in far distant provinces. It is only possible for him to be long-suffering, on the supposition, that, if he will, he may instantly punish. Thus also with God. Whatever the creature which apostatizes from God, whether standing high or low in the scale of intelligence, beyond all question, the power of God can reach and restrain and crush this creature. It may, indeed, be that the creature is permitted to go on in rebellion, and that thus no direct evidence is given of the supremacy of God. And it might be that rebellion would run along every order of being, and God be opposed by the whole body of his creatures, and those creatures be left, to all appearance, alone, to frame their schemes, and wage their battles. Wherein, then, would lie the proof of God's power? Simply, in God's long-suffering. Long-suffering is the greatest exhibition of power on this side the day of judgment. It is our evidence that God now possesses all that God shall then exercise. And when I am told that God is long-suffering, and no limitations are placed on the attribute, you bring before me a picture as overpowering in its details, as stupendous in its outlines. I see at once, that, if God be long-suffering, then God can punish every sin. What then? vice may seem to carry it over virtue; and I may search in vain, through all that is passing on a disordered creation, for tokens that a moral government is still upheld in its vigour; and the infidel may tauntingly refer to the triumph of evil, and infer that God has been compelled to abandon one world at least to the dominion of his foes; but, fastening on the long-suffering of the Creator, I am proof against all doubts as to the power of the Creator: He could not be long-suffering unless He could punish: He could not punish unless he were supreme.

And then observe, secondly, that God can pardon every sin. Of all extraordinary truths, perhaps the most extraordinary is, that sin can be forgiven. We may have accustomed ourselves to think lightly of sin: if we would be honest in searching our feelings, we should probably confess ourselves surprised at the vehement terms in which it is characterized. Yet, let reason herself sit in quiet and undisturbed judgment upon sin, and her verdict would be that sin is unpardonable. We were bound, as creatures, to serve God with all our faculties, whether of body or soul. And if we swerve, in a single particular, from this uniform consecration, we have kept back a fraction, no matter how trifling, of the tribute due from us to God; and though, for long after years, there might be no fresh deficiency, still, since God's right is to all at all times, the obedience of a century could never make up the arrears of a moment. Thus there must be always an outstanding debt; and unless God's justice shall relax in its claims—unless, that is, God shall cease to be God—there is no discernible mode in which the debt can be discharged; so that reason, sitting in judgment on the very lightest of sins, must be driven to the conclusion that sin is unpardonable. And if the providing, or making possible, a pardon for sin, be exactly that which would have seemed to us impossible, we may fairly take the pardon, when planned and perfected, as the highest demonstration of the power of God. That, which reason would have decided impossible to be effected, becomes, when effected, the noblest of all proofs of the power of the Accomplisher.

I do not know that there is any other work of the Creator, whose performance, if beforehand submitted to reason, would have been judged to be impossible. Even had man stood alone, the solitary result of the creative energies of God, his reason, judging from the magnificence of his own constitution, would have decided that an universe, unmeasured in its sweep, and full, to the overflow, of the sublime and the beautiful, might arise at the bidding of Him whose word had already given life. It would have seemed possible to man, whilst surrounded by no tokens of God's wonder-working might, thrown on the evidences of his own flesh and spirit—it would, we say, have seemed possible to man, the single inhabitant, save the Eternal One Himself, of immensity, that innumerable worlds, each possessed by an innumerable tenantry, should start out of nothingness and walk the firmament in a bright and rejoicing companionship. And thus creation is not to man the greatest demonstration of God's power. Creation does not go beyond what reason would have thought possible; and it is only the pardon of sin which reason, unaided in her search, would have set down as impossible. Reason, uninformed as to the possibility of God becoming man, must have pronounced the impossibility of God forgiving transgression. And is it not most accurate to say, that the achievement, which man would have accounted impossible, is a stronger proof to him of the power of the Achiever, than any other which his own calculations would have classed amongst the possible? So that we set it before you as not to be controverted, that the fact that God can pardon sin contains the strongest of all evidences to the power of God. And forasmuch as the long-suffering of God takes for granted that God can pardon sin, it follows that God's long-suffering is the very mightiest demonstration of God's power.

It may be a bold thing to say; but, if you examine carefully, you will see that there is a strong sense in which it may be said, that long-suffering is not natural to God.

No, not natural. For was God long-suffering without an effort? Could He be long-suffering without preparation? He could be long-suffering only as He had resolved to give up his well-beloved Son to the fiercest of agonies and the foulest of wrongs. He could be long-suffering, only as a covenant had been entered into, that, in the fulness of times, He who was from all eternity his equal would assume the rebellious nature of the fallen, and fight therein a battle in which victory must be death. He could be long-suffering, only if He would bow the Heavens, and surrender a Divine person to the scorn and the loathing of men. And He did this. He bade the sword awake against his fellow; and, rendering it possible, through the sacrifice of his Son, that sin might be forgiven, He rendered it also possible that Himself could be long-suffering. And when I think on the difference between God's creating a world, and God's pardoning a sin—the one done without effort, the other demanding an instrumentality terribly sublime; the one effected by a word, the other wrought out in agony and blood, on a quaking earth and beneath a darkened heaven—oh, the world created is as nothing by the side of the sin blotted out: that God can pardon is at the very summit of what is wonderful; and therefore then, O Lord, do I most know Thee as the Omnipotent, when I behold in Thee the long-suffering.

We have shown you that, if God be long-suffering, He can punish every sin, and He can pardon every sin; and arguing supremacy in power, both from the punishment and the pardon, we bring home to you the conclusion, that the supremacy is shown by the long-suffering. And thus, to recur once more to the statement of our text, let the scorner come forward and object, that the threatenings of God must hitherto have failed of fulfilment, because the power of God is not adequate to their execution, then I shall not point him to the marvels of creation, to the stars, and the forests, and the mountains, in order to display to him that power which he questions or denies: I shall say to him, "The Lord is not slack concerning his promise, as some men count slackness;" and I shall think it enough to rebuke all suspicion as to the slackness resulting from weakness, to add, "He is long-suffering to us-ward, not willing that any should perish, but that all should come to repentance."

Now, we trust you will all carry with you the idea which we have been most anxious to exhibit, that it is chiefly in showing Himself long-suffering that God shows Himself powerful. Take any other instance of power, and you can, perhaps, imagine a greater. Point out to me the sun, and I may suppose a yet mightier luminary, rejoicing as a giant to run a race. Point out to me the stars, and I may suppose a yet more brilliant troop walking the magnificent canopy. But tell me of forbearance, of long-suffering, of patience, and you tell me of a power (if it be not paradoxical thus to speak) which is greater than infinite. God delaying to take vengeance is God showing his power over Himself, power, that is, over the Omnipotent. So that we can well understand how the patience may be connected with the power of God, as though the one attribute were the great cause or evidence of the other. That the Divine Being can be insulted and not avenge Himself; that He can be defied, blasphemed, and not at once strike down the daring offenders; that, day after day, year after year,

He can suffer the wicked to go on in their wickedness, their every action showing scorn of Him, their every word hatred; and yet, that, all the while, He has engines at his disposal through which He might turn them into terrible monuments of his righteous indignation—oh, there is far greater demonstration of might in this, than in any of those exhibitions, to which men ordinarily refer, when they would declare the supremacy of God: every one of us, a living thing, and yet a sinful, outdoes the earth with all its wonders, and the firmament with all its hosts, in proving the Creator surpassing in his strength.

We must make a close and practical application of so surprising a fact, even though we should but repeat our foregoing statements. Children though ye be of weakness, and heirs of corruption, we may address you in terms loftier than we could dare apply to the sun when marching in his brightness, or to the gorgeous retinue of the deep rich midnight. Monuments the most illustrious of the might of the Almighty, I speak to you as to beings upon whom are gathered the regards of the Angel and the Archangel. That you are still amongst the living; that it has been possible for you to be rebellious, days and weeks and months and years; that you have been spared to insult God, to receive his favours with coldness, to break his commandments, to make light of his threatenings, to put contempt on his promises—where is the prodigy which can half as much amaze the holy creatures who have held fast their allegiance? Each amongst us is a witness that God is long-suffering, and therefore that God is Omnipotent.

But what use have we made of the Divine long-suffering? to what purpose have we turned it? Have we reason to account with the Apostle that the "long-suffering of God is salvation?" has it led us to repentance? Would that it might be so. God bears with us in love, not in wrath; bears with us, because it is yet possible that we may escape from death, and enter into life. In God's long-suffering I read this fact, salvation is within reach of all whom I address. He does not spare you to increase your condemnation: perish the thought: He spares you only because yet there is hope, yet there is grace, yet there is room; and all—which of you can be willing to be left out?—all may be sheltered, when the storm of wrath is in the Heavens, and the sheet of fire round the earth. Let us take heed, therefore, in the words of St. Paul, that we "despise not the riches of his goodness and forbearance and long-suffering, not knowing that the goodness of God leadeth us to repentance." Long-suffering, as we have shown you, proves power in two ways—as presupposing that God can punish sin, and also that God can pardon sin. There is, therefore, encouragement in long-suffering; but, at the same time, there is warning. It forbids any to despair: it allows none to presume. Since God spares me, I know that He can punish; and, therefore, I might be startled at my very preservation. But I know also, on the same account, that God can pardon; and, therefore, let me flee to Him through Christ, whilst He may still be addressed in the already quoted words of our Collect, "O God, who declarest thy Almighty power most chiefly in showing mercy and pity."

LECTURE XVI.

Sowing the Seed.

MARK iv. 26–29.

"And He said, So is the Kingdom of God, as if a man should cast seed into the ground; and should sleep, and rise night and day, and the seed should spring and grow up, he knoweth not how. For the earth bringeth forth fruit of herself; first the blade, then the ear, after that the full corn in the ear. But when the fruit is brought forth, immediately he putteth in the sickle, because the harvest is come."

YOU are all, no doubt, aware that the phrase "the Kingdom of God," or "the Kingdom of Heaven," with which so many of our Lord's parables are introduced, denotes ordinarily the Gospel dispensation, or the Divine method of dealing under the covenant of grace. In general, these parables have a twofold signification: they delineate the Gospel, either as making way in the world, or as acting on an individual. The remarkable parable, which we have just read to you, would most probably admit this double interpretation: it may be, that is, that the history of the Church as a body, and the history of every believer in particular, illustrates, or is illustrated by, the figurative sketch here given of the sowing of the seed, and of the springing of the blade. We shall not, however, attempt so lengthened an inquiry. We will confine ourselves to the individual case; and, without further preface, we ask your close attention, whilst we examine how the kingdom of God is like unto seed cast into the ground, and which springeth up, the man knoweth not how; and then, with what truth it can be said, that, when the fruit is brought forth, the sickle is immediately put in, because the harvest is come.

Now you observe that the parable under review derives, like many others, its figures from the processes of agriculture. When the husbandman has once cast the seed into the ground, there is little or nothing more that he can do towards ensuring a harvest. He will therefore employ himself on other business, leaving to the vegetating powers of the seed, and the influences of the sun and the shower, the covering his fields with the rich livery of plenty. It is this representation which is furnished by the first two verses of the parable. The kingdom of God is likened to a man who casts seed into the ground, and then sleeps, and rises night and day—that is, betakes himself to other occupations—and the seed springs and grows up, he knoweth not how. He has nothing to do with the seed after he has sown it. Nay, in place of being able to help on the springing up of the corn, he is profoundly ignorant of the secret operations of nature; there is not to him a greater mystery than that of the buried grain reproducing itself, a hundredfold multiplied.

We have in this a most simple, yet striking, representation of the business, and, at the same time, of the helplessness, of the spiritual husbandman. Unto the ministers of the Gospel, who are the great moral labourers in the field of the world, there is entrusted the task of preparing the soil, and of casting in the seed. And if they bring to this task all the fidelity and all the diligence of intent and single-eyed labourers; if they strive to make ready the ground by leading men to clear away the weeds of an unrighteous practice, and to apply the spade and ploughshare of a resistance to evil, and a striving after good; and if, then, by a faithful publication of the grand truths of the Gospel, they throw in the seed of the word; they have reached the boundary of their office, and also of their strength; and are to the full as powerless to the making the seed germinate, and send forth a harvest, as the husbandman to the causing the valleys to stand thick with corn. And, indeed, in the spiritual agriculture, the power of the husbandman is even more circumscribed than in the natural. With all the pains, with which a minister of Christ may ply at the duties of his office, he can never be sure that the ground is fit for receiving the grain: he must just do always what the tiller of the natural soil is never reduced to do, run the risk of casting the seed upon the rock, or of leaving it to be devoured by the fowls of the air.

So that, after all, the office of a minister of the Gospel, though the very noblest with which man can be charged, is, in every respect, singularly limited. It is not the office of the sculptor who takes the rude block, and, fashioning it, day by day, with industry and skill, leaves it not till it emulates the loveliness of life. It is not the office of the artisan, who, with his apparatus of tools, and his assemblage of material, toils sedulously at his occupation—each portion of the work depending equally on his care and his handicraft—till the finished piece of mechanism counts the hours, and tells the minutes. The minister of Christ can do little more than scatter the seed; and he may live and die altogether ignorant, whether much, or whether any, have sprung up into a harvest of righteousness. And even if he be privileged to behold the ground covered with a luxurious produce, he cannot be said to have been otherwise instrumental to so beautiful a result, than as having strewed the earth with the grain entrusted to him by the great Proprietor of the soil. To him, as well as to the natural husbandman, the vegetation of the seed will ever be a deep and impenetrable mystery. It springs and grows up, "he knoweth not how." Wonderful and unapproachable is the Creator in all his dealings; but in none more so than in the conversion and renewal of sinners. There can be no question, that the method, which He ordinarily employs, is the preaching of the word. You come to the sanctuary week after week; and this gathering together of the children of immortality presents the surface on which the husbandman is to labour. And, if he be faithful to the work entrusted to his performance, he brings out, from the granary of Scripture, the seeds of wholesome truth and pregnant doctrine; and, with prayer unto Him, who can alone give the increase, casts them on the ground which he hath been appointed to cultivate.

And it may be, that, though a vast quantity of this seed falls by the wayside, and is utterly lost, whilst another portion, deposited on a light and insufficient soil, sends up quickly a produce which as quickly withers, yet some is received into a well-prepared heart, and there waits the influence of the shower and the sunshine. But who shall scrutinize that agency by which the word is applied to the conscience? Who shall explain how, after weeks, it may be, or months, or even years, during which the seed has lain buried, there will often but unexpectedly come a moment when the preached word shall rise up in the memory, and a single text, long ago heard, and to all appearance forgotten, overspread the soul with the big thoughts of eternity? It is a mystery, which far transcends all our power of investigation, how spirit acts upon spirit; so that, whilst there are no outward tokens of an applied machinery, there is going on within a mighty operation, even the effecting a moral achievement which far surpasses the stretch of all finite ability. We are so accustomed to that change which takes place in a sinner's conversion, that we do not ascribe to it, in right measure, its characteristic of wonderful. Yet wonderful, most wonderful, it is—wonderful in the secrecy of the process, wonderful in the nature of the result. I can understand a change wrought upon matter. I have no difficulty in perceiving that the same substance may be presented under quite different aspects; and that mechanical and chemical powers may make it pass through a long series of transformations. But where is the mechanism which shall root from the heart the love of sin? where the chemistry which shall so sublimate the affections that they will mount towards God? It is this internal revolution, which we have no power of scrutinizing except in its effects. "The wind bloweth where it listeth, and thou hearest the sound thereof; but canst not tell whence it cometh, nor whither it goeth; so is every one that is born of the Spirit." We observe that some thorough change has been effected. The things, which were once delighted in, are now shunned; whilst those, which were disliked, are cherished as most precious. There is a clear and direct opposition to the desires and inclinations which were formerly and naturally uppermost; whilst motives, by which humanity seems ordinarily incapable of being stirred, operate overpoweringly on every faculty and feeling. But if we would look in, and behold the appliances by which this change is wrought out; if we would survey, as it were, spirit handling spirit, refreshing, remoulding, or, rather, actually recreating it—oh, it were even easier to dive into the secrecies of nature, and investigate, with curious accuracy, what goes on in her hidden laboratories, than, by all the strivings of thought, to imagine to ourselves this life-giving process.

The mystery is great of the natural seed, which must rot in the earth, and become, to all appearance, wasted and worthless, before it can reward with an increase the husbandman's anxieties. "That which thou sowest is not quickened, except it first die." But the mystery of the spiritual seed—a solitary verse, it may be, sinking, unobserved and unfelt, into the heart; lying there, unperceived or unregarded, whilst evil passions are still holding their court, and carrying on their revelry; and then, sending out suddenly fibres and roots, which occupy the space, and twine themselves, like chains, round the former possessors—this, though it be taking place every day, so that long usage has familiarized us to the fact, remains, to every inquiring and right-thinking mind, amongst the most inapproachable of marvels; and the simple verdict of the parable contains the decision of all who pour forth their attention on this moral prodigy, "It springs, and grows up, he knoweth not how."

But, if we are ignorant of the method, we are well acquainted with the result. The parable goes on to describe this result. "The earth," it saith, "bringeth forth fruit of herself"—not through the skill of the tiller, but through virtues wherewith God hath endowed it—"first the blade, then the ear, after that the full corn in the ear." You have here an account of successive stages of Christian experience. There is first the convert in the young days of his godliness—the green blade, just breaking through the soil, and giving witness to the germinations of the seed. This is ordinarily a season of great promise. We have not, and we look not for, the rich fruits of a matured and well-disciplined piety. But we have a glowing and verdant profession. Every thing looks freshly. The young believer scarcely calculates on any interruptions; and, as though there were no blighting winds, no nipping frosts, and no sweeping hail, to be expected and feared in the spiritual agriculture, the tender shoot rises from the ground, and glistens in the sunshine.

Next comes the ear; and this is the season of weariness and watching. Sometimes there will be a long interval, without any perceptible growth. Sometimes the corn will look sickly, as though blasted by the mildew. Sometimes the storm will rush over it, and almost level it with the earth. And all this takes place in the experience of the Christian. The spiritual husbandmen, and the natural, have the like anxieties in observing the ear, of which they have sown the seed. How slow is sometimes the growth in grace! how slight are the tokens of life! how yellow and how drooping the corn! The sudden gust of temptation, the fatal blight of worldly associations, the corroding worm of indwelling corruption—all these may tell powerfully and perniciously on the rising crop, so that often there shall scarcely seem reason to hope that any fruit will finally be yielded. Who would recognise in the lukewarm, and dilatory, and half and half professor, the ardent, and active, and resolute convert? Who would know in the stunted and shrivelled ear, the green blade which had come up, like an emerald shoot? We do not indeed say, that in every case, there will be these grievous interruptions and declensions. You may find instances, wherein godliness grows uniformly, and piety advances steadily and even rapidly towards perfection. A Christian will sometimes ripen for Heaven, as though, in place of being exposed to the cold air, and the wild rain, he had been treated as an exotic, and always kept under shelter. But generally even with those who maintain the most consistent profession, the earing time is a season of anxiety and uncertainty: and if it were not that there are gracious promises, assuring him that the bruised reed shall not be broken, nor the smoking flax quenched, often must the spiritual husbandman mourn bitterly over the apparent disappointment of all his best hopes, and surrender himself to the fear, that, when the great day of harvest breaks on this creation, the field which had once worn that lovely enamel, which gives fair promise of an abundant ingathering, will yield nothing to the reapers but the dry and parched stalks, fit only to be bound in bundles for the burning.

"Every plant," said Jesus, "which my heavenly Father hath not planted, shall be rooted up;" and we believe also in the converse of this saying, that every plant which God hath planted, shall at last yield fruit as a plant of righteousness and renown. It is not every blade which springs from the agriculture in which God Himself is the husbandman. The seed sown by the wayside, yields a blade. But the blade does not go on to become the ear; conviction does not deepen into conversion. This then is not the renewing work of the Holy Ghost; every blade which God Himself causes to spring, He causes also to grow till fit for the sickle. The growth may be hindered as we have explained to you; and there will necessarily be uneasiness in those who are watching it, lest, after all, the planting be not of the Lord. But God has his eye on his own field, and the parable next declares, that when the fruit is brought forth, or when the fruit is ripe, immediately He putteth in the sickle. There is no marked change of agency; though it is certain that the sower and the reaper are not strictly the same. God however is Himself the husbandman; and though He may act in one part by man, and in another by angels, the idea of his supremacy and superintendence must always be preserved, as it is by the language before us.

God then putteth in the sickle so soon as the fruit is ripe. No believer is left upon earth, after he is ready for Heaven. We are often inclined to wonder that trial after trial should be allotted to Christians, who seem to us much further advanced than others who have been gathered to their rest. When we look upon aged believers who appear to have been long ago fitted to depart hence, and to be with the Lord, we almost marvel that they are not called home, and that God still exercises them by a discipline of affliction. But of this we may be sure—the ear is not full, otherwise it would be plucked. We are poor judges of meetness, or fitness, for the inheritance of the saints in light. And there is such a difference, a natural difference, between the subjects of grace, that the amount of discipline which fully prepares one, may leave another with a vast deal to be done. The resistance of some hearts is unspeakably greater than that of others. The churlish, and rugged, and irritable dispositions will require more time ere they are subdued by religion, than the amiable, and mild, and forgiving. Besides, all are not intended for the same eminence in glory. There are to be degrees of happiness; and these we doubt not will be proportioned to degrees of holiness. And it were therefore most rash, if we decided the amount of fitness for death; seeing that, if prepared for one degree of enjoyment, there are higher and nobler, for which long years of fresh trial and warfare would still leave us unprepared. One believer is cut off in the prime of his natural strength, whilst another lingers on through a weary winter, and overpasses the natural age of mankind. Both when they die are fit for Heaven; and neither attains that fitness until the hour of dissolution; "when the fruit is brought forth, *immediately* he putteth in the sickle."

So that we have no other feeling, when standing by the sick bed of one who has been enabled to fix faith upon Christ, but that there is fruit before us which is rapidly ripening, but which, however it may strike us as already wearing the golden hue of maturity, is not yet ripe. We do not say that any defined period must necessarily elapse between justification and salvation. It is out of all question, that, whensoever a justified man dies, he enters into Heaven. But if there were needed fresh argument to demonstrate the improbabilities of death-bed repentance, we should fetch it from the Scriptural fact, that, after we are justified, there must be inwrought in us a fitness for glory. It is not God's ordinary course—we dare not limit Him in the extraordinary—it is not God's ordinary course, to bring close together the seed time and the harvest time; so that the filling of the ear shall follow instantly on the sowing of the grain. The natural husbandry typifies the spiritual; and we look not in the one for that abruptness, and that blending of results, which we find not in the other. And, therefore, if we observe a man disposed to delay, calculating that the whole work of religion may be condensed into an hour, and that, too, the very last of mortal existence, we would simply say to him, "The earth bringeth forth first the blade, then the ear, after that the full corn in the ear." And dost thou expect the three all at once? If thou art saved, it must be by a kind of annihilation of time; a year, with all its seasons, must pass in a minute. And if again we find a true Christian, who, harassed with trouble and pain, longs with somewhat of impatience for the hour of dismissal from the flesh, we say to him, Take heed how you desire the moment of gathering to precede the moment of ripeness; that you live is our proof that you are not yet fit for death; "when the fruit is brought forth, immediately (mark that), immediately he putteth in the sickle." We must dwell a moment longer upon this: it is a matter full of interest and instruction. It seems often, as we have hinted, to excite surprise both in the sufferer himself, and in others, when a Christian, who has long been eminent for piety, and whose faith has been conspicuous in his works, lingers for months, perhaps even years, in wearisome sickness, as though, notwithstanding the preparations of a righteous life, he needed protracted trial to fit him for the presence of God. But there is, we believe, altogether a mistake in the view which is commonly taken of old age, and lingering sickness. Because a man is confined to his room, or his bed, the idea seems to be that he is altogether useless; that, in the ordinary phrase, he is quite laid by, as though he had no duties to perform, when he could no longer perform those of more active life. Was there ever a greater mistake? The sick room, the sick bed, has its special, its appropriate, duties—duties to the full as difficult, as honourable, as remunerative, as any which devolve on the Christian, whilst yet in his unbroken strength. They are not precisely the same duties as belonged to the man in health: but they differ only by such differences as a change in outward circumstances and position will always introduce. The patience which he has to cultivate, the resignation which he has to exhibit, the faith which he has to exercise, the example which he has to set: oh, talk not of a sick man as of a man laid by! harder deeds it may be, ay, and deeds of more extensive usefulness, are required from him who lingers on the couch, than from many a leader in the highest and most laborious of Christian undertakings.

Is there then any cause for surprise, if a Christian be left to linger long in sickness, to wear away tedious months in racking pain, or slow decay? Is it at all in contradiction to the saying, that, "so soon as the fruit is ripe, immediately he putteth in the sickle?" Not so—the fruit is not necessarily ripe, the man's work is not necessarily done, because he is what you call laid by, and can take no part in the stir and the bustle of life. It is they who turn many to righteousness that are to shine as the stars on the firmament. And is there no sermon from a sick bed? Has the sick man nothing to do with publishing and advancing the Gospel? Nay, I think that an awful, a perilous trust is committed to the sick Christian. Friends, children, neighbours, the Church at large, look to him for some practical exhibition of the worth of Christianity; if he be fretful or impatient, or full of doubts and fears, they will say, Is this all that the Gospel can do for man in a season of extremity? If, on the other hand, he be meek and resigned, and able to testify to God's faithfulness to his word, they will be taught—and nothing teaches like example—that Christianity can make good its pretensions, that it is a sustaining, elevating, death-conquering religion.

And who shall calculate what may be wrought through such practical exhibitions of the power, the preciousness of the Gospel? I, for one, will not dare to affirm that more is done towards converting the careless, confirming the wavering, or comforting the desponding, by the bold champion who labours publicly at the making Christ known, than by many a worn-down invalid who preaches to a household, or a neighbourhood, by unruffled patience, and simple unquestioning dependence upon God. I, for one, can believe that he who dies a death of triumph, passing almost visibly, whilst yet in the exercise of every energy, from a high post of usefulness, into the kingdom of glory, may have fewer at the Judgment to witness to the success of his labours, than many a bed-ridden Christian, who, in the beautiful quietness of a godly submission, waited year after year his summons to depart. God has particular lessons to give, and particular ends to answer, when He calls away one of his servants in the midst of his strength, and with every indication of triumph, and when He leaves another to spend not only years in labour, but months, and even years, in the solitariness of his chamber, a prisoner on his couch. Dismiss then the thought, that there is any thing strange in the lingering sicknesses, the long-delayed deaths, of Christians who have given full evidence of their faith and their piety. They are ready, they are fit, to die, if by readiness, if by fitness, you mean such a spiritual state that hope might justly plant itself by their grave, and smile beautifully as they were committed to its cold embrace. But God putteth not in the sickle, because He has still work for them to do, and Heaven has still prizes for them to win. Therefore do they live. Therefore is the lamp so long in going out. They live that they may preach, they live that they may practise, Christianity. The lamp yet burns, that the flickering light may guide some wandering or wavering spirit, and add another sparkle to the crown of righteousness which shall be awarded at the Judgment. O, then, marvel not that death comes so slowly; the mercy is that it comes not more quickly. And whenever the old and worn-down man falls sick of the sickness whereof he must die, look not on him as he lingers, as on one who can be of no further use; rather regard him as still an efficient labourer in the highest of causes.

The aged believer, whose closing scene has been regarded as furnishing only material of melancholy contrast, whether with his own more active days, or with the more rapid and joyful transition of many brethren in the flesh, so debilitated has he been by long sickness, "My heart is smitten and withered like grass, so that I forget to eat my bread;" he often wins after death a testimony to his usefulness which may well compensate the darkness which seemed to cloud his decline. The good deeds wrought by him in his protracted illness, may not immediately appear. But, afterwards, we learn that he did not linger in vain, that he did not die in vain. The example is remembered, the patience, the meekness, remembered by children, by servants, by friends, by neighbours. It is remembered, to be imitated, in their own day of sorrow, their own hour of dissolution. Then it administers courage, constancy, hope. Oh! we may suffer much, we may linger long; no burning rapture may characterize our going hence. But if there be patient submission to the will of the Lord, our memory may survive, and be instrumental to the victories of religion. Ah! then, who has any thing to say as to the inconsistency of our text with the known experience, the protracted sufferings, the tedious old age of many of the righteous? Useful to the last moment, doing God's work in dying as well as in living, nay, winning it may be a higher throne, and a richer crown, at the very instant of breathing out the soul, why it is not more true, that "the earth bringeth forth first the blade, then the ear, after that the full corn in the ear," than that, "when the fruit is put forth, immediately he putteth in the sickle."

Now we said that we would not enter on the illustration of the parable, considered as delineating the history of the Church. We should not have space for the inquiry. We will only remark that the Church, from the first, has been God's witness upon earth, and that, when her testimony shall have been fully delivered, the end will have come, and the dispensation will be closed. The ripeness of the Church will be, when it shall have witnessed for all the truths which are to be opposed by the heretical and the infidel. Already has the protest been uttered on behalf of those doctrines, referring both to man and the Mediator, which are nothing less than the life's blood of Christianity. If you trace heresy downwards, from the Apostles' days to our own, you find it fastening itself successively on the several truths of our faith, so that there is scarce a fraction which has not been assaulted, and in defence of which the Church has not shown itself Protestant. What then remains to the rendering the Church fully ripe? We find from the Scriptures that one great feature of the last times shall be disbelief or denial of the second Advent of Christ. As in other days of the dispensation, so in the concluding, there shall be abroad the covetous, the blasphemers, the traitors, the high-minded, and all those manifestations of evil which have ever called forth the protest of the Church. But, over and above these forms of wickedness, scorners shall be walking the earth, arguing, from the apparent fixedness of things, to the improbability of Christ's interference, and tauntingly asking, "Where is the promise of his coming?" Here, it may be, will be the last and most energetic demand on the witness. The Church must oppose itself to this new and desperate infidelity. She must protest for the Advent of the Lord against the denial and reviling of a profligate generation. And when the Church shall have done this, witnessed that Christ is about to re-appear, and invoke a scoffing world to prepare for his approach, then, it may be, will her perfect ripeness be reached, and then, in accordance with the parable, the fruit being brought forth, Christ shall "immediately put in the sickle," gather in the corn, and house his elect, ere vengeance be let loose on the impenitent and unbelieving.

But we will not pursue this inquiry further. For an instant we would recur to that application of the parable which has to do with yourselves as the field, and with a minister as the husbandman. We have spoken of the utter weakness of the spiritual labourer, a weakness so great, that, though he may rise night and day, and spare no pains, and decline no toil, he cannot ensure one shred of produce; but, after planting and watering with all the carefulness of one, who knows himself admitted to an office of awful responsibleness, must leave altogether with God the giving an increase. It would accord better with the feelings and the wishes of nature, if the sower might do more than thus ply assiduously at the business of husbandry; or if, at the least, he might have an assurance that some portion of the seed which he scatters shall "take root downwards, and bear fruit upwards." But, whilst even this is denied him, and he may perhaps toil on, year after year, without sensible evidence of a blessing on his labours, he has the consolation of remembering that, when the grain is sown, he has done his part, and that, whatever the barrenness, it shall be no witness against him at the great day of account.

How striking are the words in the prophecies of Ezekiel, "Nevertheless, if thou warn the wicked of his way to turn from it, if he do not turn from his way, he shall die in his iniquity, but thou hast delivered thy soul." When shall we make you feel that there are, in strict truth, but two parties in religion, God and the soul? What saith Solomon? "If thou be wise, thou shalt be wise for thyself; but if thou scornest, thou alone shalt bear it." Too often if a man be spoken to of his eternal interests, if he be entreated to attend to them, and not to put from him the gracious offers of the Gospel, he will receive his adviser as though he were asking some personal favour, and as though an obligation would be conferred by his acting on the suggestion. But remember, we beseech of you, that if the minister be faithful, he is in a great degree independent. Let him sow the seed, and whether there come up the tares or the wheat; whether the field be wholly sterile or richly productive; he has done that which it was his duty to do. And though, if he "turn many to righteousness," those many shall make up his diadem, yet if it be no fault of his that he hath turned none, who will think that he must be without a crown through Eternity? The working out salvation is a business which every man must carry on on his own account—remember ye that. I cannot conduct it for you: you cannot conduct it for me. The prayers and tears of parents may do much, the warnings and entreaties of friends may do much, towards bringing the sinner to a pause: but parents cannot save the soul for you, friends cannot save the soul for you: it lies between you and God; "every man shall bear his own burden." May the Holy Spirit make you feel this, and drive you to the tillage of your own hearts, to the ploughing now, that you may reap hereafter!

LECTURE XVII.

The Great Multitude.

REV. vii. 9.

"After this I beheld, and, lo, a great multitude, which no man could number, of all nations, and people, and kindred, and tongues, stood before the throne, and before the Lamb, clothed with white robes, and palms in their hands."

TAKING this vision in the order in which it occurs amongst the visions vouchsafed to St. John in his exile, it probably delineates the happy estate of those who had adhered to Christ during the fierce persecutions which preceded the establishment of Christianity by Constantine. There can be no doubt that the book of Revelation is, in the main, a continuous prophecy, its several parts belonging to several seasons which follow successively in the history of the Church. But without disputing that, in its primary import, our text may relate to events which have long ago occurred, it were not easy to doubt, that in its larger and more comprehensive bearings, it may be taken as descriptive of the heavenly state, that condition of repose and triumph which shall be ours, even ours, if we be faithful unto death. Admitting that the great multitude, on which the Evangelist was permitted to gaze, "clothed with white robes, and palms in their hands," must be regarded as the company of those, who, during the early days of Christianity, witnessed manfully for the truth, they must still, both in number and condition, be emblematic of the Church in its final glory and exaltation; and we may, therefore, safely dismiss all reference to the first fulfilment of the prophecy, and consider heaven as the scene on which the Evangelist gazed, and "just men made perfect" as constituting the great multitude drawn together from all parts of the earth.

It is, therefore, on such notices of the heavenly state as the words before us may furnish, that we design to discourse on the present occasion. We would refresh you and animate you, wearied as you may be by the conflicts and struggles of earth, with glimpses of things within the veil. We do not indeed mean to address ourselves to the imagination: if we did, there are more dazzling passages in the book of Revelation, and we might strive to set before you the New Jerusalem, the heavenly city, with its gates of pearl, and its streets of gold. But we think to find notices in the words of our text, which, if not so resplendent with the gorgeous things of the future, shall yet go closer home to the heart, and minister more comfort to those who find themselves strangers and pilgrims below. We will not anticipate what we may have to advance. We shall only hope that we may meet with what will cheer and sustain us amid "the changes and chances of this mortal life," what will keep alive in us a sense of the exceeding greatness of "the recompense of the reward," of the desirableness of the inheritance reserved for us above, as in dependence on the teachings of the Holy Spirit, we apply to our future state the words of the Evangelist John, "I beheld, and, lo, a great multitude, which no man could number, of all nations, and kindreds, and people, and tongues, stood before the throne, and before the Lamb, clothed with white robes, and palms in their hands."

Now, when these words are set before us as descriptive of the heavenly state, it can hardly fail but that the first thing on which the mind shall fasten will be the expression, "a great multitude, which no man could number." It is so in regard of parallel sayings, "In my Father's house are many mansions." "Many shall come from the east and west, and shall sit down with Abraham, and Isaac, and Jacob, in the Kingdom of Heaven." "A great multitude," "many mansions," "many shall come." But what are "many," in the Divine arithmetic? Doubtless thousands, and tens of thousands; yea, an innumerable company. Many are the worlds scattered through immensity —who shall reckon them? Many are the leaves of the earth's forests—who shall compute them? Many are the grains of sand on the sea shore—who shall count them up? Neither may we think to compass the multitude that St. John saw "before the throne, and before the Lamb;" indeed, he tells us this, when he adds, "which no man could number." But it is a comforting thing to be told that "a great multitude," not "great" on a mere human estimate, but "great" on a Divine, shall press into the inheritance purchased by Christ's blood. Then not only is Heaven no narrow, no contracted spot; but, on the contrary, spacious enough for myriads upon myriads of happy beings: but these myriads upon myriads shall be there: the vast expanse shall not stand empty, but shall be occupied by a rejoicing and adequate assembly.

It is a refreshing thing to look away for a moment, from the strife and uncharitableness of human systems and conclusions, each disposed to narrow Heaven within its own pale and party, and to behold "a multitude, such as no man could number," entering by the gate into the everlasting city. There is something unspeakably cheering in the contrast between the representation furnished by our text, and that derived from the exclusive systems of a miscalled theology. If Heaven were to be peopled according to the estimate of self-opinionated sects; if human judgment were to settle who shall be privileged to find place within its precincts; not "many," but "few," it may be very few, would constitute the celestial assembly. But, whilst we may justly rejoice in being able to appeal from human judgment to Divine, in having the authority of Scripture, for not only assigning vast capacity to Heaven, but for regarding it as the home of an interminable throng, we are to take heed that we lower not the conditions of admission, as though the entrance must be easy, because a great multitude shall be there. The great, the solemn truth remains, that "there shall enter into the city nothing which defileth," "neither whatsoever worketh abomination, or maketh a lie, but they that are written in the Lamb's book of life." It may be that human judgment is vastly at fault, and that human bigotry, magnifying or idolizing its own tests, would exclude numbers from the celestial abode, who shall be found amid its glorified occupants. But whilst this is immeasurably comforting to those, who, wearied, and almost terrified by theological strife, can retire within themselves, and humbly venture, after due searching and probing of the heart, to exclaim with Peter, "Lord, thou knowest all things, thou knowest that I love thee," it affords no groundwork on which others may build, who are practically neglecting the great salvation. For because God "seeth not as man seeth," because He may find in many a meek, and contrite, and retiring spirit, that vital Christianity which is not to be detected, nay, which may even be denied, on the bringing it to the coarse touchstones of human systems and sects, this surely is no encouragement to the wicked, to the careless, to the indifferent: if man's intolerance, or man's ignorance, leave not sufficient to make up the "great multitude," at least the deficiency will not be supplied by man's impenitence, obduracy, or contempt of religion.

And a glance at the context should suffice to keep down any rising thought, that, because there shall be "a great multitude" in Heaven, and, therefore, perhaps numbers whom their fellow-men never expected to be there, some may find admission who have taken no pains to secure so great a blessing. "What are these," it is asked, "which are arrayed in white robes, and whence came they?" The answer is, "These are they which came out of great tribulation, and have washed their robes, and made them white in the blood of the Lamb." So far then from there being any thing for you to reckon upon, ye who are not striving after a moral fitness for Heaven, in the alleged vastness of the multitude which is to occupy Heaven, there is much to admonish and warn you: if ye know nothing of the "great tribulation," of the warfare with "the world, the flesh, and the devil," ye may forfeit your places, the places which were made yours, when God graciously admitted you into his Church: but those places will not stand empty: "God is able of these stones to raise up children unto Abraham;" and He will not be reduced, through the want of faithful disciples, to the admitting into his presence the rebellious and unclean. And Christendom, with all the advantages which it has long enjoyed, may not furnish a population for the New Jerusalem: but other nations and tribes and tongues, continents, and islands, long, and even still, oppressed with ignorance and superstition, shall receive gratefully the Gospel of Christ, and swell the ranks of his Church.

Yea, and over and above there being a warning to us in the fact, that Heaven shall be peopled to the full, even should we ourselves come short of the inheritance, is it not an animating thing to be told of all "nations, and people, and kindreds, and tongues," as contributing to the occupancy of the majestic abode? The heart of the true Christian is sorrowful within him, as he thinks of the dominion of Paganism. He grieves over the vast and rich districts of the earth, which are inhabited by the worshippers of idols, and could almost despair—so inveterate and deep-rooted appears the empire of Satan—of the spread and triumph of the kingdom of Christ. But "lo, a great multitude, of all nations, and people, and kindreds, and tongues." The purpose of the Lord is fixed: "the idols he shall utterly abolish:" the march of Christianity may have been slow and impeded; but the truth shall yet prosper and prevail; and faith, guided by the sure word of prophecy, may even now behold the wild children of the desert, the wanderers whose hand is against every man, and every man's hand against them, the slaves of bloody rites, the victims of fearful delusions, sitting at the feet of Jesus, "clothed and in their right mind," and "made meet for the inheritance of the saints in light." O glorious society which shall thus be gathered from all ages, all ranks, all countries! There is beauty in diversity, there is majesty in combination. I kindle at the thought of there being "a great multitude" in Heaven: I kindle yet more at that of this multitude being drawn from every nation, and tribe, and tongue. What a throng to join! what a company with which to associate, and enter into fellowship! The righteous of past days, of present, of future—those who, under earlier dispensations, caught faint glimpses of the star of Bethlelem; those who, possessing but the few and brief notices of traditional religion, felt after God, and proved that He had never left Himself without witness; Jews who deciphered the types, and gave substance to the shadows of the law; Gentiles on whom shone, in all its effulgence, the light of the Gospel; the mighty gatherings of that splendid season, when "the knowledge of the glory of the Lord shall cover the earth, as the waters do the sea"—what a multitude through which to move, with which to make acquaintance, with which to hold converse!

Even now, it is felt to be an ennobling, inspiriting association, if the eminent of a single Church, the illustrious of a solitary country, be gathered together in one great conclave. How do meaner men flock to the spot: with what interest, what awe, do they look upon persons so renowned in their day: what a privilege do they account it, if they may mingle a while with sages so profound, with saints so devoted: how do they treasure the sayings which reach them in so precious an intercourse. And shall we think little of Heaven, when we hear of it as the meeting-place of all that hath been truly great, for of all that hath been truly good; of all that hath been really wise, for of all that hath yielded itself to the teachings of God's Spirit; from Adam to his remotest descendant? Nay, "let us fear, lest, a promise being left us of entering into that rest, any of us should seem to come short." There is a voice to us from the "great multitude," who flock with a sound, like the rush of many waters, from all nations and tribes. "A great multitude"—there is room then for us. "A great multitude"—there will be no deficiency without us. We can be spared: the loss will be ours: but, oh, what a loss; and what an aggravation of that loss that, perhaps, as we go away into outer darkness, "where shall be weeping and gnashing of teeth," we shall see those who were once strangers and aliens, flocking into the places which might have been ours, and be witnesses to the literal accomplishment of the vision, "Lo, a great multitude, which no man could number, of all nations, and people, and kindreds, and tongues.'

But it is not merely as asserting the vastness of the multitude which shall finally be gathered into Heaven, that our text presents matter for devout meditation. We are not to overlook the attitude assigned to the celestial assembly, an attitude of rest and of triumph, as though there had been labour and warfare, and the wearied combatants were henceforward to enjoy unbroken quiet. "They stood before the throne, and before the Lamb, clothed with white robes, and palms in their hands." This exactly answers to the assertion already quoted, that they had come "out of great tribulation," and denotes—for such is the inference from the robes which they wore, and the palms which they carried, both appertaining to conquerors—that all warfare was at end, and that there remained nothing henceforward but the enjoyment of deep repose in the presence of the Lord. The imagery of the passage is derived, you observe, from the triumphs of victors. Spiritual things can only be shadowed forth to us by material; and without pretending to decide that the material is never to be literally taken,—for who, remembering that man is to be everlastingly compounded of body and soul, will venture to determine that there shall be nothing but what is purely spiritual in the future economy? who, when he reads of new Heavens, and a new earth, will rashly conclude, that, for such a being as man is to be, there cannot be reserved an abode rich in all the splendours of a most refined materialism, presenting correspondences to the golden streets, and the jewelled walls, and the crystal waters, which passed in such gorgeous and beautiful vision before the Evangelist?—but, waving the consideration that there may be something more than mere figure, something of literal and actual import, in these Scriptural delineations of Heaven, the robe, the palm, the harp, we may all feel how expressive is the imagery of triumphant repose after toil and conflict, when applied to the state reserved for those who shall be faithful unto death. Not that by repose we are to understand inactivity, for Scripture is most express on the continued engagement of every faculty of a glorified saint in the services of the Creator and Redeemer. The great multitude stand before the throne—the attitude implying that they wait to execute the commands of the Lord; and they join in a high song of praise and exultation, "Salvation to our God which sitteth upon the throne, and unto the Lamb." No idleness then, though there is perfect repose. But rest, as opposed to any thing that is painful or toilsome in employment—repose, as implying that there shall never again be weariness, exhaustion, difficulty, or danger, notwithstanding that there shall be the consecration of the whole man to the work of magnifying the Lord—this it is which is promised as the portion of the righteous; and this it is which is imaged by the palm in the hand, and the song upon the lip.

Take even that figure which is so common in Scripture, that of reclining at a banquet, as emblematic of Heaven; and the figure does not portray idleness, though it largely does repose. Even guests at a feast are not necessarily idle, nor necessarily intent on mere luxurious indulgence. Amid all the pomp and bravery of the gorgeous entertainment, there may be the lofty discussion, and the keen play of intellectual power, and the collision of mind with mind, producing new and rich sparks of thought, and the circulation of profound discoveries in science, or of important occurrences in the world—so that a man may depart from the festival as from a field of mental encounter and improvement, on which he has taken many a forward step in power and in knowledge. And whilst we believe of Heaven, that there shall be all that disengagement from laborious effort, or oppressive occupation, which seems expressed in the figure of reclining at a banquet, or standing before the Lamb, clad in white robes, with the palm in the hand, we believe also that there shall be no cessation from a service which is perfect freedom, and none from an employment which will itself constitute happiness.

But what an attractive, what an animating view of heaven, is that of its being a state of repose, as contrasted with our present state of warfare and toil—the white robe, in place of the "whole armour of God;" the palm, in place of the sword, in the hand. He must be, I will not say a strange man, but certainly a strange Christian, who is never conscious of a painful pressure from the duties and trials of life, who is never inclined to exclaim with the Psalmist, "Oh that I had wings like a dove; then would I flee away and be at rest." I cannot enter into the experience of that Christian, his life is a mystery to me, for whom there is no soothing, heart-touching sound in the words of the Apostle, "There remaineth, therefore, a rest for the people of God." For let the course of the Divine dealings with any member of the Church be the very smoothest that is compatible with a state of probation, still, compassed about as we all are with infirmity, called upon to do many things to which we are naturally disinclined; which we can neither perform without painful effort, nor omit without sinful neglect; exposed to temptations from the world, the flesh, and the devil; bearing about within ourselves a principle of corruption, which continually strives to regain the ascendancy, and which is not to be kept down but by prayer without ceasing, watchfulness without fainting—indeed, it were hard to understand how any believer could often be other than "weary and heavy laden," and required to take heed against that impatience at the burdens of life, which would show itself in undue eagerness for the repose of eternity. It is not that he would give up the service of God, but that he would be able to serve God without weariness. It is not that he would rest from holy employment, but that he would have employment entail no necessity for rest. It is not that he would be released from the struggle with corruption, but that he would have no corruption to struggle with, the final touches of sanctification having been given, so that he is "without spot, or wrinkle, or any such thing." It is not that he would make peace with spiritual enemies, but that he would be surrounded with none but spiritual friends.

And such a state of repose awaits us in heaven. There shall be no weariness there—"they rest not day nor night," employing every power on the doing God's will, and yet sensible to nothing but the delightfulness of the employment. There no evil nature shall ply the believer with temptations to sin. There no subtle adversary shall lie in wait to deceive, no roaring lion seek whom he may devour. O blessed estate! There is more of music in that one word "rest," than in all that pealing anthem which, taken up in St. John's hearing by "every creature which is in heaven, and on the earth, and under the earth, and such as are in the sea," filled the temple in the midst of which was the throne of the Almighty. And I ask not to be told what those palms may be which the victors carry in their hands, nor what those shining robes wherein they are arrayed—for, as yet, I may be poorly fitted to understand, to appreciate, heavenly happiness. But I can feel something of the comforting power of the sublime announcement,

"Blessed are the dead which die in the Lord: yea, saith the Spirit, for they rest from their labour, and their works do follow them." I can gaze on the "great multitude," as they flock from all nations and tribes; and I can long and pray to be found at last in their number, not because I know precisely what the joys are of which they are about to partake; but because, at least, I know that they are exchanging warfare for peace, danger for security, tumult for quiet, corruption for incorruption—yea, I know of this multitude, that they are to stand "before the throne, and before the Lamb, clothed with white robes, and palms in their hands."

There is another distinguishing feature of the heavenly state which may be gathered from our text. You cannot fail to observe, that, though the great multitude is collected from all nations and tribes, there is perfect concord or agreement; they form but one company and join in one anthem. The representation is much the same as is furnished by the saying of our Lord, "In my Father's house are many mansions." There are "many mansions," you observe—just as St. John beheld "a great multitude:" but there is only one house. As though Christ had said, There is room for as many as will enter, and there shall be but one roof over all. There is something very beautiful in the representation of the innumerable company of the redeemed as constituting, through eternity, only one household. It is melancholy to think how the visible Church of Christ has been divided and rent, so that the aspect of those who equally profess Christianity is as far removed as possible from the aspect of a family. The slightest causes seem to have been sufficient for violations of that brotherhood, which ought to have subsisted amongst men, and, yet more, amongst Christians; so that there has not been a thousandth part of the zeal in avoiding offences, as in magnifying into importance whatever might be an apology for a division. But the words of our text assure us that nothing of these differences and separations shall follow us through eternity. The redeemed are to constitute one rejoicing company. Nay, and the representation may almost be said to go beyond this. How are they to constitute this one company, associated by close ties, and joining in the same song, unless they are to know one the other hereafter? When Christ speaks of many as coming from the east and the west, He speaks also of their sitting down with Abraham, and Isaac, and Jacob. But this were apparently no privilege, unless they are to know these patriarchs. So also if men of all nations and tribes and tongues are to make up one family, it can hardly be doubted, that every one will know every other. And if they are to be known, the one to the other, who have been utterly separated upon earth, we may be sure as to that of which some have doubted, and on which many have longed for more express revelation, the recognition of one the other in the world above, by those who have been friends or kinsmen below.

We need not say to you that it is a very interesting feature in heavenly happiness, that of the renewal of the acquaintances and associations which have been our chief joy on earth. There is no fear of our not dwelling with delight on such a feature: the fear is rather the other way, of our suffering the mind to be engrossed with the prospect of re-union with the dead, as though the again meeting those whom we have loved were what should especially make Heaven desirable. This cannot be the right view of Heaven. Whether or not we can feel or understand how such a thing may be, it is evident that Heaven must be independent on earthly associations, independent in the sense that its happiness will be perfect, even should a saint stand alone, as perhaps many will stand, without kinsman, without friend, in the shining assembly. But the certainty that Heaven will not require, in order to its being a place of perfect happiness, the presence of the objects of earthly affection, is quite consistent with the belief, that, if friends and kinsmen meet above, they shall know one the other, and derive from their meeting new elements of rapture and joy. That God Himself will so supply the place of the absent as that they shall not be missed—this is noways at variance with the truth, that, when those who have been parted below find themselves fellow-heirs of the kingdom, they shall experience intense gladness in renewing their friendship, in again becoming bound the one to the other, though in a high and pure and happy association, such as was hardly even imaged by the most affectionate upon earth.

There is no need, in order to our excluding from our pictures and anticipations of Heaven the selfishness and contractedness of human families, that we should deny all play hereafter to the best charities of our nature, and seek to persuade those, who are weeping for the dead that have died in the Lord, that because "in the resurrection they neither marry, nor are given in marriage," therefore, in the resurrection, the stranger shall be all the same as the friend, and the friend all the same as the stranger. There is no need, even now, that, if a man grow more benevolent and philanthropic, enlarging as it were his heart, so that he daily embraces within its affections more and more of his kind, he should therefore become less warmly attached to his more immediate family—on the contrary, we may believe, that, in proportion as he came the nearer to the loving all men as himself, and sent out, in wider and wider expatiations, the sensibilities of his nature, he would find a deeper deliciousness and delight in his own domestic nest, and cling all the more tenderly to those, whom God had given him to give sunshine to his home. And hereafter, if—as we may be thoroughly sure will be the case—there shall be an universal affectionateness, the myriads of the redeemed making up but one family, each knowing, each known and loved by, every other, there may yet be only the more intimate, though the more hallowed, intercourse with those with whom on earth we had taken sweet counsel; and the heart, which has grown large enough to leave out none in the interminable throng, may have but the wider and the warmer abode for such as were its companions in the house of its pilgrimage.

And this doctrine, the doctrine of the renewal in Heaven of the intimacies and associations of earth, may certainly be considered as derivable from the text; for if, as we have said, the great multitude, beheld by St. John, constitute one family, though gathered from all nations and tribes, it cannot be doubted that those, who, here below, were strangers the one to the other, become associated and acquainted above; and it were incredible that men shall know those to whom they had been strangers on earth, and yet be strangers to those to whom they had been friends. Still, they way in which the doctrine of future recognition is delivered—not broadly stated, but left to be inferred from other announcements—should lead us to think more of Heaven as of a scene of enlarged association, the meeting-place, not merely of divided households, but of the believers of every generation, of the elect of God from the beginning to the end of time. It argues a heart still bound up in selfishness, if it be nothing, if it be little, to us, that, admitted into heaven, we are to be freed from all petty bounds and distinctions, and to form part of one close, but countless, community. The soul should be stirred within us, as we think of patriarchs, and prophets, and priests, and kings—of apostles, confessors, and martyrs; of the illustrious, not by earthly achievements, which too often dazzle by a false glare, and are dimmed with the tears of the wronged and afflicted; but the illustrious in the fight of faith, the patience of hope, the labour of love—and not only of the illustrious whose names go down in Christian biography, the precious legacy of age to age, watchwords to the Church when she would rouse her fainting children, and keep them to their posts; but of that unknown, that unremembered multitude, the good, the godly, of successive generations, who, in the quiet privacies of ordinary life, have served their God, and their Redeemer, whose names have perished from every book but that in which to be enrolled is to have the citizenship of earth, sea, air, the past, the present, the future—for "He," saith Christ, "that overcometh shall inherit all things"—oh, I say, the soul should be stirred within us, as we think of such an assembly, and hear ourselves invited to join it, and are told that we may have the friendship of each and every one in the interminable gathering.

I ask not to be told of the splendid adornments with which the roof of Heaven shall be inlaid—enough for me that, according to words already quoted, there is to be but one roof over all the inhabitants. The representations of the future, which address themselves most to the heart, are not those which are gorgeous with the gold and precious stones: these are the most dazzling, but not the most penetrating. The heart is to be reached by what breathes most of the tranquillities of universal love. And poetry, in its longings for something on which to pour the splendour of its imagery, might seize on the white robes, and on the palms, with which the ransomed are decked: but if the soul's deepest chords are to be swept, then must we hear of the repose of a home, and the hallowed charities which weave themselves into a family; and all this is intimated to us—oh, that we may be incited to make it our own!—by the vision vouchsafed to St. John, "I beheld, and, lo, a great multitude, which no man could number, of all nations, and people, and kindreds, and tongues, stood before the throne, and before the Lamb."

"Before the Lamb"—yes, the glorified humanity of the Redeemer fixes by its presence the position of Heaven, and at the same time gives it its magnificence. We know not what Heaven, or the place of separate spirits, might have been, ere the mystery of godliness was revealed, and the Word had been made flesh, and effected man's redemption. But it could hardly, if we may venture the expression, be considered the same place as now: for until it contained the Lamb which had been slain, it contained not what makes Heaven to those who had forfeited their immortality. Christ ascended triumphantly the mediatorial throne, that He might be the wellspring of joy, and the fountain of glory, to the great multitude which He had purchased with His blood. There could be no Heaven to such as ourselves without Christ: Heaven would be no Heaven without Christ: so that, in entering Heaven, Christ prepared, as He promised, a place for his disciples.

There are possibly other characteristics of the heavenly state which might be drawn from the words which form our subject of discourse. But we have gone far enough. We have adventured thus far, because it may be a wholesome and refreshing thing, to withdraw occasionally from the mazes of controversy, the cares of life, and the toils of conflict, and to meditate on the portion reserved for the righteous. But we will not pass beyond what may be practical and personal. It is not the Heaven which may dazzle your imaginations, but the Heaven which may stimulate your efforts, which we are anxious to present to you. Is not this Heaven, this place of perfect and beautiful repose, this meeting-place of the children of God—is not this worth striving for, worth the surrender of a few poor indulgences, worth the endurance of a few brief trials? For shame, that you can hesitate. For shame, that, with a Redeemer at your side, ready to impart all the assistance which can be needed to your obtaining the inheritance, you can linger amid earthly entanglements, and be so slow in securing possession, if not so indifferent as to letting it slip. For shame, that, whilst so many are pressing in from all nations and tongues—pressing from the burning east, man's earliest home: from the distant west, so long an undiscovered world—you, the children of the kingdom, with every advantage of country and churchmanship, can manifest so little earnestness, allowing it to be inferred, from your apparent preference of the shadows and braveries of earth, that you count it but a poor monarchy, of which Christianity has conveyed to you the promise.

Let us rouse ourselves, lest, what we pursue so languidly, we miss eternally. The time is at hand. The Judge standeth at the door. Already has Heaven gathered within its circuit the spoils of many generations. Patriarchs are there, and prophets, and priests, and kings. The young are there, the old are there; the men of every clime have pressed into the spacious dwelling. But the gate is still open: "yet there is room:" all of you may enter Heaven: we will not be content that any should be outcasts. I want to meet you all in a better land: I wish that we might spend eternity together. Therefore do I summon the careless to penitence, and the penitent to diligence. It may be but a little while, and the number of the redeemed will be accomplished: it can be but a little while, and our own portion will be fixed. "The violent," saith our Saviour, "take the kingdom by force"—oh, that we may not be of the indolent who lose it by sloth!

LECTURE XVIII.

The Kinsman Redeemer.

RUTH ii. 20.

"And Naomi said unto her daughter-in-law, Blessed be he of the Lord, who hath not left off his kindness to the living and to the dead. And Naomi said unto her, The man is near of kin unto us, one of our next kinsmen."

YOU can hardly need to be told that a connection the very closest may be traced between the Jewish and the Christian dispensations. But sometimes this connection is overlooked, and requires to be carefully examined and explained. This is specially the case in regard of Redemption. There was Redemption, a process through which things and persons were redeemed, under the Jewish dispensations, as there is under the Christian; but we are not perhaps so much in the habit of associating them as we ought to be. Yet, one and the same character of a Redeemer is kept up through the whole of the Bible. The Redeemer under the law is most accurately the type of the Redeemer under the Gospel. There may be no broad or distinct allusions to Christ. But whenever you meet with a transaction of Redemption, whether it be a Redemption of land or of person, you will find that the matter is so ordered as to be most strictly typical—the features of our Redemption through Christ being unequivocally stamped on the legal arrangements which come under review.

It will be the chief object of our discourse to make good this assertion. We count it an instructive and interesting thing to trace Redemption as kept always in sight; so that the Jews were taught, even through the common dealings of life, the great spiritual deliverance that was wrought out in the fulness of time. We are persuaded, that, in proportion as the Jewish code is diligently examined, will it be found to teem with notices of our Redemption by Christ. God so constructed this code that it should be virtually a system of references to Christ, and that thus the devout Jew, whether engaging in the solemnities of the Temple worship, or busying himself with temporal occupations, might have his attention turned to that "seed of the woman," who, in the fulness of time, was to put away sin by the sacrifice of Himself. We do not indeed mean, that, with the change of dispensation have passed away all these mementoes of the manner of our salvation. We rather agree with those who hold that there is still much in the arrangements of Providence, which may serve to remind us of God's dealings in grace. There is perhaps nothing over-fanciful in the thought, that the food on which we chiefly subsist should constantly suggest the idea of our Redemption through Christ. Is it to be denied that since the use of animals for food, and those principally which were made choice of in sacrifice, the world literally subsists by shedding of blood, so that the death of the innocent is every day the life of the guilty? The meat which perisheth may well thus remind us of that meat which endureth unto life everlasting; and the slaying, for the support of the body, of those beasts which were once offered in typical sacrifice, is no slight memento, that, for the support of the soul there died a victim whose "flesh was meat indeed, and whose blood was drink indeed."

But to return to the Jewish dispensation, and to that keeping up the character of a Redeemer, upon which we desire to fasten your attention. We bring you a text from the book of Ruth, in which, though the word "kinsman" is used by our translators, the marginal reading, as you will observe, is "one that has the right to redeem." Naomi is speaking of Boaz, who had shown great kindness to Ruth, whilst gleaning in his fields. Here and elsewhere, she calls Boaz "the kinsman;" but the word used in the Hebrew is "the Redeemer." It was the law amongst the Jews, that if a man died childless, his widow should become the wife of his brother. If there were no brethren, the law seems to have been extended to the nearest relations, so that the next of kin became the husband of the widow. Now Chilion, the husband of Ruth, had died in the land of Moab; and Naomi, her mother-in-law, being thus left without a son, there was no husband's brother to take Ruth from her widowhood. The law therefore gave Ruth a marriage claim on the nearest of kin, and she urged this claim upon Boaz. There was indeed a kinsman who stood nearer in relationship than Boaz: but he, refusing to perform the part of a kinsman, conceded to Boaz the right of inheritance. Boaz then honourably answered the marriage claim of Ruth, and receiving her as his wife, gave occasion to the friends of Naomi to exclaim, "Blessed be the Lord, who hath not left thee this day without a kinsman," or literally without a Redeemer. But if we examine this history a little more attentively, we shall perceive that it was not exactly his marrying Ruth which gained for Boaz the title of Redeemer. His challenge to the man who stood in closer relationship, was, that he should buy a parcel of land which Naomi was about to sell. The nearer kinsman refusing, Boaz himself bought the land, or, as the Scriptural phrase is, redeemed the land; and it was this purchasing the inheritance, and so preventing it from passing to strangers, which caused Boaz to stand in the position of Redeemer.

And if we look into the law of Moses, we shall find three states which are marked out as requiring the interposition of a Redeemer. If there had been forfeiture of inheritance, or if there had been loss of liberty, or if there had been shedding of blood—in each of these cases it was enjoined that the Goel—for such is the Hebrew name—this Goel or Redeemer being always the nearest of kin, should interfere on behalf of the distressed individual. And our desire is to show you, that, whenever the law directed the interposition of the Goel or Redeemer, it gave a typical lesson on the offices of Christ. The occasions which produced the interference of the legal Redeemer, and the manner in which that interference was conducted; these bear so accurate a reference to the Gospel Redeemer, that we cannot doubt it to have been the mind of the Spirit, to keep the grand scheme of human Redemption always present to the people of Israel. We will take in succession the three cases in which the Goel or Redeemer was bidden to interfere—the forfeiture of inheritance, the loss of liberty, the shedding of blood—and, examining each transaction under its legal description, strive to show you the fidelity with which it imaged the deliverance wrought out for us by Christ—Christ, of whom we may most emphatically say, in the language of our text, "The man is near of kin unto us, one of our next kinsmen," "Blessed be he of the Lord, who hath not left off his kindness to the living and to the dead."

We begin with the forfeiture of inheritance. You will find in the twenty-fifth chapter of the book of Leviticus directions given for the interference of the Goel. If an Israelite had become poor, and had sold away some of his possession, the nearest of kin, called the Goel or Redeemer, was directed, if possible, to purchase or redeem the land. In this case it became the property of the Goel until the year of Jubilee, when it went back to the original proprietor. The alienated or forfeited possession might, at any time, be redeemed by the first owner, supposing him able to pay the price of Redemption. But if he were not able, then none but the Goel could redeem it for him; and if the Goel came not forward, no stranger might interfere; the possession must remain unredeemed.

Now there can be no difficulty in at once discerning the typical character of this transaction. We fasten, first of all, upon the fact—a fact which is learned equally from each of the three cases of legal Redemption—that none but a kinsman could fill the office of Goel or Redeemer. It was not enough that an individual might be ready to come forwards on behalf of the impoverished Israelite. Had he the rights of the closest kinsmanship? If not, the law altogether refused to allow the interposition: its fundamental principle, in all such cases, appearing to have been, that kinsmanship was indispensable to the constitution of a Redeemer. And who sees not, that, in laying down and adhering to such a principle as this, the law taught impressively the lesson, that He who should arise, the Goel of a lost world, must be bone of their bone, and flesh of their flesh? It would have been nothing, that rank upon rank of celestial intelligence should rush eagerly forwards, and, compassionating the ruined estate of our race, offer to devote their magnificent energies to the improving its condition. Were they the kinsmen of the lost? could they make out relationship? could they prove that there existed between themselves and the fallen any of that alliance which results from community of nature? Then, an angel, not being a kinsman, could not be a Redeemer. None but a man could be the Goel of man—such was the truth which the law emphatically taught, when refusing, in any case, to concede to a stranger the right of Redemption.

And is not this the truth which was literally acted upon in the appointment of a "Mediator between God and man?" "Forasmuch as the children are partakers of flesh and blood, He also Himself likewise took part of the same." And shall we ever hesitate to say that the comforting and sustaining thing to the followers of Christ, is that the Goel, the Redeemer, is, in the strictest sense, their kinsman? That Christ was like myself in all points, my sinfulness only excepted; that his flesh, like mine, could be lacerated by stripes, wasted by hunger, and torn by nails; that his soul, like mine, could be assaulted by temptation, harassed by Satan, and disquieted under the hidings of the countenance of his Father; that He could suffer any thing which I can suffer, except the remorse of a guilty conscience; that He could weep every tear which I can weep, except the tear of repentance; that He could fear with every fear, hope with every hope, and joy with every joy, which I may entertain as a man, and not be ashamed of as a Christian—there is our creed respecting the human nature of Christ; and if you could once prove that Christ was not perfect man (always bearing in mind that sinfulness is not essential to this perfectness), there would be nothing worth fighting for in the truth, that Christ was perfect God; the only Redeemer who can redeem our lost heritage, being necessarily our kinsman; and none being our kinsman who is not of the same nature, born of a woman, of the substance of that woman, our brother in all but rebellion, ourself in all but unholiness.

Such we know abundantly from the testimony of Scripture, and from the very nature of the case, it was needful should be the Goel, or Redeemer, of men. And when, in all cases of Redemption, the law peremptorily refused to admit any one but the kinsman to the office of Redeemer, can it be questioned that there was perpetually inculcated on the Israelites the great truth of the human nature of the Mediator? Has there not throughout been the maintenance of that character of a Redeemer, which, putting our deliverance far beyond the power of angel or archangel, makes brotherhood indispensable to the effecting atonement; or renders it needful that we should be able to say, "The man is near of kin unto us, one of our next kinsmen," if we are ever to declare of any being, in the full and comprehensive meaning of the words, "Blessed be he of the Lord, who hath not left off his kindness to the living and to the dead?"

But there is nothing in these remarks which applies to one case of legal Redemption more than to another. We have only argued from the general requirement of kinsmanship, without attending to the particular features of the instance brought under review. But if you wish to describe man's natural condition, and the change effected in that condition by the interference of Christ, whence could you fetch better terms than from the directions of the law in regard of a forfeited inheritance? Who is the Israelite that has grown poor, and alienated from him the possession of his fathers, if it be not man, originally the chosen of God, rich in a birth-right which gave him a glorious world for his dwelling-place, and Immortality for his life-time; but who, afterwards, by yielding to temptation, stripped himself of all his wealth, and made himself heir to nothing but corruption? A magnificent creation was our possession; and we sold it to Satan; making it over to the ravages of the destroyer, who rifled its beauties, and let loose upon it the long train of wrath and calamity. The image of the Almighty was our possession; and we parted with this, destroying it by an act of rebellion. An eternity of happiness was our possession; and we threw away this; bringing down on ourselves the curse of death, of death alike to body and soul. And we became poor—who shall measure to us the spiritual poverty of man? have we a solitary fraction to pay down for the Redemption of the land? The way is open, as it was with the Israelites, if the man himself be able to redeem it, let him redeem it. But can we buy this creation back from Satan ? can we sweep together the costly and the precious, and tender an equivalent for the image of God ? can we accumulate the purchase-money for a bartered Immortality ? And if the effort be hopeless, must the inheritancc be forfeited for ever ? No, God's appointment with our race is just what it was with the Israelites, "the land shall not be sold for ever." Who then shall redeem it ? who but the Goel, the kinsman, the brother ? God will provide a Redeemer. There shall arise a man, yet, oh, infinitely more than a man ; and his human nature shall give Him the right, whilst his Divine gives Him the strength —the right of kinsmanship, the strength of payment—and the blood of this mysterious person shall be poured forth in ransom ; and He shall buy back the land which the rebellious have lost.

This was the achievement, which, in the fulness of time, the Goel effected. He literally redeemed man's inheritance. He snatched materialism itself from the dishonours of the fall, securing the dawning of a day, when new heavens and a new earth, sparkling with a richer than the early beauty, shall succeed to those which sin hath profaned. He gained for man the renewing influences of the Spirit; and thus brought us into such a position, that we may be cast, as it were, once more into the mint, and come forth with a fresh impress of the likeness of God. He purchased the bartered Immortality ; for did He not "abolish death, and bring life and Immortality to light by his Gospel ?" Thus the Goel, the kinsman, redeemed the land. But what He redeemed, He did not instantly restore. He has gained the right over the land ; but, for a while, He keeps possession of that right, and gives not back at once the whole forfeited inheritance. And was it not thus with the Goel under the law? He redeemed the land; but then he retained it until the year of Jubilee. In the year of Jubilee the original proprietor came forth, and the Goel restored him all which he had forfeited. With the blast of a trumpet throughout the land was ushered in the Jubilee year of the Israelites. With a mightier trumpet-peal, heard on the mountains, and in the deserts, and in the cities, and in the sepulchres, shall commence the Jubilee year of this creation. Then shall the Goel, appearing in his majesty, and yet retaining all the tokens of his kinsmanship, call up the new heavens and the new earth from the wreck of the old. Then shall He portion out eternal glories to those who have clung to Him as their surety, and restore, in all its splendour, the long-lost inheritance.

Thus, without entering into minuter particulars on the law of Redemption, we make good, as we think, the alleged typical connection between the Redemption of land under the law, and the Redemption of mankind, as revealed to us by the Gospel. We show you, that, by and through the person and office of the Goel, God was perpetually informing the Israelites as to the character and work of the Messiah. And when we have pointed out to you the impoverished Jew, spoiled of the possession of his fathers, unable of himself to do any thing towards regaining the inheritance—and have then turned your attention on a kinsman Redeemer paying down the ransom, bringing back the land into the family, keeping it in his own hands until the Jubilee trumpet sounded, and then restoring it to the original owner—we think that we have furnished you with so vivid a sketch of Paradise lost through human apostacy, regained by the purchase of a Kinsman, and given back on the day when the archangel shall lift his trump, and blow the blast at which the sheeted dead shall start, that it must on all hands be confessed that the Goel of the law was pre-eminently a type of the Redeemer of the Gospel—yes, all must be ready to look upon Christ as shadowed forth in these words of Naomi, "This man is near of kin to us, one of our next kinsmen. Blessed be he of the Lord, who hath not left off his kindness to the living and to the dead."

Now we have spoken at so much length on the first case of legal Redemption, where there had been forfeiture of inheritance, that a brief notice will suffice for the second, where there had been loss of liberty. The cases are so far alike, that they may be regarded as different exhibitions of one and the same condition; and whatever, therefore, we have advanced in respect to the former instance, applies, with only a slight change in the imagery, to the present. You will find, by reference to the twenty-fifth chapter of Leviticus, from which we have already quoted, that, for the discharge of debt, or the procurement of subsistence, an Israelite might sell himself either to an Israelite or a stranger. If he became the servant of an Israelite, there appears to have been no right of Redemption: he must remain in the house of his master till the year of Jubilee. But if he became the servant of a stranger, then there was a case for the interposition of the Goel; and the law ran, "After that he is sold, he may be redeemed again; one of his brethren may redeem him."

As in the instance of the redemption of land, if the man were able, he might be his own redeemer. But if he had no ability to pay the ransom himself, then either one of his kinsmen must interpose on his behalf, or the man must remain unredeemed; the law still holding good that no stranger could discharge the office of the Goel.

You will observe the peculiarity, that the Goel had no right to interfere, unless it were to a stranger that the Israelite had been sold. If the master were an Israelite, the servant was in no sense alienated from God's people; and the exigence was not such as to warrant the Goel's interference. But if the master were a stranger, then the servitude became typical of man's bondage to Satan. It might be said in a degree to have withdrawn the servant from the congregation of Israel; and thus a case was made out for the kinsman Redeemer; the Goel might come forward, and the servant might be free. You will perceive at once, that, in its typical character, this transaction is identical with that already reviewed. Is it not the Scriptural representation of man by nature, that he is "the servant of sin, led captive by Satan at his will?" The Israelite hath sold himself to the stranger; and not one farthing can he advance towards buying back his freedom. Must he then languish for ever in bondage? Must the chain be for ever upon him? Must he groan for ever beneath the load of oppression? There advances a mighty one who proclaims Himself his Kinsman and Goel, made of a woman, made under the law, and bearing the likeness of sinful flesh. He pays down in suffering the price of Redemption: He strikes the chain with his cross, and it is broken into shivers: He bids the prisoner come forth, and walk in the glorious liberty of the children of God.

We will not however enlarge upon this: the typical correspondence is too obvious to be overlooked. We rather proceed to the third case of the Goel's interference, a case which differs considerably from those already examined. It was the office of the kinsman, the Goel, to interpose, not only when there had been forfeiture of inheritance, or loss of liberty, but also when there had been shedding of blood. You will find the account of this third office of the Goel in the thirty-fifth chapter of the book of Numbers, which particularly describes the appointment of cities of refuge. It is here, indeed, easy to overlook the kinsman Redeemer, and not to observe that he is introduced into the discourse. Our translation speaks only of the "avenger," or the "revenger of blood." But the original word marks simply the Goel—so that the Goel, the kinsman Redeemer, was, in virtue of kinsmanship, the avenger of blood. If murder had been perpetrated, the prosecution and execution of the murdered devolved on the nearest of kin to the murdered party. He must pursue the murderer; and if he overtook him before he reached the city of refuge, he might take summary vengeance for the death of his relative. But if the Goel were not at hand when the crime was committed, it would seem that no stranger had right to arrest or follow the criminal. He betook himself unmolested to the nearest city of refuge, and remained there in safety until the cause was tried before the judges of the land. So that, in this case, as well as in the others, the interference depended on the kinsmanship. Nothing else could warrant a man in undertaking the office of the Goel; and thus that distinguishing feature of the Goel, which made him throughout the type of our Redeemer, the feature of kinsmanship to the party requiring interference, stands out as prominently when blood was to be avenged, as when land was to be redeemed, or liberty regained.

But wherein, in this instance, lies the typical resemblance between the offices of the Goel and of Christ? We suspect that wrong interpretations have been advanced of the figurative meaning of a portion of the law, through men's not observing that the "avenger of blood" is the Goel, the kinsman Redeemer. It is the common idea, that the cities of refuge were typical of Christ; and that the manslayer, who fled thither for shelter, was the human race, pursued by the justice of the Almighty. We are far from implying that there is no fidelity or beauty in such a figure; or that, under certain limitations, it may not be lawful to reckon as antitype and type, our Redeemer and the city of refuge. But we have adduced, we hope, no inconsiderable proof, that the fixed and standing type of Christ under the law was the Goel, the kinsman Redeemer; and that the offices of this Goel gave the clear outlines of those of the Messiah. Whenever, then, we find mention of an interference of the Goel, we seem bound, by all fair laws of interpretation, to search for something analogous to the interference of the Christ; and we may well hesitate, after having heretofore found man's advocate in the Goel, to assent to a commentary which, in this case, would find his adversary. We will not, therefore, seek the figure of Christ in the city of refuge. We look for Christ in the Goel; and since the

Goel is here "the avenger of blood" we will search for Christ in "the avenger of blood."

We wish you to bear in mind that our only business lies with the office of the Goel. If you follow the murderer into the city of refuge, you might find circumstances inconsistent with that designation of the murderer, which we are about to advance. But this touches not the question of the office of the Goel, and has therefore no right to be introduced into the debate. There would be just as much objection against the supposing Christ typified by the city of refuge. Those who were really guilty fled in vain to the city, and must be delivered up to the punishment due to their crime. Who can find in this any emblem of the flying of sinners to Christ, and of the succour afforded to those who have deserved hell by their many offences? We are bound to be always careful not to overstrain types. But, in the case of the Goel, let attention be only limited, as it ought to be, to the person and office, and the resemblance is so perfect that it might be hardly possible to exaggerate the figure. We have now, therefore, only to do with the Goel as the avenger of blood; and we keep out of sight the arrangements connected with the cities of refuge.

If murder were committed, the Goel alone, the kinsman Redeemer, could pursue the murderer. Such is simply the typical exhibition—and who does not find in it the representation of the office of Christ? Created deathless and imperishable, was not the human race slain by Satan, when he wrought up our first parents to an act, prohibited by the words, "In the day that thou doest it, thou shalt surely die?" We suppose it to have been with reference to this slaughter of mankind, that Christ said of the devil, "he was a murderer from the beginning." It was clearly through the instrumentality of Satan, that death, whether of body or of soul, gained footing in this creation. But, if done through his instrumentality, it may justly be ascribed to his authorship. And we count it, therefore, most correct to describe Satan as the great manslayer. He it is that hath shed human blood; and all that vast mowing down of successive generations, which keeps the sepulchres replenished with fresh harvests of the dead, must be referred to that awful being, who hath been "a murderer from the beginning." And if we can thus find the manslayer in Satan, cannot we find the avenger of blood in Christ? Who pursued the murderer! Who, so soon as man lay wounded and bleeding on the earth, snatched up the sword, and followed the track of that malignant spirit, whose blow had prostrated the world's population? Who, century after century, unwearied and undiverted, opposed Himself, in every quarter, and by every weapon, to the shedder of blood; till, at last, meeting him front to front in one dread struggle, He took on him a vengeance which drew the wonder of the intelligent universe, and "through death destroyed him that had the power of death?" Who was it, that, sorrowing over the wretchedness of the stricken race, put on righteousness as a breastplate, and clothed Himself with zeal as a cloak, and then, equipped for conflict, sprang forth to grapple with the assassin? Who but the Goel? Who but the Kinsman Redeemer? Who but that seed of the woman, predicted to bruise the serpent's head? Who but that Son of man, the brother of the slaughtered ones, who "spoiled principalities and powers, and made a show of them openly, triumphing over them in his cross?" Oh, it is certain, that, though Satan for a while may still be permitted to roam over this creation, there has been gained a mastery which reduced him into the bond-slave of our Kinsman. It is certain that One who sprang from amongst ourselves, allied to us by oneness of nature, associated by all the linkings of brotherhood, has gone after the man-slayer, and overtaken him, and spoiled him of his strength; and that, though He allow him, in subservience to the mighty purposes of God, still to walk this globe with the slaughter-weapon in his hand, He is only reserving the full taking of vengeance till the year of Jubilee arrives; and that then, reckoning with the murderer for all the blood with which the earth has been drenched, He will hurl him headlong into the lake of fire, and thus call forth an acknowledgment from congregated intelligences, that the Goel of man has been the avenger of man's blood.

Yes, we thus show you, that, when the Goel rose up at the sight of the corpse of his kinsman, and rushed forth in pursuit of the assassin—just as well as when he interfered to redeem his kinsman's land, or his kinsman's person—he was the figure of that illustrious deliverer, who, in process of time, should undertake the championship of his brethren, regain their inheritance, burst their chains, and avenge their blood. We may consider therefore that the point at which we have been labouring, is sufficiently established; that we shall carry with us your assent, when we take it as an ascertained truth, that there was a standing type of Christ under the legal dispensation, a type which would be presented to the Jew in the various transactions of life, and that this type was the Goel, the Kinsman Redeemer.

It is over the grave and the separate state, as well as over this earth with its duties and trials, that our Goel extends his care and protection: having guarded his people through life, He forgets them not in death, He forsakes them not after death; and therefore of Him, Him who "is near of kin unto us, one of our next Kinsmen," may it be said with an emphasis, which could never, comparatively, have been used of any other Goel, "Blessed be he of the Lord, who hath not left off his kindness to the living and to the dead."

We shall not presume to say that we have examined every case in which the Goel interfered. We have certainly taken the chief instances; and if others occur, a similar process of reasoning will bring out, we are persuaded, a similar result. And do not suppose, that, in pleading for the typical character of the Goel, we plead for the existence of a figure which was hidden from the men of the old dispensation. When Job exclaims, "I know that my Redeemer liveth," it is, "I know that my Goel, my Kinsman, liveth." And if the holy ones amongst the Jews could describe Christ as the Goel, would they not naturally turn to the offices of the Goel, in order that they might ascertain the offices of Christ?

Kinsmen of Christ—for ye are all his kinsmen—kinsmen of Christ, shall your Goel have thus mightily interfered, and will ye put from you, through unbelief, the benefits of his interference? He made himself the Kinsman of each one amongst you. Bear that, we beseech of you, in mind. Who is there that is not the kinsman of Christ? The kinsmanship resulted from his taking human nature; and it is enough therefore to be a man, and I know myself Christ's kinsman. And as He is the Kinsman of all, He is the Goel of all. He tasted death for every man. He redeemed every man's inheritance. He regained every man's liberty. He avenged every man's blood. If not, how was He the Goel of the race? But then He imposes a condition—"If ye will not believe, surely ye shall not be established." If ye will not believe, the land, though I have ransomed it, shall not come back to you; and the liberty, though I have purchased it, shall not be bestowed on you; and upon your own heads shall be your own blood. We give you thus the simple, glorious Gospel; and may God send it to your hearts. The Goel has interposed: He hath performed all the offices of the Kinsman: and now unbelief, and nothing but unbelief, can exclude the poorest, the meanest, the most wicked amongst you, from a full and free share in the perfect Redemption.

Can any of you think of being his own Goel, of effecting for himself the salvation of his soul? There are chains to be broken; there is Paradise to be regained; there is Satan to be trampled under foot. And which of us is sufficient for these things? Who will undertake them in his own strength? It can hardly be that you will not shrink from what so manifestly surpasses human power. Then close at once with your Goel: take the Redemption which is proffered, without money and without price: you will find Christ "able to save to the uttermost all who come unto God through Him." And when enabled to say, in the language of faith, "The man is near of kin unto us, one of our next kinsmen," your experience of his preciousness will lead you continually to exclaim, both here and hereafter, "Blessed be he of the Lord, who hath not left off his kindness to the living or the dead."

LECTURE XIX.

St. Barnabas.

ACTS xiv. 22.

"Confirming the souls of the disciples, and exhorting them to continue in the faith, and that we must through much tribulation enter into the kingdom of God."

THESE words relate what was done by Barnabas and Paul, on revisiting Lystra, Iconium, and Antioch, cities where they had preached the Gospel, and planted Churches. We take them as our subject of discourse, because our Church devotes this present day to the commemoration of St. Barnabas, the Apostle, whom she defines in her collect "as endued with singular gifts of the Holy Ghost." His name was originally Joses; he was of the tribe of Levi, but born at Cyprus. This latter circumstance explains what is said of him, on his first mention in the book of the Acts, "Having land, he sold it, and brought the money, and laid it at the Apostles' feet." You will remember, that, according to the law of Moses, the Levites were not allowed to possess estates of their own in the promised land: but this did not prevent their acquiring property in other countries: Joses then, possessing land in Cyprus, was at liberty to sell it, and throw the proceeds into the common fund, which was then applied to the sustenance of poor Christians; and, on his doing this—for he may have been amongst the first or most liberal contributors to so charitable a design—he seems to have received from the Apostles the surname of Barnabas, which is interpreted by St. Luke, "the son of consolation."

We have but little information as to the life and labours of Barnabas. We read of his having been sent by the Apostles to confirm the new Christians at Antioch, who had received the faith on the preaching of those "which were scattered abroad upon the persecution that arose about Stephen." When Barnabas came and had seen the grace of God, "he was glad, and exhorted them all, that, with purpose of heart, they would cleave unto the Lord." The Evangelist then adds a testimony, which fully bears out the expressions in the collect of the day, "For he was a good man, and full of the Holy Ghost and of faith." He then became, for a considerable time, the coadjutor of St. Paul; but even those great lights were men of like passions with us: dissensions arose between Barnabas and St. Paul: they separated, but still laboured in the same cause; each chose a field for himself; and both strove, with like zeal, to win converts to the faith of their common Lord. There is little further known in regard of Barnabas. But it is generally agreed that "his last labours were employed in his native country, and that, by the malice of the Jews, he was tumultuously assaulted, and stoned to death at Salamis, the principal city of Cyprus."

And now, in taking our text as a fit subject of discourse on the feast of St. Barnabas, and in commenting especially, as we design to do, on its latter clause, "We must through much tribulation enter into the Kingdom of God," we feel as though you may think that more consolatory words might have been looked for from "the son of consolation." Has Barnabas only to tell us of "much tribulation?" Has he no more cheering tidings, by which to vindicate his name? Nay, my brethren, if he speak of "much tribulation," he speaks also of that tribulation as a way of entering into the "Kingdom of God." Is it not consolatory to be told by St. Paul, that "our light affliction, which is but for a moment, worketh for us a far more exceeding and eternal weight of glory?" Of course, the consolation does not lie in the being told that there are afflictions which must be borne, but in the being assured that these afflictions shall be instrumental to our everlasting good. It might scarcely consist with the name of Barnabas, that he should speak only of the multiplied sorrows which fall to the true believer's lot; but we recognise the voice of the "son of consolation," when those sorrows are represented as preparing us for Heaven. And often as, in one way or another, this truth comes before us, it seems always to take a more than common hold of the mind: cares and griefs are so numerous, so varied, so oppressive, that nothing falls more gratefully on the ear of a Christian assembly, than the mention of afflictions as fitting us for glory.

But we must take care lest we misapply the exhortation of Barnabas. The very readiness with which numbers hearken to a discourse upon sorrow, the soothing sound which there evidently is in words which tell how the Lord chasteneth his people, should suggest the importance of having it rightly understood, that though the kingdom is to be entered "through much tribulation," there may be "much tribulation" which does not lead to the kingdom. And this single remark may serve to show, that there is room for great practical mistakes in regard of sorrow, as well as of other divine orderings and appointments; so that the subject should occasionally be brought forward in the pulpit, not in order to the exhibiting the comforts and consolations which God hath graciously provided for them that mourn in Zion, but rather for the correcting what may be erroneous in men's views, and the placing in its true light the moral discipline wherein affliction has so large a share. Such then is our design on the present occasion. It is the feast of St. Barnabas, and you expect only soothing things from the son of consolation. But whilst we wish you, and mean you, to have these, we must also labour that you take not comfort on insufficient grounds; therefore let us now see—and may God's Spirit assist us in the search—whether the emphatic declaration of St. Peter, as to Scripture being wrested to their own destruction by the unlearned and unstable, may not be applied even to the words of Barnabas in our text, that, "we must, through much tribulation, enter into the Kingdom of God."

Now let us give you something of a parochial minister's experience: let us make you accompany him, as he goes one of his week-day rounds, and introduce you to certain cases of sickness or suffering. Our first visit shall be to a person afflicted with great bodily disease, enduring racking pains, which threaten to be of very long continuance, neither likely to be alleviated by medicine nor terminated by death. This is a most affecting and melancholy case:

no one of common sensibility can look on a fellow-creature, thus sorely tried, and not long to say something to him which might be cheering and soothing. And it is evident that this is hardly to be done, unless reference be made to another state of being: the case is clearly beyond the ordinary and worldly expressions of hope and condolence; so that it were better to keep silence, in fear of being thought to be only trifling with misery, if we may not introduce the mention of a better land, where tears are wiped away, and pain is unknown. But it is the clergyman's business, and it is also his privilege, to point the afflicted to Heaven; and the natural impulse will be, as he gazes on the stricken and disconsolate man, to say to him in a voice of the most thorough sympathy, "Be of good cheer; we must, through much tribulation, enter into the Kingdom of God." And perhaps the words are evidently apprehended and relished by the sufferer: you can see, by the faint smile which gleams for an instant on features distorted by pain, that the reference to the ends and objects of affliction, tells on the feelings, and offers the kind of comfort on which the heart is eager to seize.

But we must examine a little into the state of mind of this sufferer: however harsh and unkind it may seem, to distress him with questions, and run the risk of destroying even that small measure of support which our salutation gave, we are not to leave him under a possible delusion, but must endeavour to ascertain whether it be on right grounds that he regards present sorrow as instrumental to future happiness. Alas, it is not needful to put many questions, or elicit many statements, in order to the discovering how confused, yea, how false, are the afflicted man's notions. Ask him whether he know himself to be a sinner, and that God's law hath denounced grievous punishment upon sin; and he will tell you, yes, he knows himself a sinner, and therefore liable to the heavy wrath of God: but he will probably add, that, having so much of stern suffering to endure in this life, he hopes that, in the next, he shall find himself at rest. How often, how lamentably often, has the parochial minister to listen to some such statement as this—the sick man implying that he regards his sufferings as the punishment of sin, so that what he now undergoes is so much taken off from future penalties, and may even be so great as to leave nothing to be endured after death.

But what can be more fatally erroneous than any such notion? Admitting, as of course we do, that all suffering is a consequence of sin; for had not sin entered the world, suffering could have had no place; what men endure now, can be at most but the temporal punishment of sin, and must leave the eternal undiminished. It is not indeed for us to decide why one man has so much more to endure than another. The Judge of all the earth will do right: and hereafter there shall be such ample explanation of every dealing as will prove it to have been both in wisdom and goodness, that, for years, excruciating pain was the lot of this individual, whilst unbroken health attended upon that. But one stern truth we are bound to deliver without compromise and without hesitation, and this is, that there is nothing whatsoever, in the present sufferings of the one, or the present freedom from suffering of the other, from which to argue, that when the two die, they may not have precisely the same amount of suffering to undergo through Eternity, the same portion to receive in that terrible state, where "the worm dieth not, and the fire is not quenched." O fearful aggravation of present affliction, to think that it may all go for nothing, that the being, who lies before you distracted by pain, and whose cries might pierce a heart of stone, may, all the while, have standing against him the vast debt under which sin has brought him to the justice of God; so that, if, in one of those throes of agony which it is agony to witness, the immortal spirit were to escape from its worn, distracted tenement, it would be doomed to that inconceivable, interminable wretchedness, which must be the heritage of such as are not found in Christ.

But who shall doubt that this might be the case? There is no expiatory power or virtue in our sufferings. They make no atonement. If endured patiently, they leave in full force the incurred penalties of God's Law; if impatiently, they but incur fresh. Let this be remembered by you all; for we will not undertake to say how far the notion, which the parochial minister so often finds, in its grosser forms, amongst the sick and suffering poor—the notion of enduring all one's pains in this life, and therefore finding ease and happiness in the next—may obtain place in more refined shape, and under some specious disguise, in those whose opportunities of knowing better should have secured them against such delusion. A life of misery is no security against an eternity of torment. You may lose both worlds, wretched here, and wretched hereafter. Sorrows may be heaped upon you; you may be forced to drain the very dregs of the cup of trembling. But throughout the most severe and terrible allotments, there may be the same unsubdued heart, the same centring of the affections upon earthly things—ay, and, from what we have now been observing, a growing opinion, that God is exacting from you here the penalties of his law, that He may be able to acquit you when brought to his bar. And our present business is with the urging on you, that you take heed how you infer that the path of tribulation must be the path to glory. You are not to think, that, because God "scourgeth every son whom He receiveth," therefore every one whom He scourgeth must be a son. You are not to think, that, because "many are the troubles of the righteous," every one who has many troubles must therefore be righteous. Oh, not so; sorrow may be the frequent accompaniment of godliness; but there may be multiplied and intense sorrow, where there is no godliness to accompany. You must look for other proofs and evidences of piety than sufferings, "whether in mind, body, or estate:" for however commonly piety and sufferings may be combined, it does not show that there is no piety, that there is no special suffering; and far less does it show that there is piety, that there is special suffering.

Be careful then of any misinterpretation or misapplication of the words of our text. For events may apparently come alike to all. God may rebuke a wicked man in his wrath, and a righteous man in his love: but the dealings may wear the same aspect, though there is so wide a distinction in the originating cause. And whilst all are sinners, and whilst sorrow is fastened to sin, whether in the way of appointed judgment, or of natural consequence, it may, yea it must, be continually happening that calamities beset those who, all the while, are living in alienation from God, that tears are the portion, night and day, of men who have no Scriptural ground for hope, that God will finally wipe away tears from their eyes; and nevertheless the proposition of our text may be unimpeached, as announcing an ordinary, if not invariable, appointment, that "we must, through much tribulation, enter into the Kingdom of God."

Now we trust that you will have thoroughly understood the drift of the foregoing remarks. We have seen so much tendency among the sick and the suffering, to the taking the being visited with affliction as an evidence or proof of being God's children, that we are very anxious to point out what ought to be too manifest to need any showing, that, though God's children are commonly afflicted, all that are afflicted are not God's children. "Whom the Lord loveth, He correcteth," is a Scriptural proposition. But "whom the Lord correcteth, He loveth," is a very different sentiment; he who is a son may expect, that, being such, he shall be chastened; but he who is chastened must not, on that account, conclude himself a son.

There is however a wholly different, though an equally erroneous, inference, which may be drawn from our text and from other passages of Scripture, which, in like manner, associates suffering with piety. When one man, to whose share fall more than common troubles, reads the saying, that "we must through much tribulation enter the Kingdom of God," there will be danger of his hastily concluding, Then, surely, I have one great sign of being on the way to the Kingdom, for "much tribulation" is given as my lot. But when another who is not called to extraordinary trials, whose course of life, on the whole, is one of evenness and peace, reads of entering the Kingdom through "much tribulation," there is great likelihood of his suspecting that he is destitute of a chief evidence of being a child of God; The children, he will say, are chastened and corrected; can I then be a child, who experience little or nothing of this fatherly discipline? This is a case which comes under the parochial minister's observation, if not as frequently as the former, yet sufficiently often to render it right that we give it a careful consideration. There is hardly a shape or form which doubts may not assume; if the greatness of trouble distress and harass one Christian, the very want of trouble may be a trouble to another. And certainly one may observe many cases, in which, for many years, God seems to have done to an individual or a family what Satan alleged as the producing cause of the piety of Job, "Hast thou not made an hedge about him, and about his house, and about all that he hath on every side? thou hast blessed the work of his hands, and his sustenance is increased in the land." Every thing goes smoothly and brightly; the party is an object of great respect and esteem: death makes no inroad into the household: there is prosperity in business: children grow up "in the nurture and admonition of the Lord;" and the whole domestic aspect, or picture, is that of a choice and curtained spot, which the Almighty Himself has marked off for exemption from those rough visitations which so often lay waste the homes and hearts of the children of men.

How natural for an individual, whatever his earnestness and sincerity in religion, when he observes how he thus seems defended and shielded, to experience something like uneasiness on hearing or reading our text! how natural for him to say, Can I indeed be on my way to God's Kingdom, when thus exempted from those "many tribulations," which an Apostle asserts to be the necessary entrance? Ah, my brother, life is not finished yet; there may remain time enough for many reverses, many funerals, many disappointments, many calamities. Be not impatient for the coming of trial; but keep always praying, that, when it comes, you may have patience for its endurance. It will come soon enough, sooner perhaps than you will be ready to meet it. It does not take long to darken the brightest sky, when God has once "commanded the clouds from above:" when He restrains not his east wind, there is no need of years, moments suffice, to blight the sweetest flowers, and nip the choicest buds. And in the mean time, thou canst not justly say, thou hast no trial: the want of trial is thy trial; unbroken sunshine may be a trial as well as continued storm—ay, why not even a greater, as making thee doubtful of thy "calling and election?" for an old writer justly says, "Pain of the body is after all but the body of pain;" it is the pain of the soul which is the soul of pain: and certainly to one, who truly loves God, there cannot be a severer thing, than that, whatsoever it be, which causes him to doubt whether God loves him. He might more readily welcome troubles which brought witness of his being a son, than preserve exemptions which breed suspicions of his being an alien. So that long uninterrupted prosperity may be the portion of a wicked man: it may also be the portion of a righteous man; with the wicked it will nourish presumption and indifference to religion; with the righteous it will suggest fears as to acceptance with God; and these fears, springing from the thought that the believer has not trial enough, may themselves constitute no common trial.

Though, in all honesty, there is another view which should be taken of the question, Can I be a true Christian, when I have so little of tribulation? We might meet the question with another, Why have I so little tribulation? Do you think that the "much tribulation," spoken of in our text, is made up exclusively of what the world counts disasters and calamities? Nay, not so, else how could our blessed Lord speak of our taking up the cross "daily," and following Him? The "tribulation" consists greatly in conflict with our own evil hearts, in the grief occasioned by our frequent fallings into sin, in the sorrow and the shame of finding the lines of the Divine image so faintly traced within, the power of corruption still so strong, the will so biassed, and the affections so depraved. And know ye nothing of this tribulation? Alas, that were tribulation indeed. He who cannot find trouble enough inside, has stronger ground for fears as to his spiritual condition than the finding none outside. Though, it must further be inquired, how comes there to be no external tribulation? The tribulations of which St. Paul spake, were, we know, to arise mainly from the persecutions to which the bold profession of Christianity would then expose the converts from idolatry. But has the offence of the cross ceased? Is there no longer any such thing as the being "persecuted for righteousness' sake?" Nay, if true religion have never made you an enemy, be not too sure that you are not an enemy to it. The offence of the cross cannot wholly cease, because it is the heart, as it is human, rather than man, as he is heathen, by which the prejudice is felt. The world must dislike genuine piety, as that by which it is opposed, reproved, condemned; and it ought to make us doubt whether our piety be genuine, if it never cause a clashing between the world and ourselves. Do you say that you know nothing of "tribulation" as occasioned by religion? But are you quite sure that you have done your duty as a religious man? Have you been faithful in the reproving sin, in the not suffering sin upon your neighbour? Have you drawn the line with due breadth and distinctness, between the world and yourself? No wonder, if the world do not persecute you, when you do not openly separate from the world. No wonder, if you have not incurred much obliquy, dislike, and contempt, if you have been conceding to the world, handling its faults with the greatest possible gentleness, and practically slurring over, so far as you could or dared, the distinguishing characteristics which mark off its votaries from faithful followers of Christ.

Suppose you were to make an experiment, ye who are ready to express wonder and fear at having so little of trial and tribulation, the experiment of being more rigid and conscientious in the practice of Christian duties, of being more faithful in telling men of their faults, more zealous in seizing opportunities of defending and displaying the doctrine of the Cross, more earnest in showing what are the real and every-day doings and demandings of vital religion. Ah, perhaps the result of such an experiment would be the rapid removal of every ground of misgiving, that your path was too easy to be the path of God's Kingdom. I do not mean that the experiment might bring trouble upon you in the shape of loss of property, or of the frequent funeral, or of the bitter disappointment, or of the carking care. But the cold dislike, the scornful laugh, the ill-disguised contempt, the broken friendship, the keen resentment, the injurious speech—these, which are the weapons with which the world wages war, when and where Christianity has the patronage of the State—these, which, be ye well and thoroughly assured, are always brought into exercise by the uncompromising display of Christian principle and practice—these would sufficiently destroy the character of your path, as being too comfortable, too smooth, too much strewed with flowers, too little set with thorns, to be the path to Heaven. Oh, there may be riches, there may be health, there may be domestic enjoyment, there may be prosperous circumstances; but let a believer labour earnestly at the doing his duty in that station of life wherein it hath pleased God to place him, his duty in and to himself, his duty to the Church and to the world, and we can be confident that he will not long find or fancy in his experience any exception to the rule, which St. Barnabas laid down in our text, that, "we must, through much tribulation, enter into the Kingdom of God."

Now we have not thus so much either defended or examined the assertion of our text, as considered two cases in which a wrong use may be made of the passage—the one, that in which the having to endure tribulation is unwarrantably taken in evidence of the being truly religious; the other, that in which comparative exemption from tribulation is, as unwarrantably, thought to prove the not being on the way to the Kingdom of Heaven. On the one hand, we have wished to guard you against a false comfort; on the other, against a false fear—false comfort, which men may draw from their griefs; false fear, which they may ground on their blessings.

But let us not forget that the Church commemorates this day the son of consolation; and let us now, therefore, observe that the text affixes a particular character to afflictions, as the ordinary instruments through which God fits his people for their glorious inheritance. For you may clearly see, from the mode of expression which he adopts, that Barnabas does not merely assert a fact, that we shall have "much tribulation:" he alleges a suitableness, that this "much tribulation" is the due preparation for the kingdom. "We must,"—it behoves, it is needful for us. He gives much the same representation as is given in the verse already quoted from St. Paul, "Our light affliction, which is but for a moment, worketh for us a far more exceeding and eternal weight of glory." But how "worketh for us?" The Apostle cannot mean that the affliction produces the glory, in any thing of the sense in which a cause produces an effect. It does not work for us glory, as if it made satisfaction for sin, and opened to us Heaven. This is the error that has been combated in an earlier part of our discourse; and again and again be it said, that no amount of suffering here can be taken in substitution for suffering hereafter. O ye children of sorrow, dream of any thing rather than of what ye endure now excusing you from future punishment, or giving you a sort of title to rest beyond the grave. But affliction "worketh for us glory" in the sense of preparing, or fitting, us for glory: God thereby disciplines his people, detaches them from earthly things, refines their affections: it is in the furnace of trial that He makes them holier, using the trial to burn out, so to speak, the indwelling corruption; and whatsoever tends to increase present holiness, tends equally to increase future happiness; there being, as we are taught, an appointed proportion between the two, or rather, the one containing in it the germ, or even the very essence of the other.

And thus, also, as affliction worketh for us glory, working in us meetness, or fitness, for glory, so is it necessary that, through much tribulation, we enter the Kingdom. Not indeed that the tribulation is indispensable; for God, if He pleased, could make us ready for the Kingdom, through some other process than that of "much tribulation;" but the "much tribulation" is his ordinary course; so that, as a general rule, we "must" endure it, we must look to endure it, if we hope for final entrance to a land of light and life. And what a character does this give to tribulation! I understand from this what St. Paul means when he says, "We glory in tribulations." Glory in them! was then the Apostle a Stoic? did he profess to make light of pain, and to count it no evil? Nay, it was no Stoic that could say, as he said of Epaphroditus, "He was sick nigh unto death; but God had mercy on him, and not on him only, but on me also, lest I should have sorrow upon sorrow." And in place of accounting pain no evil, this same Apostle hath elsewhere distinctly said, "No chastening for the present seemeth to be joyous, but grievous." Yea, and you should carefully observe that our text is so constructed as to show that Barnabas and Paul were not laying down a rule for others, from which they were to be exempted themselves. There is a sudden change of persons in the verse. You observe that, the third person having been used, whilst mention is made of the Apostles as "confirming the souls of the disciples, and exhorting them to continue in the faith," the first person is employed when the discourse comes to turn on the tribulations which would have to be endured. "We must, through much tribulation, enter into the Kingdom of God." It is as though Barnabas and Saul, when they had to speak of suffering, from which nature is most averse, were careful to have it understood, that they were speaking of that in which themselves had full share: it is as though St. Luke, when recording the exhortation for the instruction of the Church in every age, was directed to throw it into such form, that no one should ever be able to read the latter part, without being reminded that it included himself.

But if St. Paul thus identify himself with tribulation, and if, from expressions already quoted, he were no Stoic, but thoroughly sensitive to tribulation, how are we to explain his glorying in tribulation? how could he "glory in tribulation," and yet reckon chastening not to be "joyous but grievous?" This is easily explained. He reckoned tribulation grievous in itself; but he gloried in it as a preparation for Heaven. He felt it to be an evil; but he would not have been without it for any thing which you could have offered him; it was making him ready for the blessed abode which Christ had made ready for him; and he knew that the one preparation was just as needful as the other—what availed it that the place should be prepared for the inhabitant, unless the inhabitant were also prepared for the place? Heaven can be Heaven to those only who are made meet for Heaven: should he then glory in the rearing of the palace, and in the throwing open its doors? and should he not also glory in what schooled him to pass the gates, and find a home in the magnificent structure? He gloried then in tribulation—not from him would come congratulatory speech on beholding a Christian apparently exempt from visitations of trouble. His congratulations were more likely to have been heard, when sorrow had broken, as an armed man, into a household, and grief had set up its abode, like one who did not mean to be speedily or easily dislodged. "We glory in tribulations, knowing that tribulation worketh patience, and patience experience, and experience hope." Who then can wish to be without tribulation? It were caring but little for the Kingdom, to care much for the tribulation through which we must enter it.

Nay, and this is but a half statement: this is as though tribulation were only a something to be passed through; whereas it is a preparation: it is that out of which glory is to grow: tears turn to jewels in the crown; sighs to songs upon the harp; poverty becomes wealth; bereavement, possession; contumely, triumph. Again, therefore, we ask, who would wish to be without tribulation? Whilst indeed God is pleased to keep sorrow from your doors, it is not for you to seek it, but rather to take thankfully the blessing and the brightness so graciously bestowed: and, whilst you have the heart to keep with all diligence, and sin to reprove with all faithfulness, you will always, as we have shown you, have trouble enough to employ you, and to exercise. But do not shrink, if there be signs as of the disturbing of the external peacefulness, if the clouds begin to gather, and God seem about to give you "the bread of adversity, and the water of affliction." Rather prepare to bid sorrow welcome. Rather receive it with a solemn joy, with a thankful submission. There are other forms which attend its sad and measured march, besides those of anxiety and anguish. As it approaches, palled in deep night, there are other voices, which fall on the listening ear of faith, besides those which swell the shriek and mingle in the dirge. The spirits of the departed righteous throng about calamity, as it turns its fatal step towards the believer's door. Their utterance it is, which is so distinctly and sweetly heard, amid the murmurings of the gathering storm, "O child of God, wouldst thou be without chastisement, whereof all are partakers?" wouldst thou forget thy Master's word, "In the world ye shall have tribulation, but be of good cheer, I have overcome the world?" wouldst thou be an exception to an experience whereof all we are witnesses—ay, and the son of consolation it was who spake the words—that, "through much tribulation must men enter into the Kingdom of God."

LECTURE XX.

Spiritual Decline.

GALATIANS v. 7.

"Ye did run well; who did hinder you that ye should not obey the truth?"

IN a recent discourse, we took occasion, from what is recorded of Asa—that his heart was perfect, though the high places were not removed out of Israel—to speak to you of the possibility that there might be decay at the heart in the matter of religion, though as yet the life gave no signs of spiritual decline. But we have since felt as if we had not gone sufficiently into so important a matter, as if we had not examined with due accuracy the symptoms of the insidious disease, as if we had not exposed with due faithfulness how frequent its occurrence, and how fatal its tendency. And as I purpose leaving you to-day for a brief period of necessary relaxation, I should not feel easy if I did not go at greater length, and with greater minuteness, into this matter of spiritual decline—for how possible it may be—ought I not even to say, how probable?—that there are some amongst you who have begun well in a Christian course, but who have been gradually growing slacker and slacker, less earnest in duty, less fervent in affection; and to whom therefore may fitly be addressed the pathetic remonstrance of St. Paul to the Galatians, "Ye did run well; who did hinder you that ye should not obey the truth?" Perhaps we shall only be repeating—at all events, only amplifying—the statement in a former discourse: but better do this, better weary you with repetition, than run any risk of leaving you with vague and indefinite notions, where it so much concerns your safety that you should be alive to your danger. Observe then, that, if we take as our topic of discourse what is called spiritual declension; if we endeavour to examine the symptoms, and expose the peril, of that moral disease which eats away religion in the soul; we are not to be regarded as speaking only to those—though such are not excluded—who prove, by outward and undeniable signs, that they are forsaking their God and Redeemer—the disease is rather one which, like that fatal malady, which leaves the cheek beautiful and the eye brilliant, whilst it rapidly undermines the strength, may allow external appearances to continue specious and flattering, though the work of death is fast going on within. Observe, for instance, what is said, in the Book of Revelation, of the Ephesian Church. "I know thy works, and thy labour, and thy patience; and how thou canst not bear them which are evil; and thou hast tried them which say they are Apostles, and are not, and hast found them liars; and hast borne, and hast patience, and for my name's sake hast laboured, and hast not fainted." Here, by a reduplication, and even a repetition, of epithets, the idea is strongly conveyed of an active, persevering, and patient religion—a

Church, of which all this could be said, must have been distinguished by great readiness both to do and suffer in the cause of God and his Christ. Yet the next words are, "Nevertheless I have somewhat against thee, because thou hast left thy first love." It is not laid to the charge of the Ephesian Christians, it is not even insinuated, that they laboured less than at first—but it is distinctly asserted, that they loved less, as though that, which alone can give the action any worth, may be on the wane whilst in the action itself there is no perceptible difference.

Let us set ourselves, then, to the examining whether men may not have a name to live whilst they are dead in God's sight. May God enable us to be at once faithful and affectionate in detecting and exposing the signs of a disease, under which, as we have said, it is but too possible that some amongst you may be labouring, the disease of religious decline. May his Spirit, without which there can be no right understanding of the things of religion, be our guide whilst we endeavour to show you, in the first place, how you may find out whether, according to the words of our text, you are ceasing to "run well;" and in the second place, what reasons there are for regarding the condition so described as one of pre-eminent danger.

Now we have already pointed out to you that there certainly was spiritual decline in the case of the Ephesian Christians—they no longer had that ardent affection which they had felt and displayed when first converted from idolatry: they were not as warm in their love towards God and the Saviour; and they are plainly told, that, unless they repented, and did the first works, they should quickly be visited with the removal of their candlestick.

But in the last also of the Apocalyptic Epistles, which is that to the Church of the Laodiceans, you have a denunciation of lukewarmness, the being neither hot nor cold in religion, and an assertion of such indignation as felt in consequence by God, as you can scarcely perhaps find expressed in any other part of Scripture. This lukewarmness which is charged on the Laodiceans, can be only a greater degree of that leaving their first love which is charged on the Ephesians; and the utter loathing, with which the lukewarm are spoken of, must indicate, that, where spiritual declension has gone far, the man who is its subject is held of God in perfect abhorrence. The language in our text will apply to any or all of the stages of the disease—for the ceasing to run well may indicate a slight, and almost imperceptible, decline of speed, and extend also to the slow and hesitating step which can scarcely be said to make any progress in the heavenward path. Thus there may be various stages of the disease; from that of the man, in whom love is not quite as ardent as at the first, to that of another, in whom it scarce retains any thing of its original fervour. Amongst those who have really "run well" in religion, and who still, to all outward appearance, are true servants of Christ, we may have many who are wasting away through the spiritual consumption—some on whom the malady has only just gained a hold, and others whom it has already reduced to little more than moral skeletons. But whilst we endeavour to lay before you certain of the symptoms of spiritual decline, you must be honest and fearless with yourselves: if you will not, as we proceed, search into your own cases, and see how far they answer to our description, in vain might we depict with a most thorough accuracy the signs and stages of insidious disease. Come then, let conscience do its part, and we may, by God's help, assist you in determining this most momentous of questions, Might St. Paul say of us, as of the Galatians of old, "Ye did run well; who did hinder you that ye should not obey the truth?"

Now the first test, to which we would bring the professing Christian, anxious to determine whether he is ceasing to run well, is that furnished by secret prayer, and the study of God's word. When a man is first brought to a sense of the evil of sin, and of the graciousness of the deliverance wrought out for him by Christ, he is frequent and fervent in prayer, and he reads with great earnestness the pages of Scripture. And if he go on "running well" in religion, he will be increasingly diligent in these private duties, finding, every day, more and more against which, and for which, to pray; and feeling the Bible to be a store-house of instruction from which it is his privilege continually to draw. But now suppose, that, in place of this, the Christian grows remiss in spiritual exercises, glad of an excuse for shortening his devotions, easily satisfied with any reason for omitting them, and speedily wearied when he engages in their performance—what are we to say of him, if not that he presents one great symptom of spiritual decline? Prayer is not inaptly called the breathing of the soul; and you may be sure, that, where this grows shorter and more difficult, there is no healthful play in the organs of life. If any one of you is beginning to abbreviate his seasons of private devotion, reading a chapter or two less of the Bible, spending fewer moments in meditation, in self-examination, and in supplication for others and himself—and all, not because he has actually less time at his disposal, but less will to devote it to such occupation—let that man look at once to his state: the fervency is departing from the love: the disease has already made inroad on the spiritual constitution: he "did run well;" alas, what has hindered him that he is no longer obedient to the truth?

And as one great symptom of spiritual declension may be gathered from the more private means of grace, so may another from the more public. The Christian, in whom vital religion is in a healthy estate, attaches great worth to the public ordinances, finding it vastly for his edification and comfort to join the worshipping assembly, to listen to the preaching of the Word, and to receive those sacred elements which both represent and convey the body and blood of his Redeemer. He would not willingly absent himself from the congregation; for he has learnt to exclaim with one of old, "How amiable are thy tabernacles!" "I was glad when they said unto me, Let us go into the house of the Lord." He does not require to have the messages of the Gospel adorned for him by human rhetoric: it is the simple, beautiful truth, which he loves, and which came home to him so thrillingly when first brought to know the Lord; and this he recognises and prizes, however humble the garb under which it is presented. Neither can he be content with occasional communion, neglecting as frequently as he attends the most solemn rite of our religion; he knows his need of that flesh which is meat indeed, and of that blood which is drink indeed; and thankfully avails himself of every opportunity of obtaining spiritual sustenance. Such is the Christian when his first love is in its strength, when he is "running well," with the first vigour of dedication to God. But suppose him to become less assiduous, and more formal, in the public duties of religion; suppose that he easily finds excuses for staying away from church—a degree of sickness, or a state of the weather, which would never keep him from any worldly engagement, keeping him from public worship—suppose that he get satiated with the simple Gospel, and cannot be contented, unless he have flowery and oratorical preaching: suppose, yet further, that he reduces his sacramental attendances to certain high festivals, communicating at Christmas, Whitsuntide, and Easter, but finding no inconvenience from spiritually fasting all the year besides—what are we to say of him, if not that he has ceased to "run well?" he is losing the spiritual appetite, so that he no longer "hungers and thirsts after righteousness"—can we doubt then the progress of the spiritual decline?

But let us take other symptoms, equally decisive, though perhaps more easily overlooked. There is no feeling stronger in a genuine Christian, than that of a desire to promote God's glory, and the salvation of his fellow-men. The consciousness of having received vast and unmerited benefits, the sense of gratitude for his own deliverance from condemnation, the apprehension of the greatness of that wrath which will overtake the impenitent—these constrain him, whilst warm with first love, to the counting nothing too costly or laborious, so that Christ may be magnified, and those who are sitting in darkness may see a great light. But suppose him to become comparatively indifferent to the diffusion of the Gospel—not indeed withdrawing his subscriptions from societies, but taking little or no interest in their failure or success; not declining all part in the enterprises of Christian philanthropy, but engaging only so far as there is bustle, and show, and excitement—so that it is not with the heart, though it may be with the purse and the hand, that he helps forward the cause of the Redeemer—ah, who will say that there is no abatement in the "running well?" who will deny the spiritual declension?

And again—there is a broad line of separation between men of the world, and men of religion. Those who have been renewed in the spirit of their minds, and those who are still in the alienation of nature, differ immeasurably the one from the other, and cannot unite, except as the former abandon their principles, or the latter undergo a great moral change. And the healthful Christian is quite aware of this. He knows that separation from the world must be his distinguishing characteristic; and he guards accordingly, with godly jealousy, against any such conformity as would do violence to his profession. His conscience is tender; and whensoever there may be doubt as to what is lawful for him, and what unlawful, he will always take the safe side, feeling it better for him to give up what he might have retained, than to retain what he ought to give up. But there may be, and often is, a great change in these respects. The man of religion comes to view the world with less fear and repugnance. He fancies that he has been hitherto overstrict, and that he might safely conform, more closely than he has done, to the customs and fashions of the ungodly. The conscience grows more accommodating; and now the calculation is, how far he may venture, how much of earthly pleasure he may allow himself, how nearly he may sail on the same tack with the world, without actually steering for the same port. Alas, this is among the strongest of symptoms, that the man has ceased from "running well:" he who is less and less scrupulous as to the being "conformed to this world," must be already far gone in spiritual decline.

And not unlike the symptom of making light of the difference between the religious and the worldly, is that of the making light of differences between various creeds. The peculiar and distinguishing doctrines of the Gospel are prized by the genuine and ardent Christian, as treasures without which he were unutterably poor. It is not as the tenets of the Church to which he belongs that he values them—he rests on them all his hopes of everlasting happiness; and he, therefore, who attacks them, seeks to rob him of his all, and leave him bankrupt for eternity. Hence he looks with abhorrence on Socinianism: it would strip Christ of divinity; and this, he feels, were to strip himself of immortality. He looks with dread upon Popery: by its fables and falsehoods, though mixed with fundamental truths, it keeps the sinner from the Saviour, and substitutes dross for gold; and whatever obscures the mediatorial work involves him in a darkness from which he can find no escape. But this repugnance to error may not continue. Whilst thoroughly orthodox in his creed, he may be less alive to the importance of its doctrines. He may come to look more leniently upon heresy, confounding bigotry with the honest attachment of truth, and mistaking for charity a growing indifference to falsehood. And wherever there is any of this lowered sense of the indispensableness of fundamental truth, and of an increasing disposition to think lightly of wrong systems of religion—as though, after all, the heretical and orthodox, the reformed and unreformed, if there were but a few mutual concessions, might meet on the same ground, and shake hands as brethren—you may be sure that the Christian course is ceasing to be "well run:" whilst that proceeds vigorously, the relish for truth is shown by a loathing of falsehood; but when that grows languid, the taste is less keen; error is no longer nauseated: the world applauds the Christian for having become liberal, whereas he should grieve over himself as having become lukewarm.

These, then, are certain of the symptoms, by which you may detect the presence of spiritual consumption. Though all should moreover remember, that it is against the very nature of religion to suppose a man stationary; so that any one who sees no reason to hope that he is advancing, has reason for fear that he is declining. Judge then yourselves, ye who would know whether ye are the subjects of spiritual declension—can ye find cause to hope, after a rigid process of self-examination, that ye are the subjects of spiritual advancement? Are you more humble than you were, more sensible of your sinfulness, stronger in faith, warmer in love, less attached to earthly things, more attracted by heavenly? Is it a greater privilege to you to pray, a less labour to be obedient? Have you a firmer command over your passions? is the will more in harmony with the divine? is the conscience more sensitive, and is the judgment prompter in deciding for the right against the agreeable? In prosperity, have you less of pride and self-confidence? in adversity, have you more of patience and acquiescence? Indeed, if you have cause to conclude that you have stood still, you have verily cause to conclude that you have gone back.

But we have now spoken sufficiently on the symptoms of spiritual decline, sufficiently, we mean, for every practical purpose—our object being that of enabling the sick man to determine whether he have the disease, and not that of curiously noting down every sign and shade of the malady. It is our business to endeavour to come down amongst you, as a physician, with his instruments in his hands, that we may determine, if possible, whether the lungs be yet sound, and whether consumption may not lurk where there is no taint as yet on the outward appearance. We apply our instruments, or rather, we entreat you to apply them for yourselves. It is nothing to us that your profession is still that of godliness, and that you have not visibly returned to the world and its iniquities. It is an insidious disease, of which we are in quest—not open apostacy, which all might discover and denounce,—but secret declension, which may be scarcely detected, till it have reached its last stage. We try you by what you are when on your knees: we try you by what you are when brought into God's house, and by what, when exposed to the cold winds of the world. We listen for the beatings of the heart: we inquire what lassitude is produced by exercise, and what food taken with appetite. And with all frankness, but yet with all affection, we assure those of you who may be making a Christian profession, that, if they have fallen into habits of shortening their season of private devotion—and, much more, if they have no such seasons at all—if they have comparatively no relish for the simple Gospel, but must have it garnished up by man, before it can be palatable; if they can do without the Sacrament, except on high festivals; if they can conform themselves to the world as nearly as they dare, and are always calculating how small a sacrifice will serve for religion if they think; less of the differences between error and falsehood, and reckon it charitable to become latitudinarian—ay, and even if, on a careful review of past years, they cannot judge themselves to have advanced in spiritual-mindedness, and those various graces which are the fruits of the Spirit—we tell them, that if they find, not all, but any, of these symptoms in themselves, they ought to conclude that disease has begun, if it have not already made fatal progress: they may still be able to appeal to their works, their labour, and their patience; but they ought to feel that St. Paul, were he on earth, would address them as he addressed the Galatians, "Ye did run well; who did hinder you that ye should not obey the truth?"

And here we come to the considering the dangerousness of the state which is thus metaphorically described—for some of you might be disposed to say, Well, what if we be not running as well as we did, we may still be running sufficiently well to reach Heaven at last. But if you remember how our Lord reasoned in regard of salt which lost its savour, you will be forced to the conclusion, that he who has the disease on which we discourse, must almost be considered as having entered "the valley of the shadow of death." "If the salt have lost his savour, wherewith shall it be seasoned? It is neither fit for the land, nor yet for the dunghill, but men cast it out." It is not the difficulty of infusing salt at first, on which these words bear;

but the difficulty, when salt has been infused, and its strength has evaporated, of restoring the savour which it originally possessed. And in like manner the grand difficulty is not that of producing Christian love at the first, but of restoring its heat, when it has been suffered to grow cold. But why should the difficulty be greater? might it not be thought that it would even be less, seeing that the man, who has only degenerated, is not, at least, insensible to the claims of religion, and has proved himself not invulnerable to moral attack? We reply that, even amongst ourselves, and in reference to human attachments, the difficulty of reviving a decayed affection is almost proverbial. The party who has loved, and then ceased to love, is, of all others, the least likely to love again. If the fire of affection have once gone out, it is of all things the hardest to re-illumine the embers. And the difficulty which is experienced in the revival of a human affection must be looked for, when it is the love of God and of Christ which has grown languid. You are to observe that a great deal must have been done for the man in whom the love of God has once been kindled. The Spirit of God must have striven with this man, striven with him successfully, so as to have roused in him the dormant immortality, and brought him to some experience of the power of the Gospel. But this Divine agent will not persist in working where there is no earnestness in holding fast what has already been wrought. If He have given some measure of spiritual warmth, and you expose yourselves to damp, or unnecessarily permit the cold winds of temptation to beat on you, He will work with less and less energy, or communicate less and less of animating grace.

It is very mainly on this account that we look with so much apprehension on any case of spiritual decline. It is not the actually irreligious man on whom the disease can fasten. It must be a man on whom religion has had a hold; and in the weakening of that hold is our great evidence of his danger. For that hold could not have been weakened, except through compliances with the world, or omissions of known duty, for which the man himself is wholly answerable, and which not only loosen what has already been fastened, but alienate that Spirit which can alone restore firmness. And we cannot but suppose that this Spirit is more displeased when neglected by one in whom He has effectually wrought, than when resisted by another with whom it has striven in vain.

There is treachery in the first case, the cutting slight, and the base ingratitude, which will be far more likely to grieve the Divine agent than the open opposition which distinguishes the last. And if every one of you who may be the subject of spiritual declension, can only have become so through provoking the withdrawment of the renewing influences of the Holy Ghost, what marvel if we look upon him with no common alarm? How is it that the love has lost its fervour, except that that Spirit, which alone can keep it ardent, has withdrawn its holy fires? and how shall it be made to burn again, if its very dimness be as much a proof of your having driven away that Spirit, as an evidence of his departure? the lost heat can be restored by none but God's Spirit, and it would not have been lost, had not that Spirit left man, in just judgment, to himself. Oh then, there may be none to prove to you that you are in danger of eternal destruction, because you have manifestly gone back to the world, because you have visibly restored the empire to evil, and returned to open enmity with righteousness—yet know ye of a truth, that, as involving the alienation of the Holy Ghost, it is to stand within a hairbreadth of everlasting ruin, to stand in such a position that an Apostle might say to you, as to the Galatians of old, "Ye did run well; who did hinder you that ye should not obey the truth?"

But, you will say, the Spirit may be recalled, and then the smothered flame may be rekindled, the lost speed recovered. We will not deny it—God forbid that we should. We are not required to make the case out hopeless, but only full of difficulty. But this we must say—and we say it mainly for the warning of those who are still "running well"—that the very circumstance of the having been concerned as to religion, and then grown indifferent, is wondrously calculated to prevent the use of those means, through which the Spirit may be induced to resume his abode in the soul. The man is lukewarm; and Christ exclaims in the Epistle to the lukewarm Laodiceans, "I know thy works, that thou art neither cold nor hot; I would thou wert cold or hot." If this mean any thing, it must mean that Christ had more hope of the cold than of the lukewarm—one thing or the other, cold or hot, He emphatically wishes for, implying special abhorrence of that which was neither. And we are not surprised at this. The man who has cooled gradually down, but who yet retains some measure of spiritual heat, will be the last to allow or suspect any danger: feeling yet a degree of warmth, he will conclude himself as zealous in religion as religion requires, and count it enthusiasm to pretend or desire to be more. It was thus with the Laodiceans. "Thou sayest, I am rich, and increased with goods, and have need of nothing, and knowest not that thou art wretched and miserable, and poor and blind, and naked." They were self-complacent, and self-complacency was amongst the worst features of their state, because exactly calculated to keep them what they were, to prevent them from discovering, and therefore from attempting to correct their degeneracy. The lukewarm will have ordinarily just heat enough to keep him from perceiving the cold; and so, whilst the fire is going out, he will be quite pleased with its blaze. Here then the question presses with fresh force, how shall the half-extinguished flame be rekindled? I know that the Spirit of God, through its irresistible fires, could restore the love to its pristine condition. Yea, I know that this Spirit, however grieved and provoked to withdraw its influence, is ready to return, if there be only contrition, and an earnest desire to regain the lost ardour. But it is the very property of the diminished heat to seem hot enough; and therefore, not because there is no power to warm, but no wish to be warmed, is there a fearful probability that the subject of spiritual decline will never be recovered, but continue deteriorating day by day, though up to the very last he may not only pass with others for a genuine Christian, but be unsuspicious himself that he has no right to the character.

And if this decaying of the first love, this declining from the first speed, go on, so that we have the form of godliness with none of its power, indeed there are perhaps no terms too strong for the describing what the professor becomes. Take away the life from religion, leave us nothing but formality—and there is not on the face of the earth an individual so useless to others and himself, as the one in whom love remains, but remains in its ashes, and not in its fires. We are not speaking of actual apostacy The man who makes profession of religion, and then openly abandons that profession, is indeed chargeable with aiming a heavy blow at Christianity; for he publicly declares, that, having put the thing to the proof, having made trial for himself, he has ascertained it to be better and wiser to take side with the world than with God. But the apostate is not the man in whom the love has merely lost its warmth, or the spiritual step its speed; he is the man who has cast out the love altogether; there is no disguise about him; whatever his disease, the symptoms are all external; whatever his danger, it is plain to every eye. And this is not the case which we now have in hand. We are now upon love which is dying away; and we affirm the lukewarm man useless to himself and to others—to himself, for such religion as his will never save him; to others, for such religion will not enable him to be instrumental to the saving his fellow-men. "He that hath ears to hear, let him hear what the Spirit saith unto the Churches." There is no subject on which you can be addressed of greater difficulty and importance than that which is now engaging your attention. We have endeavoured to put you in possession of the symptoms and dangers of spiritual disease, before leaving you for a few weeks; but we are still quite dissatisfied; for we seem to have altogether failed in expressing our own sense, whether of the commonness, or of the fearfulness, of the disease, which we have wished to expose.

We have striven to be simple and faithful, avoiding all such speech as might have diverted the mind from the solemn points in discussion, and dealing with you just as a medical practitioner would deal with those in whom he feared that a secret poison might be at work, and whom he was anxious to instruct in the detecting its presence. And yet, before leaving you, we could almost wish to go over the whole ground again, fearing that we have not been plain enough, or not explicit enough, or not earnest enough. For how can we be sufficiently energetic and faithful, when it is but too possible, that, even amongst the apparently righteous and consistent of our hearers, there may be going forwards a process of decay? so that whilst, Tuesday after Tuesday, we summon the wicked to forsake his way, and the unrighteous man his thoughts, those to whom the summons is not addressed, and who would never dream of applying it to themselves, may be wasting down into the mere wreck of Christianity, losing all the strength of religion, and suffering all its essence to escape.

Or if—in place of speaking especially to the unconverted—a class of which we dare hardly doubt that it constitutes a large section of our hearers, we dilate on the privileges of believers, on the freeness of their justification, on the promises made to them by "God who cannot lie," and on the inheritance reserved for them in Heaven; how can we be otherwise than startled as the conviction comes over us, that the discourse may be admired and appropriated by some who never doubt its close reference to themselves, though all the while they may be ceasing to "run well," and may therefore be becoming the lukewarm, whom Christ declares that He holds in utter abhorrence? It is, as we have several times intimated, the insidiousness of the disease, which makes it so difficult to cope with, and so likely to be fatal. The analogy or resemblance is continually forced on us, between what our medical men call consumption, and what our theological call spiritual decline. You know very well that the presence of consumption is often scarcely suspected, till the patient is diseased past recovery. The worm has been eating out the core of life; and yet its ravages have been overlooked —for the victim hardly seemed to languish—and if the hectic look may have occasionally excited a parent's fears, they have been quickly allayed by assurances that no pain was felt, and by smiles which appeared prophetic of life. And even when no doubt can exist in the minds of others as to the presence and progress of the malady, it is, we might almost say, one symptom of the complaint, that it flatters the patient, so that often he will be expecting recovery on the day of his death. Every clergyman who visits the sick has seen much of this. It is not an unfrequent feeling in young persons, that they should like to die of consumption, because they suppose this lingering mode of quitting life well adapted to preparation for the last dread account. But they little know with what difficulty the consumptive patient is brought to look death in the face; there is perhaps no disease which less tells its victim what its fatal errand is; you know how beautifully brilliant it often makes the eye and the cheek—alas, this is but emblematic of what it does upon the heart, flushing it with hope, and suffusing it with light, when the winding-sheet is woven, and the evening shadows are falling.

But this disease, so insidious, so flattering, so fatal, is the exact picture of spiritual decline. Indeed, there is one point of difference; but it only makes the moral malady the more formidable of the two. It may be hard to make the consumptive patient see his danger—but that danger is apparent enough to others; friends and neighbours, however unsuspicious at first, become well aware of the painful truth as disease is more confirmed. But where there is spiritual decline, it may be unsuspected to the last. Ministers and kinsmen may perceive no difference in the man—equally regular in the public duties of religion; equally large in his charities; equally honourable in his dealings; equally pure in his morals. This was the case, as we showed you, with the Ephesian Church. They were the same in their patience, in their labour, in their works, and nevertheless they had left their first love. They had ceased to "run well." The fatal symptoms may be all internal; and because they are not such as to draw observation, there will be no warning given by others; and the sick man, not examining himself, and not finding that his religious friends suppose his health on the decline, will be all the more likely to feel persuaded of his safety, and to learn his disease, alas! only from his death.

"He that hath ears to hear, let him hear." We would not willingly, at any time—more especially when leaving, as we now do, for the few next weeks, our accustomed place—do that which is spoken of in the Prophet, "make the heart of the righteous sad whom God hath not made sad." But in an age of great religious profession, and when moreover we have not the fires of persecution to furnish tests of the strength and fervency of our love, we ought to take frequent opportunities of setting before you the fearful probability, that many are backsliders who are thought to be steadfast, and that many have let go the spirit, who still retain all the form of devotion. See to it, men and women, whether or not there be amongst you this spiritual canker. Ye may find out, by the symptoms which we laboured to exhibit, whether or not you are in any measure ceasing to "run well." Ye must be honest and bold with yourselves; the case is not one for trifling, and you are not to shrink from proving yourselves diseased. Go down into your hearts; try the pulse *there;* use the thermometer *there;* stay not upon the surface where a thousand things may preserve the appearance of animation, and induce what will pass for the glow of life and health; but descend into yourselves, search into yourselves, and be content with no evidence but that of an increasing love of God, and an increasing hatred of sin.

And if the freshness have gone out of your love, and you detect the degeneracy; if the heat have diminished, and you ascertain the lukewarmness; if the lungs are affected, and you prove the unsoundness—it is not despair, but effort, which we preach to you; we do not leave you for a season, bidding you reckon all lost, but bidding you strive that all may be recovered—for even to the Laodiceans, the Laodiceans of whom He had spoken in terms of absolute loathing, our blessed Redeemer could say, "I counsel thee to buy of me gold tried in the fire, that thou mayest be rich; and white raiment, that thou mayest be clothed; and anoint thine eyes with eyesalve, that thou mayest see."

HOOKER'S LIST OF BOOKS.

CHARLES HARDWICK, M.A. History of the Articles of Religion. 8vo.................... 2 00
REV. WILLIAM ADAMS, D.D. Elements of Christian Science. Third Ed. 8vo......... 1 75
REV. E. BICKERSTETH, M.A. Treatise on Baptism. 12mo.................................. 75
REV. M. MAHAN, D.D. On Faith. 18mo.. 38
REV. RICHARD CHENEVIX TRENCH. Hulsean Lectures. 12mo.......... 88
REV. RICHARD CHENEVIX TRENCH. Star of the Wise Men; being a Commentary on Second Chapter of Matthew. 12mo.. 50
ROBERT A. HALLAM, D.D. Lectures on the Morning Prayer. 12mo.................... 1 00
HUGH DAVEY EVANS, LL.D. An Essay on the Episcopate of the Protestant Episcopal Church, in the United States of America. 12mo.................................... 63
GEORGE MOBERLY, D.C.L. The Sayings of the Great Forty Days. 12mo................ 1 00
DOUBLE WITNESS OF THE CHURCH. By BISHOP KIP................ .... 1 00
ISAAC TAYLOR. Restoration of Belief. Complete. 12mo.................................. 1 00
CHARLES INGHAM BLACK. Messiahs and Ante-Messiahs. A Prophetical Exposition. 12mo.. 75
M. THE ABBE LABORDE. The impossibility of the Immaculate Conception as an article of Faith. Translated by A. CLEVELAND COXE. 12mo................................ 63
THE BOOK OF THE HOMILIES. Complete; with the Constitution and Canons of the English and American Churches. 8vo.. 2 50
THE POPULAR WORKS OF THE REV. HENRY BLUNT. In 4 vols........................... 4 00
REV. HENRY BLUNT's Family Commentary on Genesis. 12mo................................ 75
" " " " on Exodus and Leviticus. 12mo........ 75
" " " " Numbers and Deuteronomy. 12mo............ 75
Complete in 3 vols. uniform. 12mo.. 2 25
History of the Seven Churches in Asia. 12mo.. 75
PRACTICAL RELIGION EXEMPLIFIED, by Letters and Passages from the Life of the REV. ROBERT ANDERSON. 12mo.. 75
ROWLAND HILL'S VILLAGE DIALOGUES. From the Eighteenth London Edition. 2 vols. 12mo.. 1 50
THE LAST ENEMY; Conquering and Conquered. By BISHOP BURGESS. 12mo.......... 75
KRUMMACHER'S PARABLES. 12mo.. 75
QUESTIONS ILLUSTRATING THE XXXIX. ARTICLES of the Church of England, with Proof from Scripture and the Primitive Church. By E. BICKERSTETH, Curate of Holy Cross. 12mo... 50

*** This Work is regarded as one of the best Commentaries on the Articles, and as a Manual for the use of Students of Divinity has no superior.

QUESTIONS ON THE COLLECTS, EPISTLES AND GOSPELS of the Church's Year; and their Connection. By the REV. WILLIAM CROSSWELL DOANE, A.M. 18mo........... 25
CURIOUS PASSAGES from the Lives of Misers and Philanthropists; or Riches that bring no Sorrow. By REV. ERSKINE NEAL, M.A. 12mo.. 75
WARNINGS OF THE HOLY WEEK. Lectures for the week before Easter, and the Easter Festivals. By REV. W. ADAMS, M.A., author of "The Old Man's Home." 18mo.. 40
WILBERFORCE'S PREPARATION FOR THE HOLY COMMUNION. Edited by the REV. DR. COXE. Muslin, plain, 50 cents. Red edges.. 60
PORTION OF THE SOUL and CHRISTIAN LIFE, in one vol. By the REV. HERMAN HOOKER 60
USES OF ADVERSITY. By the REV. HERMAN HOOKER.. 25
LIFE OF DAVID. By REV. DR. NORTON............. 50
CHRISTIAN BALLADS. By A. CLEVELAND COXE. 10th Edition 18mo, muslin......... 60
Blue and Gold $1.00. Turkey morocco. 2 25
KEBLE'S CHRISTIAN YEAR. 8vo., with four plates. By BIRKET FOSTER. On tinted paper..price from 2.50 to 6 00
KEBLE'S CHRISTIAN YEAR, 12mo., red edges.. 1 00
" " " 18mo., plain 60 cents, gilt edges............................. 1 00
JOYS AND SORROWS OF THE ECCLESIASTICAL YEAR, being Meditations and appropriate Poetry for the Various Seasons. By MARIA G. MILLWARD. 12mo........... 1 00
Cloth, gilt, $1.25. Turkey extra, 2 50

www.ingramcontent.com/pod-product-compliance
Lightning Source LLC
LaVergne TN
LVHW020108110826
845151LV00001B/102

* 9 7 8 1 4 2 5 5 4 3 6 1 7 *